Third DialDoc Workshop on Document-grounded Dialogue and Conversational Question Answering (DialDoc 2023)

Toronto, Canada
13 July 2023

ISBN: 978-1-7138-8226-8

Printed from e-media with permission by:

Curran Associates, Inc.
57 Morehouse Lane
Red Hook, NY 12571

Some format issues inherent in the e-media version may also appear in this print version.

Printed with permission by Curran Associates, Inc. (2024)

Association for Computational Linguistics
209 N. Eighth Street
Stroudsburg, Pennsylvania 18360

Phone: 1-570-476-8006
Fax: 1-570-476-0860

acl@aclweb.org

Additional copies of this publication are available from:

Curran Associates, Inc.
57 Morehouse Lane
Red Hook, NY 12571 USA
Phone: 845-758-0400
Fax: 845-758-2633
Email: curran@proceedings.com
Web: www.proceedings.com

DialDoc 2023

Proceedings of the Third DialDoc Workshop on Document-grounded Dialogue and Conversational Question Answering

Proceedings of the Workshop

July 13, 2023

The DialDoc organizers gratefully acknowledge the support from the following sponsors.

Gold

達摩院
ALIBABA DAMO ACADEMY

Order copies of this and other ACL proceedings from:

Association for Computational Linguistics (ACL)
209 N. Eighth Street
Stroudsburg, PA 18360
USA
Tel: +1-570-476-8006
Fax: +1-570-476-0860
acl@aclweb.org

Introduction

Welcome to the Third Workshop on Document-grounded Dialogue and Conversational Question Answering (DialDoc), co-located with ACL 2023.

The DialDoc workshop aims to address the challenges of Document-Grounded Dialogue and Conversational Question Answering. In today's world, where a vast amount of content is generated across various mediums, it becomes crucial to not only make this content accessible to users through conversational interfaces but also ensure that the responses provided by models are accurate and grounded in reliable knowledge sources.

In our third workshop, we are particularly interested in exploring the theme of Factual Consistency. With the recent advancements in large language models, a significant concern arises when these systems generate responses that contain factual inconsistencies compared to external sources. This issue has implications on user trust and safety. We aim to highlight important community efforts that address the challenges associated with factual consistency, including but not limited to automatic evaluation methods, human evaluation, modeling techniques, and datasets.

The Shared Task competition primarily focuses on developing goal-oriented document-grounded dialogue systems in a multilingual setting. These systems allow users to interactively query domain-specific information based on provided documents. The task of querying document knowledge through conversational systems has gained considerable attention from both research and industrial communities due to its various applications. While previous Shared Tasks organized by the First and Second DialDoc Workshops focused on English document-grounded dialogue systems, other languages have been less explored. As a result, large communities of users are unable to access automated services and information. In order to bridge this gap, the Third DialDoc Workshop introduces a shared task that involves documents and dialogues in diverse languages. The aim is to encourage researchers to explore effective solutions for two key challenges: (1) transferring a DGD model from a high-resource language to a low-resource language, and (2) developing a DGD model capable of providing multilingual responses given multilingual documents. To evaluate the performance of response generation, the workshop adopts token-level F1, SacreBleu, and Rouge-L metrics. The score is calculated based on the sum of these metrics. A total of 71 teams participated in the Dev Phase, and for the final Test Phase, 29 teams submitted their models to the leaderboards. Many submissions have significantly outperformed the baseline, with the best-performing system achieving a score of 215.4 compared to the baseline's score of 156.0.

The workshop received a total of 19 submissions, featuring 18 paper presentations in either poster or oral format. Additionally, we are privileged to have invited talks from Greg Durrett, Hannaneh Hajishirz, Xiang Ren, and Rui Yan.

We would like to express our gratitude to all those who have contributed to the success of this workshop. Our thanks go to the authors for their valuable paper submissions, the teams for their participation in the Shared Task competition, the program committee members for their significant contributions, and the ACL workshop co-chairs for their guidance. We are also grateful to our esteemed invited speakers. Special appreciation is extended to Alibaba DAMO Academy for their sponsorship of the rewards for the Shared Task competition.

Organizing Committee

Program Chairs

Roee Aharoni, Google Research
Nouha Dziri, Allen Institute for AI
Song Feng, AWS AI Labs
Yongbin Li, DAMO Academy, Alibaba Group
Yu Li, Columbia University
Hui Wan, IBM Research AI

Shared Task Organizers

Haiyang Yu, DAMO Academy, Alibaba Group
Cam-Tu Nguyen, Nanjing University
Bowen Yu, DAMO Academy, Alibaba Group
Haomin Fu, Nanjing University
Yeqin Zhang, Nanjing University

Program Committee

Reviewer

Ankita Gupta
Chang Gao
Chulaka Gunasekara
Nico Daheim
Daniele Bonadiman
Etsuko Ishii
Hao Fang
Han He
Haomin Fu
Ehsan Kamalloo
Kun Qian
Anh-Cuong Le
Hoang-Quynh Le
Min Yang
Nguyen Cam-Tu
Pengshan Cai
Srijan Bansal
Sam Davidson
Wanyu Du
Xiangkun Hu
Xing Han Lu
Bowen Yu
Yeqin Zhang
Zichao Li
Ankita Gupta
Chulaka Gunasekara
Ehsan Kamalloo
Etsuko Ishii
Hao Fang

Keynote Talk: Assessing LLM Faithfulness: Lessons from Political Fact-checking

Greg Durrett
The University of Texas at Austin

Bio: Greg Durrett is an assistant professor of Computer Science at UT Austin. His research focuses on techniques for accessing and reasoning about knowledge in text. Large language models (LLMs) like ChatGPT and GPT-4 have dramatically advanced the frontiers in this area; currently his team is looking at where these systems succeed and fail and how to enhance their capabilities, particularly via systems that use LLMs as primitives. He is a 2023 Sloan Research Fellow and a recipient of a 2022 NSF CAREER award, among other grants from agencies including the NSF, Open Philanthropy, DARPA, Salesforce, and Amazon. He completed his Ph.D. at UC Berkeley where he was advised by Dan Klein, and he was previously a research scientist at Semantic Machines.

Keynote Talk: Reflex or Reflect: When Do Language Tasks Need Slow Reasoning?

Xiang Ren
University of Southern California

Bio: Xiang Ren is an assistant professor at USC Computer Science Department and a Research Team Lead at USC ISI. He is the director of Intelligence and Knowledge Discovery (INK) Research Lab, the Information Director of ACM SIGKDD, and member of USC Machine Learning Center. Priorly, he was a research scholar at Stanford University, and received his Ph.D. in Computer Science from University of Illinois Urbana-Champaign. Dr. Ren's research focuses on developing label-efficient, prior-informed computational methods that extract machine-actionable knowledge from natural-language data, as well as performing neural-symbolic reasoning over heterogeneous data. His research leads to a book and over 50 publications, was covered in over 10 conference tutorials, and received awards including faculty research awards from Google, Amazon, JP Morgan, Sony and Snapchat, ACM SIGKDD Dissertation Award, The Web Conference Best Paper award honorable mention, and David J. Kuck Outstanding Thesis Award. He was named Forbes' Asia 30 Under 30 in 2019.

Keynote Talk: Improved Factual Precision in Long-form Text Generation with Fine-grained Evaluation and Feedback

Hannaneh Hajishirz
University of Washington

Bio: Hanna Hajishirzi is a Torode Family Associate Professor in the Paul G. Allen School of Computer Science Engineering at the University of Washington and a Senior Research Manager at the Allen Institute for AI. Her research spans different areas in NLP and AI, focusing on developing general-purpose machine learning algorithms that can solve diverse NLP tasks. Applications for these algorithms include question answering, representation learning, green AI, knowledge extraction, and conversational dialogue. Honors include the NSF CAREER Award, Sloan Fellowship, Allen Distinguished Investigator Award, Intel rising star award, best paper and honorable mention awards, and several industry research faculty awards. Hanna received her PhD from University of Illinois and spent a year as a postdoc at Disney Research and CMU.

Keynote Talk: Recent Progress of Conversational AI in the Open Domain

Rui Yan
Renmin University of China

Bio: Rui Yan is an associate professor with tenure at Gaoling School of Artificial Intelligence, Renmin University of China. He was selected as a young scientist at Beijing Academy of Artificial Intelligence (BAAI) and a startrack young fellow of Microsoft Research Asia (MSRA). Till now he has published more than 100 highly peer-reviewed publications with more than 10,000 citations. He regularly served as an area chair/senior PC member for top-tier international conferences. He has been invited to give tutorial talks for these conferences as well.

Table of Contents

Program

Thursday, July 13, 2023

08:55 - 09:00	*Opening Remarks*
09:00 - 09:35	*Invited talk I by Hannaneh Hajishirz*
09:35 - 09:55	*Paper Presentation - Follow the Knowledge: Structural Biases and Artefacts in Knowledge Grounded Dialog Datasets*
09:55 - 10:15	*Paper Presentation - Revisiting Sentence Union Generation as a Testbed for Text Consolidation*
10:15 - 10:30	*Paper Presentation - Graph-Guided Unsupervised Knowledge Identification for Dialogue Agents*
10:30 - 10:50	*Coffee Break*
10:50 - 11:25	*Invited talk II by Rui Yan*
11:25 - 12:30	*Lightning Talks*
12:30 - 13:30	*Lunch Break*
13:30 - 14:00	*Shared Task Prizes*
14:00 - 14:35	*Invited talk III by Xiang Ren*
14:35 - 14:50	*Coffee Break*
14:50 - 15:10	*Paper Presentation - AlignScore: Evaluating Factual Consistency with A Unified Alignment Function*
15:10 - 15:30	*Paper Presentation - A Dialogue System for Assessing Activities of Daily Living: Improving Consistency with Grounded Knowledge*
15:30 - 15:50	*Paper Presentation - Ontologically Faithful Generation of Non-Player Character Dialogues*
15:50 - 16:10	*Paper Presentation - MoQA: Benchmarking Multi-Type Open-Domain Question Answering*

Thursday, July 13, 2023 (continued)

16:10 - 16:45 *Invited talk IV by Greg Durrett*

16:45 - 16:50 *Ending Remark*

Cross-lingual Data Augmentation for Document-grounded Dialog Systems in Low Resource Languages

Qi Gou, Zehua Xia, Wenzhe Du
State Key Laboratory for Novel Software Technology, Nanjing University, China
{qi.gou, zehuaxia, gowott}@smail.nju.edu.cn

Abstract

This paper proposes a framework to address the issue of data scarcity in Document-Grounded Dialogue Systems(DGDS). Our model leverages high-resource languages to enhance the capability of dialogue generation in low-resource languages. Specifically, We present a novel pipeline CLEM (Cross-Lingual Enhanced Model) including adversarial training retrieval (Retriever and Re-ranker), and Fid (fusion-in-decoder) generator. To further leverage high-resource language, we also propose an innovative architecture to conduct alignment across different languages with translated training. Extensive experiment results demonstrate the effectiveness of our model and we achieved 4th place in the DialDoc 2023 Competition. Therefore, CLEM can serve as a solution to resource scarcity in DGDS and provide useful guidance for multi-lingual alignment tasks.

1 Introduction

Document-Grounded Dialogue System (DGDS) is a meaningful yet challenging task, which not only allows content accessible to end users via various conversational interfaces, but also requires generating faithful responses according to knowledge resources.

However, in real-world scenarios, we may not have abundant resources to construct an effective dialogue system due to the low resources of some minority languages such as Vietnamese and French. Previous works only consider building a DGDS in high-resource languages with rich document resources such as English and Chinese (Feng et al., 2021; Fu et al., 2022), which is contrary to real-world situations. Extensive minority languages struggle to build well-founded chatbots due to the low resource of documents.

Therefore, how to generate evidential responses under a scarce resources setting deserves our attention. To address this issue, we propose a novel architecture to leverage high-resource languages to supplement low-resource languages, in turn, build a fact-based dialogue system. Thus, our model can not only handle high-resource scenarios but also generate faithful responses under low-resource settings.Our key contributions can be split into three parts:

- We proposed a novel framework, dubbed as CLEM, including adversarial training Retriever, Re-ranker and Fid (fusion-in-decoder) generator.
- We presented the novel architecture of translated training and three-stage training.
- Extensive results demonstrated the effectiveness of CLEM. Our team won the 4th place in the Third DialDoc Shared-task competition.

2 Related Work

Document Grounded Dialogue System is an advanced dialogue system that requires the ability to search relevant external knowledge sources in order to generate coherent and informative responses. To evaluate and benchmark the performance of such systems, existing DGDS datasets can be broadly classified into three categories based on their objectives: 1) **Chitchat**, such as WoW (Dinan et al., 2019), Holl-E (Moghe et al., 2018), and CMU-DoG (Zhou et al., 2018). These datasets typically involve casual and open-ended conversations on various topics; 2) **Conversational Reading Comprehension (CRC)**, which requires the agent to answer questions based on understanding of a given text passage. Examples of CRC datasets include CoQA (Reddy et al., 2019), Abg-CoQA (Guo et al., 2021), and ShARC (Saeidi et al., 2018); and 3) **Information-seeking Scenarios**, such as Doc2dial (Feng et al., 2020), Multidoc2dial (Feng et al., 2021), and Doc2bot (Fu et al., 2022), where the agent needs to retrieve

Proceedings of the Third DialDoc Workshop on Document-grounded Dialogue and Conversational Question Answering, pages 1–7
July 13, 2023 ©2023 Association for Computational Linguistics

relevant information from one or more documents to address a user's query.

Cross-lingual Data Augmentation has emerged as an effective approach to address the challenges of multilingual NLP tasks (Zhang et al., 2019; Singh et al., 2019; Riabi et al., 2021; Qin et al., 2020; Bari et al., 2021). Particularly in low-resource language settings, DA has demonstrated its usefulness (Liu et al., 2021; Zhou et al., 2022b,a). Explicit DA techniques mainly involve translation-based templates, such as word-level adversarial learning (Bari et al., 2020) and designed translation templates (Liu et al., 2021; Zhou et al., 2022b). Implicit data augmentation techniques, on the other hand, focus on modeling instead of expanding datasets like representation alignment (Mao et al., 2020), knowledge distillation (Chen et al., 2021) and transfer learning (Schuster et al., 2019).

3 Task Description

Formulation. We aim to improve the performance of DGDS in low-resource languages (Vietnamese and French). Formally, given labeled set $D = \{x_i, p_i, r_i\}, i \in [1, N_D]$, where N_D denotes the number of data and x_i, p_i, r_i denotes the input, grounding passage and response. Note that the input is obtained by concatenating the current turn and previous context. In addition, we have access to some high-resource language labeled datasets U with size N_U, where $N_U \gg N_D$. Our goal is to explore how to utilize high-resource datasets to enhance performance in low-resource languages (Vietnamese and French).

We have access to two large datasets, namely Multidoc2dial (Feng et al., 2021) for English and Doc2bot for Chinese(Fu et al., 2022). To fully take advantage of these high-resource datasets to enhance the performance in French and Vietnamese, we conducted translated training and generated pseudo-labeled training sets in Vietnamese and French. Specifically, we utilized the Baidu API[1] and Tencent API[2] to translate English and Chinese into French and Vietnamese, separately. Notably, English and French are Indo-European languages, indicating a common ancestral language, and Chinese and Vietnamese share historical and cultural connections and have influenced each other. Our methodology involved augmenting the training set

[1]https://fanyi-api.baidu.com/api/trans/product/index

[2]https://www.tencentcloud.com/products/tmt

data	number of turns
Chinese corpus	5760
English corpus	26506
Shared-Task/train	3446 (Vi) and 3510(Fr)
Zh-Vi	4908
En-Fr	4980
Shared-Task/dev	95(Vi) and 99(Fr)
Shared-Task/test	94(Vi) and 100(Fr)

Table 1: Statistics of provided datasets. Chinese and English corpus is provided by the third workshop committee of DialDoc. Zh-Vi and En-Fr means the number of translated data from Chinese to Vietnamese and from English to French respectively.

by translating 5000 English examples into French and 5000 Chinese examples into Vietnamese. After filtering out instances of poor quality and excessive length, we ultimately derived 4980 En-Fr and 4908 Zh-Vi pseudo examples.

Now we have three training data, cross-lingual training data D, translated pseudo data D' and downstream fine-tuning data D^t. We will show how to use these data in Section 4.4. And the statistics are presented in Table 1.

4 Methodology

We adopt the Retrieve-Rerank-Generation architecture (Glass et al., 2022; Zhang et al., 2023) and incorporate adversarial training into both the Retriever and Re-ranker components. To address the low-resource DGDS scenario, we propose a novel three-stage training approach.

4.1 Passage-Retriever With FGM

Given an input x, the retriever aims to retrieve the most relevant top-k documents $\{z_i\}_i^k$ from a large candidate pool. We follow the schema of conventional Dense Passage Retrieval (DPR) (Karpukhin et al., 2020) for passage retrieval:

$$s(q) = \text{XLM-R}_1(q)$$
$$s(z) = \text{XLM-R}_2(z)$$
$$p_\phi(z|q) \propto \text{dot}[s(q)^\top s(z)]$$

To improve multi-lingual performance further, where the encoder is initialized from XLM-RoBERTa (Conneau et al., 2019) denote as XLM-R which are used to convert question templates into dense embedding vectors for passage retrieval. Sub-linear time search can be achieved with a Maximum Inner Product Search (MIPS) (Shrivastava and Li, 2014).

In addition, inspired by FGM (Miyato et al., 2017), we extend the adversarial training to document retrieval. We apply infinitesimal perturbations on word embeddings to increase the learning difficulty by constructing adversarial examples. Based on this, the passage retriever is regularized and has better generalization performance since it has to retrieve the correct relevant documents under the attack of adversarial examples.

4.2 Passage-Reranker with FGM

Given a shortlist of candidates, the goal of Reranker is to capture deeper interactions between a query x and a candidate passage p. Specifically, the query x and passage p are concatenated to form the input for XLM-RoBERTa (Conneau et al., 2019). And the pooler output of XLM-RoBERTa is considered as similarity score:

$$P(p|q) = \mathrm{SoftMax}\left(\mathrm{Linear}\left(\text{XLM-R}([p, q])\right)\right)$$

As in the previous stage, we still employed FGM (Miyato et al., 2017) to add perturbations to word embeddings.

4.3 Knowledge-Enhancement Generation

The generator aims to generate correct and factual responses according to the candidates of passages. The key problem is how to leverage the knowledge of passage candidates as much as possible. we adopt Fusion-in-Decoder(FiD) (Izacard and Grave, 2021) as our response generator. During generation, FiD will first encodes every input with multiple passages independently through encoder, and then decodes all encoded feature jointly to generate final response. Concisely, the decoder has extra Cross Attention on more passages feature. This is significant because it is equivalent to improve grounding passage accuracy from top-k to top-n. Note that $k \ll n$ due to the CUDA memory limitation.

Since prompt-learning is effective in generation proved by previous work (Wei et al., 2021), we also adopt this way by adding the prompt to the front of input query. We choose *"please generate the response:"* as our prompt, so the final input of generator is "prompt <query> query <passage> passage", where <prompt> and <passage> are special tokens.

Model	Total
Baseline	156.42
CLEM	**201.0913**

Table 2: Performance of CLEM on Test set

4.4 Training Process

Our training process consists of three stages. In the first stage, we use all available Chinese and English training corpora to pre-train the model, aiming to develop its primary cross-lingual perception capability. We incorporate downstream fine-tuning data in this stage as well. We denote this stage as $T(D + D^t)$, where T represents training.

In the second stage, we train the model using translated pseudo data, which includes both noisy data and downstream fine-tuning data. We denote this stage as $T(D^{'} + D^t)$.

Finally, we fine-tune the model from the second stage on downstream low-resource training data. We denote this stage as $F(D^t)$, where F represents fine-tuning.

Therefore, the complete training process can be represented as $T(D + D^t)T(D^{'} + D^t)F(D^t)$. In the Experiment section, we also explore other training processes, such as two-stage training and direct fine-tuning.

5 Experiments and Results

In this section, we will introduce our datasets and baseline system. Additionally, we will demonstrate the effectiveness of each component in our methodology, such as adversarial training and the novel training process.

5.1 Datasets

We train CLEM on the given shared task datasets, containing Vietnamese (3,446 turns), 816 dialogues in French (3,510 turns) and a corpus of 17272 paragraphs in ModelScope[3], where each dialogue turn is grounded in a paragraph from the corpus. Moreover, we also utilize Chinese (5760 turns) and English (26,506 turns) as additional training data.

5.2 Baseline System

The baseline follows the pipeline of Retrieval, Re-rank and Generation. It simply uses DPR

[3]https://modelscope.cn/

CLEM	F1	BLEU	ROUGE	Total
CLEM-Full	**66.51**	**57.45**	**64.38**	**188.34**
CLEM(two-stage)	65.52	55.23	63.15	183.9
CLEM(fine-tune)	63.76	53.41	61.47	178.64
CLEM(two-stage w/o Zh-Vi)	64.24	54.51	62.18	180.93
CLEM(two-stage w/o En-Fr)	61.99	51.21	60.28	173.48
CLEM(w/o prompt)	64.34	55.12	62.31	181.77

Table 3: Ablation results of Modelon Development set. Here, the best are marked with **Bold**. Two-stage means we do not use original Chinese and English data. Fine-tune means we just use downstream training data.

CLEM	R@1	R@5	R@20	MRR@5
retrieval	0.57	0.78	0.87	0.65
retrieval†	0.62	0.77	0.87	0.68
re-rank	0.74	0.84	0.87	0.78
re-rank †	**0.76**	**0.85**	0.87	**0.79**

Table 4: Effect of FGM on Development set, where †means we use adversarial training

(Karpukhin et al., 2020) as retriever and Transformer Encoder (Vaswani et al., 2017) with a linear layer as re-ranker.

5.3 Result and Analysis

We evaluate the generation results based on token level F1, SacreBLEU and Rouge-L. The final result is the sum of them. As shown in Table 2, CLEM has a significant improvement by 28% on total result compared to strong baseline, which demonstrates the effectiveness of our method.

5.3.1 Ablation Study

We study the impact of different components ofCLEM, where the results are given in Table 3.

Training process we compare CLEM with two-stage training and fine-tuning directly. The former only contains translated corpus without original Chinese and English data, which can be denoted by $T(D' + D^t)F(D^t)$. While the latter means we only use downstream fine-tuning data denoted by $F(D^t)$. From the first three lines of Table 3, we can observe that CLEM has superior performance than two-stage training which means CLEM can leverage cross-lingual corpus to do a better language alignment for downstream training and get a better initialization. Not surprisingly, two-stage training outperforms fine-tuning directly which echos the Translated Training (Singh et al., 2019)

Different pseudo corpus As described in section 3, we leverage two translated pseudo corpus Zh-Vi and En-Fr. We also study the impact of each set with two-stage training. From 4th and 5th line of Table 3, the performance without Zh-Vi(Chinese to Vietnamese) and En-Fr(English to French) will decrease, which proved that the translated corpus is useful for shared task.

Without prompt We also run the experiments without prompt to explore the impact of prompt. From the last line of Table 3, the performance of CLEM will decrease sharply.

Without FGM We also explore the effectiveness of FGM (Miyato et al., 2017) at retriever and re-ranker. Results are listed in Table 4. We can observe significant improvements from retrieval to re-rank which prove the effectiveness of re-rank.

6 Conclusion

This paper introduces CLEM, a novel pipeline for document-grounded dialogue systems that uses a "retrieve, re-rank, and generate" approach. To address the issue of low performance due to limited training data, we extend the adversarial training to the document Retriever and Re-ranker components. Additionally, CLEM leverages high-resource languages to improve low-resource languages and develops a new training process under data-scarce settings.

Experimental results demonstrate that CLEM outperforms the strong, competitive baseline and achieved 4th place on the leaderboard of the third DialDoc competition. These findings provide a promising approach for generating grounded dialogues in multilingual settings with limited training data and further demonstrate the effectiveness of leveraging high-resource languages for low-resource language enhancement.

Acknowledgements

References

M. Saiful Bari, Shafiq R. Joty, and Prathyusha Jwalapuram. 2020. Zero-resource cross-lingual named entity recognition. In *The Thirty-Fourth AAAI Conference on Artificial Intelligence, AAAI 2020, The Thirty-Second Innovative Applications of Artificial Intelligence Conference, IAAI 2020, The Tenth AAAI Symposium on Educational Advances in Artificial Intelligence, EAAI 2020, New York, NY, USA, February 7-12, 2020*, pages 7415–7423. AAAI Press.

M Saiful Bari, Tasnim Mohiuddin, and Shafiq Joty. 2021. UXLA: A robust unsupervised data augmentation framework for zero-resource cross-lingual NLP. In *Proceedings of the 59th Annual Meeting of the Association for Computational Linguistics and the 11th International Joint Conference on Natural Language Processing (Volume 1: Long Papers)*, pages 1978–1992, Online. Association for Computational Linguistics.

Weile Chen, Huiqiang Jiang, Qianhui Wu, Börje Karlsson, and Yi Guan. 2021. AdvPicker: Effectively Leveraging Unlabeled Data via Adversarial Discriminator for Cross-Lingual NER. In *Proceedings of the 59th Annual Meeting of the Association for Computational Linguistics and the 11th International Joint Conference on Natural Language Processing (Volume 1: Long Papers)*, pages 743–753, Online. Association for Computational Linguistics.

Alexis Conneau, Kartikay Khandelwal, Naman Goyal, Vishrav Chaudhary, Guillaume Wenzek, Francisco Guzmán, Edouard Grave, Myle Ott, Luke Zettlemoyer, and Veselin Stoyanov. 2019. Unsupervised cross-lingual representation learning at scale. *arXiv preprint arXiv:1911.02116*.

Emily Dinan, Stephen Roller, Kurt Shuster, Angela Fan, Michael Auli, and Jason Weston. 2019. Wizard of Wikipedia: Knowledge-powered conversational agents. In *Proceedings of the International Conference on Learning Representations (ICLR)*.

Song Feng, Siva Sankalp Patel, Hui Wan, and Sachindra Joshi. 2021. MultiDoc2Dial: Modeling dialogues grounded in multiple documents. In *Proceedings of the 2021 Conference on Empirical Methods in Natural Language Processing*, pages 6162–6176, Online and Punta Cana, Dominican Republic. Association for Computational Linguistics.

Song Feng, Hui Wan, Chulaka Gunasekara, Siva Patel, Sachindra Joshi, and Luis Lastras. 2020. doc2dial: A goal-oriented document-grounded dialogue dataset. In *Proceedings of the 2020 Conference on Empirical Methods in Natural Language Processing (EMNLP)*, pages 8118–8128, Online. Association for Computational Linguistics.

Haomin Fu, Yeqin Zhang, Haiyang Yu, Jian Sun, Fei Huang, Luo Si, Yongbin Li, and Cam Tu Nguyen. 2022. Doc2Bot: Accessing heterogeneous documents via conversational bots. In *Findings of the Association for Computational Linguistics: EMNLP 2022*, pages 1820–1836, Abu Dhabi, United Arab Emirates. Association for Computational Linguistics.

Michael Glass, Gaetano Rossiello, Md Faisal Mahbub Chowdhury, Ankita Naik, Pengshan Cai, and Alfio Gliozzo. 2022. Re2G: Retrieve, rerank, generate. In *Proceedings of the 2022 Conference of the North American Chapter of the Association for Computational Linguistics: Human Language Technologies*, pages 2701–2715.

Meiqi Guo, Mingda Zhang, Siva Reddy, and Malihe Alikhani. 2021. Abg-coQA: Clarifying ambiguity in conversational question answering. In *3rd Conference on Automated Knowledge Base Construction*.

Gautier Izacard and Édouard Grave. 2021. Leveraging passage retrieval with generative models for open domain question answering. In *Proceedings of the 16th Conference of the European Chapter of the Association for Computational Linguistics: Main Volume*, pages 874–880.

Vladimir Karpukhin, Barlas Oguz, Sewon Min, Patrick Lewis, Ledell Wu, Sergey Edunov, Danqi Chen, and Wen-tau Yih. 2020. Dense passage retrieval for open-domain question answering. In *Proceedings of the 2020 Conference on Empirical Methods in Natural Language Processing (EMNLP)*, pages 6769–6781.

Linlin Liu, Bosheng Ding, Lidong Bing, Shafiq Joty, Luo Si, and Chunyan Miao. 2021. MulDA: A multilingual data augmentation framework for low-resource cross-lingual NER. In *Proceedings of the 59th Annual Meeting of the Association for Computational Linguistics and the 11th International Joint Conference on Natural Language Processing (Volume 1: Long Papers)*, pages 5834–5846, Online. Association for Computational Linguistics.

Xin Mao, Wenting Wang, Huimin Xu, Man Lan, and Yuanbin Wu. 2020. Mraea: An efficient and robust entity alignment approach for cross-lingual knowledge graph. In *Proceedings of the 13th International Conference on Web Search and Data Mining*, WSDM '20, page 420–428, New York, NY, USA. Association for Computing Machinery.

Takeru Miyato, Andrew M. Dai, and Ian J. Goodfellow. 2017. Adversarial training methods for semi-supervised text classification. In *5th International Conference on Learning Representations, ICLR 2017, Toulon, France, April 24-26, 2017, Conference Track Proceedings*. OpenReview.net.

Nikita Moghe, Siddhartha Arora, Suman Banerjee, and Mitesh M. Khapra. 2018. Towards exploiting background knowledge for building conversation systems. In *Proceedings of the 2018 Conference on*

Empirical Methods in Natural Language Processing, pages 2322–2332, Brussels, Belgium. Association for Computational Linguistics.

Libo Qin, Minheng Ni, Yue Zhang, and Wanxiang Che. 2020. Cosda-ml: Multi-lingual code-switching data augmentation for zero-shot cross-lingual nlp. In *Proceedings of the Twenty-Ninth International Joint Conference on Artificial Intelligence, IJCAI-20*, pages 3853–3860. International Joint Conferences on Artificial Intelligence Organization. Main track.

Siva Reddy, Danqi Chen, and Christopher D. Manning. 2019. CoQA: A conversational question answering challenge. *Transactions of the Association for Computational Linguistics*, 7:249–266.

Arij Riabi, Thomas Scialom, Rachel Keraron, Benoît Sagot, Djamé Seddah, and Jacopo Staiano. 2021. Synthetic data augmentation for zero-shot cross-lingual question answering. In *Proceedings of the 2021 Conference on Empirical Methods in Natural Language Processing*, Online and Punta Cana, Dominican Republic. Association for Computational Linguistics.

Marzieh Saeidi, Max Bartolo, Patrick Lewis, Sameer Singh, Tim Rocktäschel, Mike Sheldon, Guillaume Bouchard, and Sebastian Riedel. 2018. Interpretation of natural language rules in conversational machine reading. In *Proceedings of the 2018 Conference on Empirical Methods in Natural Language Processing*, pages 2087–2097, Brussels, Belgium. Association for Computational Linguistics.

Sebastian Schuster, Sonal Gupta, Rushin Shah, and Mike Lewis. 2019. Cross-lingual transfer learning for multilingual task oriented dialog. In *Proceedings of the 2019 Conference of the North American Chapter of the Association for Computational Linguistics: Human Language Technologies, Volume 1 (Long and Short Papers)*, pages 3795–3805, Minneapolis, Minnesota. Association for Computational Linguistics.

Anshumali Shrivastava and Ping Li. 2014. Asymmetric lsh (alsh) for sublinear time maximum inner product search (mips). *Advances in neural information processing systems*, 27.

Jasdeep Singh, Bryan McCann, Nitish Shirish Keskar, Caiming Xiong, and Richard Socher. 2019. XLDA: cross-lingual data augmentation for natural language inference and question answering. *CoRR*, abs/1905.11471.

Ashish Vaswani, Noam Shazeer, Niki Parmar, Jakob Uszkoreit, Llion Jones, Aidan N Gomez, Łukasz Kaiser, and Illia Polosukhin. 2017. Attention is all you need. *Advances in neural information processing systems*, 30.

Jason Wei, Maarten Bosma, Vincent Y Zhao, Kelvin Guu, Adams Wei Yu, Brian Lester, Nan Du, Andrew M Dai, and Quoc V Le. 2021. Finetuned language models are zero-shot learners. *arXiv preprint arXiv:2109.01652*.

Meishan Zhang, Yue Zhang, and Guohong Fu. 2019. Cross-lingual dependency parsing using code-mixed TreeBank. In *Proceedings of the 2019 Conference on Empirical Methods in Natural Language Processing and the 9th International Joint Conference on Natural Language Processing (EMNLP-IJCNLP)*, pages 997–1006, Hong Kong, China. Association for Computational Linguistics.

Yeqin Zhang, Haomin Fu, Cheng Fu, Haiyang Yu, Yongbin Li, and Cam-Tu Nguyen. 2023. Coarse-to-fine knowledge selection for document grounded dialogs. In *ICASSP 2023-2023 IEEE International Conference on Acoustics, Speech and Signal Processing (ICASSP)*, pages 1–5. IEEE.

Kangyan Zhou, Shrimai Prabhumoye, and Alan W Black. 2018. A dataset for document grounded conversations. In *Proceedings of the 2018 Conference on Empirical Methods in Natural Language Processing*.

Ran Zhou, Xin Li, Lidong Bing, Erik Cambria, Luo Si, and Chunyan Miao. 2022a. ConNER: Consistency training for cross-lingual named entity recognition. In *Proceedings of the 2022 Conference on Empirical Methods in Natural Language Processing*, pages 8438–8449, Abu Dhabi, United Arab Emirates. Association for Computational Linguistics.

Ran Zhou, Xin Li, Ruidan He, Lidong Bing, Erik Cambria, Luo Si, and Chunyan Miao. 2022b. MELM: Data augmentation with masked entity language modeling for low-resource NER. In *Proceedings of the 60th Annual Meeting of the Association for Computational Linguistics (Volume 1: Long Papers)*, pages 2251–2262, Dublin, Ireland. Association for Computational Linguistics.

A Experiments Hyperparameters

A.1 Hyper-parameters for retriever

train_batch_size=128
epochs=50
max_input_length=512
dropout=0.1
weight_decay=0.1
warmup_steps=1000
gradient_checkpoint_segments=32
optim=adam
learning_rate=4e-05
preKturns=2

A.2 Hyper-parameters for re-reanker

learning_rate=2e-5
dropout=0.1

epochs=20
train_batch_size=1
accumulation_steps=32
weight_decay=0.1
warmup_steps=1000
max_input_length=512
passages=20
preKturns=2

A.3 Hyper-parameters for generator

learning_rate=2e-4
dropout=0.1
epochs=20
accumulation_steps=16
max_grad_norm=1
train_batch_size=1
accumulation_steps=1
weight_decay=0.1
warmup_steps=1000
max_input_length=1024
max_output_length=128
beam_size=3
passages4gen=5
preKturns=2

MoQA: Benchmarking Multi-Type Open-Domain Question Answering

Howard Yen[†] **Tianyu Gao**[†] **Jinhyuk Lee**[‡] **Danqi Chen**[†]
[†]Department of Computer Science, Princeton University
[‡]Google Research
{hyen,tianyug,danqic}@cs.princeton.edu jinhyuklee@google.com

Abstract

Previous research on open-domain question answering (QA) focuses mainly on short-answered questions. However, information-seeking QA often requires various formats of answers depending on the nature of the questions, e.g., why/how questions typically require a long answer. In this paper, we present MoQA[1], a benchmark for open-domain QA that requires *building one system* that can provide short, medium, long, and yes/no answers to different questions accordingly. MoQA builds upon Natural Questions (Kwiatkowski et al., 2019) with multiple types of questions and additional crowdsourcing efforts to ensure high data quality. We adapt state-of-the-art models, and reveal unique findings in multi-type open-domain QA: (1) For retriever-reader models, training one retriever on all types achieves the overall best performance, but it is challenging to train one reader model to output answers of different formats, or to train a question classifier to distinguish between types; (2) An end-to-end closed-book QA model trained on multiple types struggles with the task across the board; (3) State-of-the-art large language models such as the largest GPT-3 models (Brown et al., 2020; Ouyang et al., 2022) also lag behind open-book QA models. Our benchmark and analysis call for more effort to build versatile open-domain QA models in the future.[2]

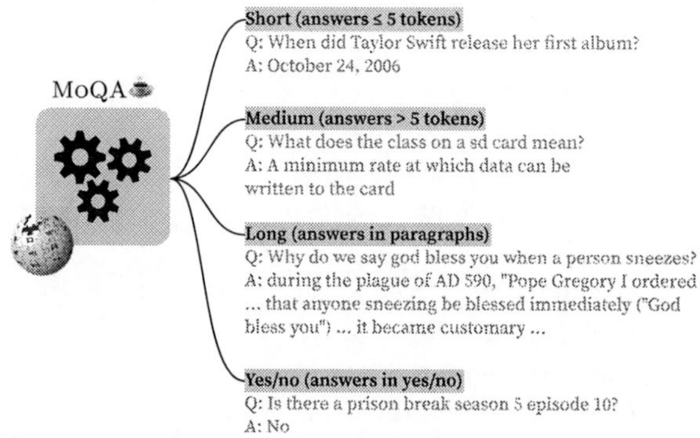

Figure 1: Examples of question-answer pairs. MoQA is designed to build one single open-domain QA system to answer various types of questions.

1 Introduction

Open-domain question answering (QA) leverages a large knowledge source such as Wikipedia to answer open-domain questions (Voorhees and Tice, 2000; Chen et al., 2017). Such a task mimics humans' information-seeking process—finding relevant documents and composing answers based on them—and has potential to become a fundamental component of next generation chatbots and search engines. An ideal open-domain QA system should be able to answer all types of questions human may ask, and provide answers in proper formats depending on the nature of questions.

However, for the ease of evaluation, most existing research on open-domain QA focuses on questions with short answers (Karpukhin et al., 2020; Lee et al., 2021; Izacard and Grave, 2020), originating from earlier work by Lee et al. (2019)[3]. This trend leaves a large portion of the open-domain QA task unattended: for example, *Why* questions often require sentence-level answers as you cannot explain "*why is the sky blue*" in a few words; yes-no questions like "*is there a Prison Break 5 episode 10?*" are also prevalent but largely neglected.

There has been recent efforts to study other forms of answers in open-domain QA (Fan et al., 2019; Stelmakh et al., 2022). In particular, GooAQ (Khashabi et al., 2021) is a benchmark consisting of different types of questions mined from Google autocomplete system and Google's answers boxes without human annotation. Nonetheless, all

[1]MoQA = Multi-type Open-domain Question Answering. It is pronounced as *mocha*.

[2]https://github.com/princeton-nlp/MoQA

[3]Lee et al. (2019) only considered answers $\leq$ 5 tokens in Natural Questions and exact match as the metric. This setting has been adopted by numerous follow-up work.

Proceedings of the Third DialDoc Workshop on Document-grounded Dialogue and Conversational Question Answering, pages 8–29
July 13, 2023 ©2023 Association for Computational Linguistics

of these works consider each type of questions *separately*. The closest work to ours is KILT (Petroni et al., 2021), which also considers different types of open-domain questions and builds one system to answer them. However, KILT is a collection of different tasks such as QA, fact checking, entity linking, etc., each with its own unique collection pipeline, which can introduce superficial cues that help the model determine the format of the answer.

Building one system for different types of questions has been studied in the reading comprehension setting (Kwiatkowski et al., 2019; Khashabi et al., 2020), where the supporting evidence is given as input. On the other hand, open-domain QA requires retrieving the evidence from a large text corpus or recalling specific facts from a model's parametric knowledge, both of which poses significantly different challenges.

Different from previous work, we bring different types of questions drawn from the same distribution together, and aim to build a single open-domain system (either open-book or closed-book QA) that can handle various types of questions with fine-grained annotations, based on a single knowledge source i.e., English Wikipedia. We further discuss the differences with past works in Section 6.

In this paper, we propose MoQA, a benchmark that requires an open-domain QA system to answer multiple types of questions (Figure 1). We build our benchmark by extending Natural Questions (NQ) (Kwiatkowski et al., 2019) into the open-domain setup, aligning each answer to a fixed-length Wikipedia passage, while keeping questions of four types: short, medium, long, and yes/no. We also use additional human annotations on the test set to filter out ill-defined long-answer questions, ensuring the high quality of MoQA evaluation.

We conduct a comprehensive set of experiments on MoQA with state-of-the-art QA models (Karpukhin et al., 2020; Izacard and Grave, 2021; Roberts et al., 2020; Brown et al., 2020; Ouyang et al., 2022), and reveal multiple interesting findings:

- Retrieving text passages for different types of questions exhibits a similar difficulty, and simply training a dense retriever (Karpukhin et al., 2020) on all types achieves overall best performance.

- However, building a single reader remains challenging. Joint training of a reader model on all types performs poorly, and it is also difficult to train a classifier to identify question types before applying individual reader models of each type.

- Finally, closed-book QA models trained on all questions as well as few-shot large language models (LLMs) without explicit retrieval significantly lag behind their open-book counterparts.

Our findings suggest building such a versatile open-domain system still has a series of unsolved challenges and call for more effort in the direction.

Type	Train	Dev	Test	Description (avg. ans. length)
Short	79,168	8,757	3,610	≤ 5 tokens (3.3)
Medium	16,668	1,853	565	> 5 tokens (15.5)
Long	19,649	2,169	201	Long answers (102.9)
Yes/No	3,154	351	99	YES/NO (1.0)
Total	118,639	13,130	4,475	-

Table 1: Dataset statistics of MoQA. Avg. ans. length is the average number of words in the answers.

2 The MoQA Benchmark

In open-domain QA, models are given a set of K passages $\mathcal{D} = \{d_1, \dots, d_K\}$ for a question q. In MoQA, the correct answer a to the question q could be a span ranging from a couple words to a paragraph, , YES, or NO. Unlike existing open-domain benchmarks that assume an answer span to be short (usually ≤ 5 tokens), MoQA does not assume a length limit and requires models to output different formats of answers considering the nature of each question.

2.1 Dataset Collection

We first build our dataset by adapting the Natural Questions (NQ) dataset (Kwiatkowski et al., 2019) into the open-domain setting while keeping all types of questions presented below[4]. We use the 2018-12-20 Wikipedia snapshot as the knowledge source and slice it to 100-word passages following Karpukhin et al. (2020). We then align each question-answer pair to a supporting passage and slightly modify the gold answers so that they could be found in the passage. Table 1 shows statistics of our dataset, and about 33% of the dataset is not short-answer questions. For more details of the dataset, and preprocessing steps, see §A and §C.

Short. The short-answer questions are defined as those having at least one short answer up to 5 tokens. It is exactly the same as Lee et al. (2019),

[4]We do not include unanswerable questions in the original NQ dataset, since many of them become answerable in the open-domain setting.

followed by most open-domain QA research. We keep our short-type questions consistent with the train/dev/test sets from Min et al. (2019).

Medium. The medium-answer questions can still be answered by span of text but contain more than 5 tokens. Most of them are noun or verb phrases or text around the length of one to two sentences, other than proper nouns, dates or numbers. For example, the question "what does the class on a sd card mean?" can be answered by "a minimum rate at which data can be written to the card", which cannot be reduced to just a couple words.

Long. The long-answer questions have paragraph-level answers and cannot be answered by a short string. We focus on long-answers that originates from paragraph as these questions tend to be inherently complex and therefore require long natural language explanations, and filter out those originating from tables and lists.

Yes/No. The yes/no-type questions can only be answered by either `YES` or `NO`. The original NQ annotations consider them as short-type questions, but we separate them since yes/no-type questions often require a different reasoning ability (Clark et al., 2019) and model design.

2.2 Mechanical Turk for Data Filtering

From preliminary qualitative analysis, we found that the original NQ long-answer annotations are noisy (many questions are marked as 'long answer' even though they can be answered by a few words), we carry out a manual filtering for the long-answer questions in the test set to ensure that these questions truly require long explanations to answer. To this end, we use Mechanical Turk (MTurk) for further data filtering, where each question is annotated by at least five MTurk workers. Each worker is shown both the question and the original long answers, and decides if the question can only be answered by the long answer, and if not, what is the shortest answer.

The Fleiss kappa between the human annotators is 0.143 when judging if a question requires short or long answer. The low agreement suggests that the length of the answer could be subjective for some questions — the annotator's familiarity with the subject may be a factor. Thus, we filter out any question that is marked as short by at least one worker. This provides a high guarantee that all human annotators agree that our long-type questions truly require long-form answers.

2.3 Evaluation

We use the original NQ development set as the test set and split the original NQ training sets into training and development sets with a $9:1$ ratio.

For retrieval, we report A@k (accuracy at top-k passages) and MRR@k (mean reciprocal rank). We consider a passage to be correct if it contains the long answer of the question. For answer prediction, we report exact match (EM) and F1 for short and medium answers, EM and ROUGE-L for long answer, and accuracy for yes/no answers. We also report the macro-averaged EM as the overall result.

Furthermore, we report the BERTScore (Zhang et al., 2019) for short, medium, and long-type answers in Table 8, and found that these metrics correlate with the F1 score and the ROUGE-L score. We also conduct human evaluation for selected models to study the difficulty of our dataset in Section 5. For more details about the metric, please refer to Appendix D.

3 Adapting QA models for MoQA

We establish multiple baselines for MoQA, by adapting state-of-the-art open-domain QA systems, including both supervised open-book QA models (Chen et al., 2017; Lee et al., 2019), supervised closed-book QA models (Roberts et al., 2020), and LLMs (Brown et al., 2020; Ouyang et al., 2022).

3.1 Open-book QA Models

Open-book QA models first retrieve supporting passages from a large corpus such as Wikipedia, and then apply a more expensive reader to predict answers using the passages. We carefully consider both components in MoQA by training both the retriever and the reader on different portions of the dataset and examine their trade-offs.

Retrievers. Retrievers return the most relevant passages from a large text corpus for a given query. We investigate the trade-offs of training one retriever on all questions together versus training a separate retriever for each question types.

We use DPR (Karpukhin et al., 2020) for the retriever component. (1) For the jointly trained model, we include all questions, and use all annotated gold passages as positive passages and passages retrieved by BM25 that are not the gold passages as hard negatives. The resulting model is DPR_{all}. (2) We also add a reference baseline, $\text{DPR}^{\dagger}$, which assumes we know the question type, and we train a DPR model on only the corresponding type of questions. See §E for more details and baselines.

Readers. Readers leverages attention across both the query and the retrieved passages to predict an answer. Similar to retriever, we are interested in the trade-offs between training a single reader model for all question types versus training separate readers for each question type.

Furthermore, we use two common types of readers: (1) An extractive reader based on RoBERTa (Liu et al., 2019), which predicts the rank of a passage and the start and the end positions of the answer span given the concatenation of the question and the retrieved passage[5]. (2) the generative reader model Fusion-in-Decoder (FiD; Izacard and Grave, 2021) based on T5-base (Raffel et al., 2019), which achieves the state-of-the-art performance on short-form answers since it is able to attend to multiple passages during decoding. We then analyze the performance of readers with different architectures on different types of questions.

For each reader model, we consider training them on all questions combined, as well as training them on each individual question type (there will be four readers in this case). For the latter, we need to train an extra **question classifier** in the pipeline to decide which individual reader to be applied. The question classifier is implemented by feeding the question into a RoBERTa model (Liu et al., 2019) and training a classifier on top of the [CLS] token (see §G for details).

3.2 Closed-book QA Models

Unlike open-book QA models, closed-book QA models entirely rely on their parameters to generate the answers. We consider both fine-tuning approach and few-shot in-context learning approach. Furthermore, we examine how the more powerful LLMs behave under the settings where the question type is either given or not given.

We follow Roberts et al. (2020) and fine-tune a T5-large model (Raffel et al., 2019) on all the questions in the training set, since the fine-tuned T5 model achieve impressive results on short-form QA and closed the gap to open-book models. See Appendix H for training details.

We evaluate the largest GPT-3 models: `davinci` (Brown et al., 2020) and `text-davinci-003` (Ouyang et al., 2022), due to their abilities to recall factual knowledge and performance on open-domain QA benchmarks. For each LLM, we use in-context learning with eight-shot ICL consisting of two demonstrations from each question type. We randomly sample one question from each type to construct sets of four demonstration, and balance the answer labels for yes/no-type questions. We also consider an oracle setting where the question type is given, and we only include two demonstrations from that question type for comparison.

Additionally, we use GENREAD (Yu et al., 2023) and prompt InstructGPT to first generate a supporting passage before outputting the final answer. Previous works showed that generating a supporting evidence improves the LLM's performance on short-form QA, and we investigate the method's robustness to different question types. For details on the prompting and examples, see Appendix H.2.

Retriever	#Train	A@1	A@5	A@20	MRR@20
Short					
DPR_{all}	89k	**36.0**	**62.8**	**77.0**	**47.6**
$DPR^{\dagger}_{short}$	56k	33.6	59.7	75.1	45.0
Medium					
DPR_{all}	89k	41.4	69.5	83.3	53.7
$DPR^{\dagger}_{medium}$	11k	**45.8**	**71.9**	**86.7**	**57.9**
Long					
DPR_{all}	89k	**37.8**	64.7	**80.6**	**49.2**
$DPR^{\dagger}_{long}$	20k	34.8	**65.2**	78.1	47.4
Yes/No					
DPR_{all}	89k	**37.0**	**64.4**	**79.5**	**49.7**
$DPR^{\dagger}_{yes/no}$	2k	35.6	57.5	72.6	45.9

Table 2: Passage retrieval results on the MoQA test set (A@k: top-k retrieval accuracy; MRR@k: mean reciprocal rank at k).

4 Results

Retriever: different types of questions have similar difficulty. We first demonstrate the retrieval results in Table 2. We can see that overall using all question type training data outperforms using the corresponding training data for each type, and the performance across different types does not differ much. We assume this comes from the nature of retrieval – because retrieval is mostly about topic, answer types do not matter much and training data can generalize to all types of questions.

[5]To support yes/no answers, we prepend every passage with two special tokens: [YES] and [NO].

Retriever	Reader	Short EM	Short F1	Medium EM	Medium F1	Long EM	Long ROUGE-L	Long BScore	Yes/No Acc.	Avg.
Oracle Question Types										
DPR_{all}	$\text{RoBERTa}^{\dagger}_{*}$	45.1	53.3	25.1	47.3	23.9	49.8	71.7	59.6	38.4
	$\text{FiD}^{\dagger}_{*}$	47.6	55.7	25.3	50.7	18.4	48.3	71.0	63.6	38.7
None	`davinci`$^{\dagger}_{*}$	20.6	30.1	0.8	21.1	0.0	20.2	51.9	54.2	18.9
None	`text-davinci-003`$^{\dagger}_{*}$	20.8	35.9	0.5	26.3	0.0	24.2	59.1	60.3	20.4
GenRead	`text-davinci-003`$^{\dagger}_{*}$	31.6	46.9	2.8	29.7	0.0	23.3	59.0	67.3	25.4
Open-book QA Models										
DPR_{all}	$\text{RoBERTa}_{\text{all}}$	43.8	52.1	**18.6**	**40.5**	**9.0**	**31.7**	**59.1**	54.6	31.5
	Cls. + $\text{RoBERTa}_{*} \times 4$	43.4	51.7	8.5	29.4	6.0	21.3	52.4	57.6	28.9
	FiD_{all}	**46.5**	**54.8**	15.0	36.0	0.0	9.5	44.3	**69.7**	**32.8**
	Cls. + $\text{FiD}_{*} \times 4$	46.1	54.5	6.9	29.3	4.5	21.8	52.2	61.6	29.8
Closed-book QA Models										
None	$\text{T5-large}_{\text{all}}$	16.4	23.0	6.0	19.2	1.5	12.7	46.5	59.6	20.9
None	`davinci`$_{\text{all}}$	17.7	27.1	0.5	17.9	0.0	16.3	51.4	29.0	11.8
None	`text-davinci-003`$_{\text{all}}$	10.9	25.7	0.3	23.6	0.0	20.5	57.5	14.8	6.5
GenRead	`text-davinci-003`$_{\text{all}}$	28.5	43.8	4.1	31.1	0.0	14.8	51.6	67.0	24.9

Table 3: QA results on the MoQA test set. BScore: BERTScore (Zhang et al., 2019). †: An oracle that assumes that the question type is known and uses a reader trained only on each individual type. Cls.: a question classifier is used, and there are four readers trained independently, either for RoBERTa or FiD. Otherwise, all questions are jointly trained. $\text{T5-large}_{\text{all}}$: a closed-book QA model trained on all questions. `davinci`$_{\text{all}}$ and `text-davinci-003`$_{\text{all}}$ are prompted with two demonstrations from each question type, and averaged across 3 randomly seeded runs. Avg. takes the macro-averaged EM of the four types.

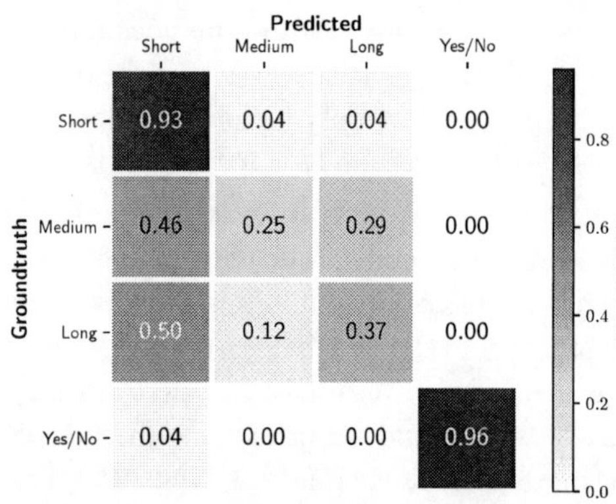

Figure 2: Normalized confusion matrix for question type predictions. For each ground truth type (row), we show the normalized prediction ratios over all types.

Reader: challenging to train one versatile reader that handles all questions. Table 3 shows the main QA results. Different from the retrieval component, we see that a single reader trained on all types of questions shows very imbalanced performance on different subsets. The single reader also significantly lags behind the oracle (marked by †) that assumes knowing the question type and applies corresponding readers. Between the extractive RoBERTa and the generative FiD, we find that FiD performs better on short-answer and yes/no questions but RoBERTa is better on medium and long-answer questions, even though in previous work FiD always prevails.

Though the oracle model is much better than the single reader, we see that training question classifier and 4 readers underperforms training jointly. This comes down to the difficulty to train the question classifier – Figure 2 shows the confusion matrix for question type prediction. It is noticeable that medium and long-answer questions are the most difficult to predict. For example, it is not trivial to understand that the question "who is covered under payment of gratuity act 1972" requires a long answer. Improving the classifier will be a straightforward to advance MoQA performance, as the current systems still have a huge gap to the corresponding type oracles. Please refer to Appendix J for qualitative examples.

Closed-book QA models significantly lag behind. Though competitive on short-answer questions as shown in previous work, closed-book QA models perform poorly on other types, especially on long-answer questions. Both the trained T5-large model as well as the LLMs lag behind open-book QA models. Our result suggests that it is still challenging to solve MoQA relying purely on parameters.

One possible explanation is the fact that more complex questions and extensive explanations require more memorization than short-form answers from the closed-book QA models, so it is harder to rely on knowledge stored in the model's parameters for this task. Furthermore, these explanations are less likely to appear in the pre-training corpus than popular entities such as people's names, famous places, and significant dates. Even for models such as GPT-3 that has been trained on an extremely large corpus, these answers still appear to be harder to recall than shorter answers.

Generating supporting passages improves performance. By first generating a supporting passage, InstructGPT can improve its performance on all question types except for long questions. Our findings are consistent with previous works that LLM can improve downstream performance with intermediate generation steps (Yu et al., 2023; Wei et al., 2022; Kojima et al., 2022). From qualitative analysis, we found that the vanilla prompting strategy results in `text-davinci-003` generating long and excessive answers, hence the low performance on short and medium-type questions. The additional generation step allows the model to output more concise and refined answers.

However, `text-davinci-003` performs worse with GenRead as its outputs becomes shorter for long-type questions. We will further analyze this behavior in Section 5.

5 Human Evaluation

5.1 Annotation Process

To further analyze the difficulty of MoQAand gain insights into how and why current models fail, we randomly sample and annotate 25 outputs from each question type on the test set for selected models: We assign two scores to each output: a correctness score and a sufficiency score, and show the results in Figure 3.

Correctness score. We first score the output on the factuality and relevance of the output: `correct` means the output is factually correct with respect to the question; `relevant` means the output is relevant to the query but not factually correct; `wrong` means the output is factually incorrect and irrelevant to the query.

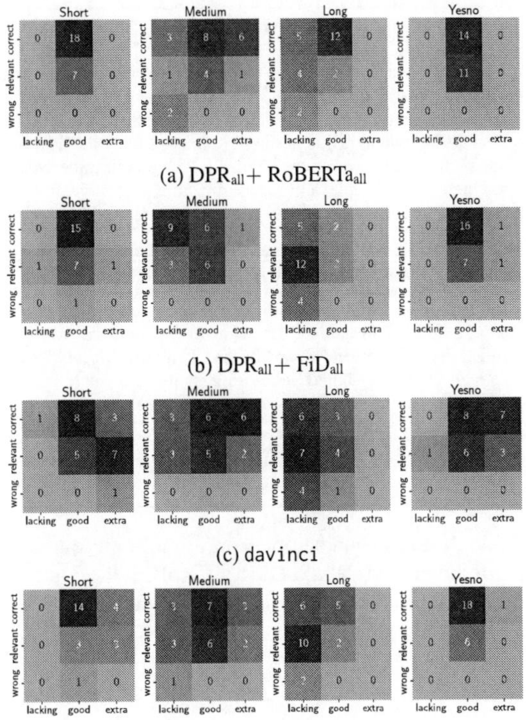

(a) DPR_{all}+ $RoBERTa_{all}$

(b) DPR_{all}+ FiD_{all}

(c) `davinci`

(d) GenRead+ `text-davinci-003`

Figure 3: Human evaluation results of 25 randomly sampled questions from the test set on select models. We plot correctness scores and sufficiency scores. Correctness score rates the output on its factually correctness and if it answers the question. Sufficiency score reflects if the output contains the appropriate amount of information required by the question.

Sufficiency score. We then determine if the output provides the appropriate amount of context: `lacking` means the output lacks the amount of explanation and context expected for the query; `good` means the output contains the perfect amount of explanation; `extra` means the output supply excessive explanation.

For more details on the human evaluation and examples of the annotations, please see §I.

5.2 Analysis

Extractive reader can adapt to short, long, and yes/no type questions. Outputs from the RoBERTa model are often both correct and contain the right amount of information. We also noticed that the model will always return either `YES` or `NO` for yes/no type questions, which supports our finding that boolean questions are relatively easy to identify. Since the outputs are always a span from the top 24 retrieved passages, they are almost always relevant to the query.

Q: Where does the expression go commando come from? A: The origins of the phrase "go commando" are uncertain, with some speculating that it may refer to being "out in the open" or "ready for action". "Slate" magazineś Daniel Engber dates the modern usage to United States college campuses circa 1974, where it was perhaps associated with soldiers in the Vietnam War, who were reputed to go without underwear to "increase ventilation and reduce moisture". However, more recently, Graeme Donald has pointed out that the US forces are "Rangers" rather than "Commandos"
DPR_{all}+ FiD_{all}: unknown
GPT-3: The term commando is derived from the Spanish word comando, meaning a "detachment" or "body of troops". In English, "commando" was originally a term for a type of soldier, but in the United States military it has come to mean a member of certain special forces units.
GENREAD+ InstructGPT: The phrase "go commando" is believed to have originated in the British military during World War II.

Table 4: Prediction samples on a long-type question from the test set. While DPR_{all} + $\text{RoBERTa}_{\text{all}}$ outputs the ground truth answer, other models' outputs lack the expected historical context.

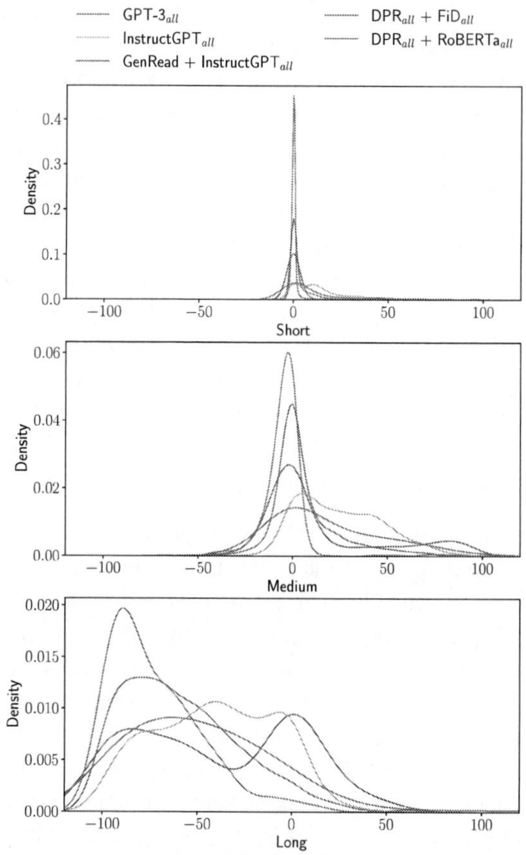

Figure 4: The distribution of Δl_i over the test set for DPR_{all}+$\text{RoBERTa}_{\text{all}}$, DPR_{all}+FiD_{all}, GPT-3_{all}, $\text{InstrctuGPT}_{\text{all}}$, and GENREAD+ $\text{InstructGPT}_{\text{all}}$. We omit yes/no-type questions since every model almost always return either `YES` or `NO`.

Generative models tend to generate shorter responses. Consider the examples shown in Table 4, where the question is inherently complex as it is asking about the historical origin of the phrase "go commando". In this example, the RoBERTa reader outputs the ground truth answer, while the other models fail in various ways. DPR_{all} + FiD_{all} simply generates "unknown", which is irrelevant to the question and does not answer it at all. `davinci` elaborates on the word "commando" but does not consider the phrase "go commando". GENREAD+ `text-davinci-003` only offers one explanation, while the complexity of the query necessitates more context given its historical background.

All models typically output relevant information. Even when the model does not output the correct answer, they often return relevant information. For instance, for the question "*who plays the woodsman in Over the Garden Wall*", the correct answer is "*Christopher Lloyd*". `davinci` returned "*Tom Kenny*", who is a voice actor involved in many animated series similar to *Over the Garden Wall.*

Furthermore, one of the main challenges of long-type questions is the complexity of the query. Generative models output incorrect answers more often on long-type questions, which suggests that *composing an answer with detailed explanations and historical contexts means more room for the model to make mistakes.*

All models struggle with the boundaries of medium-type questions. All model sometimes output insufficient or excessive explanations for medium-type questions, which suggests that the boundary between medium-type questions and the other question types are not quite clear. Indeed, this can be the case since medium-type answers may contain characteristics of both short and long-type answers. For example, the answer "Harry Potter and the Deathly Hallows" is more than 5 tokens long, but it is also a proper noun typically found in short-type answers. On the other hand, some answers such as "a transformative change of heart; especially: a spiritual conversion" is more descriptive and similar to long-type questions.

5.3 Output Length Distributions

To illustrate the issue of providing insufficient and excessive information, we show the difference between the length of the output generation and the length of the ground truth answer in Figure 4.

Specifically, let $A_i = \{a_1, a_2, \ldots, a_n\}$ be the set of n possible answers to the question q_i and $\texttt{len}(s)$ be the function that returns the number of tokens in the string s after whitespace tokenization. We define the difference in length Δl_i between output o_i with A_i:

$$\Delta l_i = (l_o - L_{\text{min}})\mathbb{1}_{l_o<L_{\text{min}}} + (l_o - L_{\text{max}})\mathbb{1}_{l_o>L_{\text{max}}}$$

where $l_o = \texttt{len}(o_i)$, L_{max} and L_{min} are the maximum and minimum of the answers A_i, respectively.

Extractive model is better at identifying the question type. Even though the RoBERTa model often returns outputs shorter than the ground truth of long-type question, its Δl_i distribution is centered around 0 for all question types. In contrast, all generative models' outputs often lack explanation for long-type questions. Interestingly, GENREAD causes `text-davinci-003` to generate shorter outputs on average as the density of the Δl_i distribution shifts left. One possible explanation for this is that `text-davinci-003` treats the final output as a summary of the generated passage. As a result, it ends up generating sequences shorter than the passage.

6 Related Work

Long-form QA. ELI5 (Fan et al., 2019) mines questions and answers from the subreddit Explain Like I'm Five[6], the answers are abstractive and are not grounded in a knowledge source. Similar to our work, ASQA (Stelmakh et al., 2022) also considers long-form answers in open-domain QA and its questions originates from NQ (Kwiatkowski et al., 2019). However, it only focuses on the questions that have long answers due to ambiguity. GooAQ (Khashabi et al., 2021) propose a dataset consisted of different question types, but these questions are mined from Google's answer boxes and therefore noisy. Furthermore, ELI5, ASQA, and GooAQ all study each question type independent of each other.

Extension of Natural Questions. Recent works leverage the original NQ beyond those with only short answers. For example, AquaMUSE (Kulkarni et al., 2020) use the long answer only questions from the original NQ for the task of query-based multi-document summarization. They consider NQ questions that only have long answers as these question "result in open-ended and complex topic answers". BoolQ (Clark et al., 2019) focuses on boolean questions that can be answered by true or false, and expands on the yes/no questions from the original NQ by collecting additional questions using the same pipeline. The authors found the task challenging and require robust reasoning ability. The unanswerable questions in NQ were explored by Asai and Choi (2020), but such questions are difficult to study in the open-domain setting and require extensive manually annotations. In contrast to these works, we study draw a diverse set of questions with different answers from the same query distribution and study these types together.

Multi-type Question Answering UnifiedQA (Khashabi et al., 2020) builds a single QA system to answer different types of questions. However, their setting is limited to the closed-domain setup, and only analyzes fine-tuned generative models.

LLMs achieves impressive performance on many knowledge-intensive tasks due to the knowledge packed in its parameters (Brown et al., 2020). They do not require any additional fine-tuning and only rely on in-context examples to adapt to different tasks. A recent line of work proposes to further improve LLMs capabilities by prompting them to generate a series of intermediate reasoning steps (Wei et al., 2022). GENREAD (Yu et al., 2023) applies a similar idea to open-domain QA, where the LLM first generates a supporting passage instead of relying on external retriever models, and then output the answer.

7 Conclusion

We propose MOQA, an open-domain QA benchmark with multi-type questions, and evaluate a range of baseline models. Our findings suggest that the main difficulty lies in the reader's task, and building a versatile reader or an accurate classifier is challenging. Competitive closed-book QA models also degrade on the new benchmark. Improving the classifier or mining more data to build a generalizable reader might be promising directions towards truly all-round systems.

[6]https://www.reddit.com/r/explainlikeimfive/

Limitations

Though our ultimate goal is to build a versatile QA system that can handle all types of questions, our benchmark mainly focuses on extractive questions – those can be explicitly answered by copying from a document in the knowledge source. We start from extractive QA because they cover a wide range of real-world questions and are easier to be automatically evaluated.

Although we addressed the issue of long-form QA evaluation with human evaluation and a range of automatic evaluation metrics, there is still much room for improvements in terms of evaluation of long-form text — human evaluation can be expensive and non-reproducible while current automatic metrics are not without faults. We encourage future work exploring various evaluation strategies of long-form QA.

Furthermore, all questions are in English and possibly collected from English-speaking users. We also use the English Wikipedia as our knowledge source. Thus, our models and dataset may under-represent the non-English speakers.

Ethical Statement

Training language models can use significant amount of energy as the process is very computationally expensive, this can come at an environmental cost. In our work, we attempt to minimize this effects by using pre-trained models like RoBERTa (Liu et al., 2019) and only doing the necessary fine-tuning to minimize the computation cost. Furthermore, to promote reproducible and accessible academic research, we will publicly release all of our dataset and code. Natural language datasets can contain biases like gender and racial stereotypes. Although this issue is not as prominent in QA datasets compared to large copra used for pre-training language models, we encourage the community to build robust QA models that are more resistant to these biases.

References

Akari Asai and Eunsol Choi. 2020. Challenges in information-seeking qa: Unanswerable questions and paragraph retrieval. In *Annual Meeting of the Association for Computational Linguistics*.

Tom B. Brown, Benjamin Mann, Nick Ryder, Melanie Subbiah, Jared Kaplan, Prafulla Dhariwal, Arvind Neelakantan, Pranav Shyam, Girish Sastry, Amanda Askell, Sandhini Agarwal, Ariel Herbert-Voss, Gretchen Krueger, Tom Henighan, Rewon Child, Aditya Ramesh, Daniel M. Ziegler, Jeffrey Wu, Clemens Winter, Christopher Hesse, Mark Chen, Eric Sigler, Mateusz Litwin, Scott Gray, Benjamin Chess, Jack Clark, Christopher Berner, Sam McCandlish, Alec Radford, Ilya Sutskever, and Dario Amodei. 2020. Language models are few-shot learners.

Danqi Chen, Adam Fisch, Jason Weston, and Antoine Bordes. 2017. Reading Wikipedia to answer open-domain questions. In *Proceedings of the 55th Annual Meeting of the Association for Computational Linguistics (Volume 1: Long Papers)*, pages 1870–1879, Vancouver, Canada. Association for Computational Linguistics.

Mark Chen, Jerry Tworek, Heewoo Jun, Qiming Yuan, Henrique Ponde, Jared Kaplan, Harrison Edwards, Yura Burda, Nicholas Joseph, Greg Brockman, Alex Ray, Raul Puri, Gretchen Krueger, Michael Petrov, Heidy Khlaaf, Girish Sastry, Pamela Mishkin, Brooke Chan, Scott Gray, Nick Ryder, Mikhail Pavlov, Alethea Power, Lukasz Kaiser, Mohammad Bavarian, Clemens Winter, Philippe Tillet, Felipe Petroski Such, David W. Cummings, Matthias Plappert, Fotios Chantzis, Elizabeth Barnes, Ariel Herbert-Voss, William H. Guss, Alex Nichol, Igor Babuschkin, S. Arun Balaji, Shantanu Jain, Andrew Carr, Jan Leike, Joshua Achiam, Vedant Misra, Evan Morikawa, Alec Radford, Matthew M. Knight, Miles Brundage, Mira Murati, Katie Mayer, Peter Welinder, Bob McGrew, Dario Amodei, Sam McCandlish, Ilya Sutskever, and Wojciech Zaremba. 2021. Evaluating large language models trained on code. *ArXiv*, abs/2107.03374.

Christopher Clark, Kenton Lee, Ming-Wei Chang, Tom Kwiatkowski, Michael Collins, and Kristina Toutanova. 2019. BoolQ: Exploring the surprising difficulty of natural yes/no questions. In *Proceedings of the 2019 Conference of the North American Chapter of the Association for Computational Linguistics: Human Language Technologies, Volume 1 (Long and Short Papers)*, pages 2924–2936, Minneapolis, Minnesota. Association for Computational Linguistics.

Angela Fan, Yacine Jernite, Ethan Perez, David Grangier, Jason Weston, and Michael Auli. 2019. ELI5: Long form question answering. In *Proceedings of the 57th Annual Meeting of the Association for Computational Linguistics*, pages 3558–3567, Florence, Italy. Association for Computational Linguistics.

Gautier Izacard and Edouard Grave. 2020. Leveraging passage retrieval with generative models for open domain question answering. *arXiv preprint arXiv:2007.01282*.

Gautier Izacard and Edouard Grave. 2021. Leveraging passage retrieval with generative models for open domain question answering. In *Proceedings of the 16th Conference of the European Chapter of the Association for Computational Linguistics: Main Volume*, pages 874–880, Online. Association for Computational Linguistics.

Vladimir Karpukhin, Barlas Oguz, Sewon Min, Patrick Lewis, Ledell Wu, Sergey Edunov, Danqi Chen, and Wen-tau Yih. 2020. Dense passage retrieval for open-domain question answering. In *Proceedings of the 2020 Conference on Empirical Methods in Natural Language Processing (EMNLP)*, pages 6769–6781, Online. Association for Computational Linguistics.

Daniel Khashabi, Sewon Min, Tushar Khot, Ashish Sabharwal, Oyvind Tafjord, Peter Clark, and Hannaneh Hajishirzi. 2020. UNIFIEDQA: Crossing format boundaries with a single QA system. In *Findings of the Association for Computational Linguistics: EMNLP 2020*, pages 1896–1907, Online. Association for Computational Linguistics.

Daniel Khashabi, Amos Ng, Tushar Khot, Ashish Sabharwal, Hannaneh Hajishirzi, and Chris Callison-Burch. 2021. GooAQ: Open question answering with diverse answer types. In *Findings of the Association for Computational Linguistics: EMNLP 2021*, pages 421–433, Punta Cana, Dominican Republic. Association for Computational Linguistics.

Takeshi Kojima, Shixiang Shane Gu, Machel Reid, Yutaka Matsuo, and Yusuke Iwasawa. 2022. Large language models are zero-shot reasoners. *ArXiv*, abs/2205.11916.

Sayali Kulkarni, Sheide Chammas, Wan Zhu, Fei Sha, and Eugene Ie. 2020. Aquamuse: Automatically generating datasets for query-based multi-document summarization. *ArXiv*, abs/2010.12694.

Tom Kwiatkowski, Jennimaria Palomaki, Olivia Redfield, Michael Collins, Ankur Parikh, Chris Alberti, Danielle Epstein, Illia Polosukhin, Jacob Devlin, Kenton Lee, et al. 2019. Natural questions: a benchmark for question answering research. *TACL*.

Jinhyuk Lee, Mujeen Sung, Jaewoo Kang, and Danqi Chen. 2021. Learning dense representations of phrases at scale. In *Proceedings of the 59th Annual Meeting of the Association for Computational Linguistics and the 11th International Joint Conference on Natural Language Processing (Volume 1: Long Papers)*, pages 6634–6647, Online. Association for Computational Linguistics.

Kenton Lee, Ming-Wei Chang, and Kristina Toutanova. 2019. Latent retrieval for weakly supervised open domain question answering. In *Proceedings of the 57th Annual Meeting of the Association for Computational Linguistics*, pages 6086–6096, Florence, Italy. Association for Computational Linguistics.

Yinhan Liu, Myle Ott, Naman Goyal, Jingfei Du, Mandar Joshi, Danqi Chen, Omer Levy, Mike Lewis, Luke Zettlemoyer, and Veselin Stoyanov. 2019. Roberta: A robustly optimized bert pretraining approach. *arXiv preprint arXiv:1907.11692*.

Sewon Min, Danqi Chen, Hannaneh Hajishirzi, and Luke Zettlemoyer. 2019. A discrete hard em approach for weakly supervised question answering. In *EMNLP*.

Long Ouyang, Jeff Wu, Xu Jiang, Diogo Almeida, Carroll L. Wainwright, Pamela Mishkin, Chong Zhang, Sandhini Agarwal, Katarina Slama, Alex Ray, John Schulman, Jacob Hilton, Fraser Kelton, Luke E. Miller, Maddie Simens, Amanda Askell, Peter Welinder, Paul Francis Christiano, Jan Leike, and Ryan J. Lowe. 2022. Training language models to follow instructions with human feedback. *ArXiv*, abs/2203.02155.

Fabio Petroni, Aleksandra Piktus, Angela Fan, Patrick Lewis, Majid Yazdani, Nicola De Cao, James Thorne, Yacine Jernite, Vladimir Karpukhin, Jean Maillard, Vassilis Plachouras, Tim Rocktäschel, and Sebastian Riedel. 2021. KILT: a benchmark for knowledge intensive language tasks. In *Proceedings of the 2021 Conference of the North American Chapter of the Association for Computational Linguistics: Human Language Technologies*, pages 2523–2544, Online. Association for Computational Linguistics.

Colin Raffel, Noam Shazeer, Adam Roberts, Katherine Lee, Sharan Narang, Michael Matena, Yanqi Zhou, Wei Li, and Peter J Liu. 2019. Exploring the limits of transfer learning with a unified text-to-text transformer. *The Journal of Machine Learning Research (JMLR)*.

Pranav Rajpurkar, Robin Jia, and Percy Liang. 2018. Know what you don't know: Unanswerable questions for SQuAD. In *Proceedings of the 56th Annual Meeting of the Association for Computational Linguistics (Volume 2: Short Papers)*, pages 784–789. Association for Computational Linguistics.

Adam Roberts, Colin Raffel, and Noam Shazeer. 2020. How much knowledge can you pack into the parameters of a language model? In *Proceedings of the 2020 Conference on Empirical Methods in Natural Language Processing (EMNLP)*, pages 5418–5426, Online. Association for Computational Linguistics.

Ivan Stelmakh, Yi Luan, Bhuwan Dhingra, and Ming-Wei Chang. 2022. ASQA: Factoid questions meet long-form answers. In *Proceedings of the 2022 Conference on Empirical Methods in Natural Language Processing*, pages 8273–8288, Abu Dhabi, United Arab Emirates. Association for Computational Linguistics.

Ellen M. Voorhees and Dawn M. Tice. 2000. The TREC-8 question answering track. In *Proceedings of the Second International Conference on Language Resources and Evaluation (LREC'00)*, Athens, Greece. European Language Resources Association (ELRA).

Jason Wei, Xuezhi Wang, Dale Schuurmans, Maarten Bosma, Ed Huai hsin Chi, F. Xia, Quoc Le, and Denny Zhou. 2022. Chain of thought prompting elicits reasoning in large language models. *ArXiv*, abs/2201.11903.

Wenhao Yu, Dan Iter, Shuohang Wang, Yichong Xu, Mingxuan Ju, Soumya Sanyal, Chenguang Zhu, Michael Zeng, and Meng Jiang. 2023. Generate rather than retrieve: Large language models are strong context generators. In *The Eleventh International Conference on Learning Representations*.

Tianyi Zhang, Varsha Kishore, Felix Wu, Kilian Q. Weinberger, and Yoav Artzi. 2019. Bertscore: Evaluating text generation with bert. *ArXiv*, abs/1904.09675.

A Dataset Statistics

We show detailed statistics about the MoQA dataset in Table 5. We also show the majority label for our yes/no questions in Table 6.

B Mechanical Turk

The annotation results of our MTurk campaign on the test set long-type questions is shown in Table 7.

C Pre-processing Steps

C.1 Original Natural Questions

Natural Question is a question answering dataset collected from the Google search engine. Real Google queries are first inputted into the Google search engine to obtain the top ranked Wikipedia page. Then, both the question and the Wikipedia article are given to annotators. The annotators first decide if a question is of good quality, in which case the annotator will attempt to find an answer to the question within the Wikipedia page. The annotators may not find a valid answer or select an HTML bounding box–typically a natural paragraph or a table–as the long answer. If a long answer is selected, then the annotator can choose to select a substring as the short answer or annotate the answer as simply "YES" or "NO". For more details about the original Natural Questions dataset, we refer readers to Kwiatkowski et al. (2019). If the annotator does not find an answer or deem the question of bad quality, then the annotator would denote the answer as "NULL".

We first obtain all the questions that are found in NQ-Open (Lee et al., 2019) and denote them as short-type questions. Specifically, these questions are all the questions that have at least one annotated answer that is 5 words or shorter.

For all other questions, we first filter out all questions where the top Wikipedia page title contains "(disambiguation)", "(disambiguation page)", "(List of .+)", "(Index of .+)", or "(Outline of .+)". Then, we use the Python library BeautifulSoup[7] to clean the HTML tags and obtain the text of each long answer(s) and short answer(s) associated with the question (if they exist).

We denote all questions with at least one short answer as medium-type questions. We denote all remaining questions with at least one YES/NO answers as yes/no-type questions. We denote all remaining questions with at least one long answer as long-type questions except for those questions where the long answer is originally from the HTML boxes "<table>", "<td>", "<tr>", or "<ol>" or if the length is shorter than 10 tokens. We do this because answers from tables and lists are often low quality after being converted to paragraph-like texts, when their structure is lost, or too short to fit the criteria of a long answer, and we discard these questions. We do not use any questions that were not annotated with a long answer.

Finally, we use the original development set as our test set, as the original test is hidden. Following the original Natural Questions, we filter out any questions in the test set that do not have at least 2 non-NULL annotations.

C.2 Long Answers

Since Natural Questions were collected at different timestamps, each Wikipedia page and therefore the long answers and short answers are from different times. This typically don't affect the short answers, because short spans of text can be easily found in different snapshots of Wikipedia.

However, long answers can be affected by minor grammar changes and the exact paragraph often cannot be found in different versions of Wikipedia. This poses a challenge for extractive models because some long answers might be unanswerable purely due to the difference in Wikipedia snapshots. Therefore, we replace every long answer with the corresponding string from the December 20, 2018, dump of Wikipedia, which is a popular version of Wikipedia dump used by many retrievers (Karpukhin et al., 2020, Lee et al., 2021). Specifically, we use the version where paragraphs are split into 100 token passages from Karpukhin et al. (2020) to minimize the variance in passage length.

To do this, we follow the matching strategy from KILT (Petroni et al., 2021). For every long answer, we first find the same Wikipedia article in our snapshot using the page title. Then, for each passage in the page, we find the span with the highest BLEU score to the long answer. We denote the passage containing the span with the highest BLEU as the gold passage, and the span as the long answer.

For long-type questions, we do an additional filtering where the best span must have a BLEU score of at least 0.5 to ensure that the matching long answer does not deviate significantly from the

[7]https://www.crummy.com/software/BeautifulSoup/bs4/doc/

Type	# Examples	% of Total	Avg. Question Length	Avg. Answer Length	Min Answer Length	Max Answer Length	Matched Long Answer
Train Set							
Short	79168	66.73	9.1	2.2	1	66	56346
Medium	16668	14.05	9.0	11.2	1	215	10891
Long	19649	16.56	9.1	76.5	4	100	19649
Yes/No	3154	2.66	9.1	1.0	1	1	2192
Total	118639	100	9.1	13.8	1	215	89078
Development Set							
Short	8757	66.69	9.0	2.2	1	37	6228
Medium	1853	14.11	9.1	11.2	2	140	1196
Long	2169	16.52	9.1	76.8	7	100	2169
Yes/No	351	2.67	8.9	1.0	1	1	234
Total	13130	100	9.0	13.8	1	140	9827
Test Set							
Short	3610	80.67	9.1	3.2	1	48	2645
Medium	565	12.63	9.0	13.0	1	62	406
Long	201	4.49	9.0	83.0	9	100	201
Yes/No	99	2.21	9.2	1.0	1	1	73
Total	4475	100	9.1	9.1	1	100	3325

Table 5: Comprehensive statistics of the MoQA dataset. Text length is calculated using whitespace tokenization. "Has Length" is the number of examples where a matching long answer was found in the 2018-12-20 Wikipedia snapshot. Recall that every example were originally annotated with at least one long answer, and the long answer matching process is descried in C.

Dataset	%Yes
Train	61.41
Dev	62.11
Test	69.70

Table 6: Percentage of YES in yes/no questions.

Annotation	Count
Long	201
Not Long	145
Total	346

Table 7: Resulting annotation of our Mechanical Turk (MTurk) campaign.

original long answer, and we discard any long-type questions where we fail to find such span.

For yes/no-type questions, we only add the gold passage and matching long answer annotation if the best span's BLEU score is 0.5, but we do not discard the questions where no matching long answer is found.

For short-type and medium-type question, we restrict the gold passage selection to only the passages where the short or medium answer is found as an exact substring, but use no BLEU score threshold when matching the long answer, because if the short or medium answer is found within the same Wikipedia page, then the long answer is likely to be found in one of the paragraphs. We also do not discard the questions where no matching long answer is found.

Therefore, every long-type question is guaranteed to have at least one matching long answer, while the other types are not guaranteed to have any matching long answer.

C.3 Unanswerable Questions

Although the original Natural Questions dataset (Kwiatkowski et al., 2019) includes questions that were not annotated with any answers, we chose not to include them in MoQA. This is because the nature of the dataset collection process does not guarantee the question to be unanswerable or truly have NULL as an answer.

Specifically, annotators are only shown the top Wikipedia result returned by the used search engine and they can only choose an extractive answer based on that Wikipedia article. However, it is not always true that the gold answer in the in top Wikipedia page returned by the search engine: they can exist in other pages.

Therefore, even though unanswerable questions are important to study (Rajpurkar et al., 2018), the questions not annotated with any answers in the original Natural Question cannot be taken as true

Retriever	Reader	Short	Medium	Long
DPR_{all}	$RoBERTa^{\dagger}_{*}$	78.8	72.4	71.7
	$FiD^{\dagger}_{*}$	80.3	74.5	71.0
None	$GPT\text{-}3^{\dagger}$	67.9(1.8)	60.2(0.2)	51.9(1.7)
None	Codex †	74.3(1.9)	62.6(0.9)	54.5(2.9)
None	$InstructGPT^{\dagger}$	68.0(0.3)	63.7(0.2)	59.1(0.2)
GENREAD	$InstructGPT^{\dagger}$	75.9(0.3)	65.2(0.6)	59.0(0.4)
DPR_{all}	$RoBERTa_{all}$	77.9	**67.2**	**59.1**
	Cls. + $RoBERTa_{*} \times 4$	77.7	61.5	52.4
	FiD_{all}	**80.0**	65.0	44.3
	Cls. + $FiD_{*} \times 4$	79.4	61.5	52.2
None	$T5\text{-}large_{all}$	64.9	56.4	46.5
None	GPT-3	63.2(2.8)	56.4(1.3)	51.4(1.3)
None	Codex	67.4(3.9)	58.7(1.5)	54.6(0.8)
None	InstructGPT	60.5(1.4)	61.5(0.8)	57.5(0.4)
GENREAD	InstructGPT	73.1(0.7)	65.6(0.3)	51.6(0.4)

Table 8: BERTScore(Zhang et al., 2019) results on the MoQA test set. For the LLMs, we show the mean and the standard deviation in parentheses across three randomly seeded runs. †: An oracle that assumes that the question type is known and uses a reader trained only on each individual type. Cls.: a question classifier is used, and there are four readers trained independently, either for RoBERTa or FiD. Otherwise, all questions are jointly trained. $T5\text{-}large_{all}$: a closed-book QA model trained on all questions. GPT-3(Brown et al., 2020): `davinci` model with two-shot ICL. InstructGPT(Ouyang et al., 2022): `text-davinci-003` model with two-shot ICL. Codex(Chen et al., 2021): `code-davinci-002` model with two-shot ICL.

unanswerable questions without significantly more annotations.

D Evaluation

For retrieval, we regard a retrieved passage is correct if the passage contains the matching long answer of the question (we exclude the questions without matching long answers in retrieval evaluation). We report accuracy@k that checks if the top k retrieved passages contains a correct passage. We also report mean reciprocal rank (MRR)@k, which averages the reciprocal rank of the top correct passage.

For the final answer, we report the exact match (EM) and the F1 score for short-type and medium-type questions, EM and ROUGE-L for long answers, and accuracy for yes/no-type questions. Although EM is often the primary metric used in open-domain QA research, we believe that the F1 and ROUGE-L scores are more suitable for medium and long answers following past work on long-form QA (Fan et al., 2019; Stelmakh et al., 2022; Khashabi et al., 2021). We also report the macro-averaged EM, which averages the EM scores across the 4 question types.

Furthermore, we also report the BERTScore(Zhang et al., 2019) on short, medium, and long-type questions. BERTScore is a model-based metrics that is better at capturing semantic similarities between long-form texts than traditional metrics. This is especially important for the medium and long type questions, since there are many possible ways of answering the question without using the exact same words. We use the authors' implementation[8] and the set-up with the best human correlation score at the time of writing: model is `microsoft/deberta-xlarge-mnli`[9] and the layer is 40[10]. We found that the BERTScore correlates with F1 scores and ROUGE-L scores on short, medium, and long type answers. This suggests that the best performing models RoBERTaall and FiDall also output the most semantically similar texts to the ground truth answers.

[8] `https://github.com/Tiiiger/bert_score`

[9] `https://huggingface.co/microsoft/deberta-xlarge-mnli`

[10] hash is `microsoft/deberta-xlarge-mnli_L40_no-idf_version=0.3.12(hug_trans=4.23.0)`

E Retrieval

We use the code repo[11] from Karpukhin et al. (2020) for our DPR experiments. We also follow all of their hyperparameter settings; specifically, we use a learning rate of 2×10^{-5}, and a per GPU batch size of 16 and a gradient accumulation of 2 on 4 80GB A100 GPUs to achieve a total batch size of 128. We train for 40 epochs, except for DPR$_{\text{yesno-gold}}$ and DPR$_{\text{yesno-DS}}$ where we train for 400 epochs due to its small train set. We then use the model with the highest validation rank loss as our final model.

Similar to the original DPR, we also explore how the final retrieval model perform when using the annotated gold passage and when using a distant-supervision annotation approach that selects the positive passage based on the answer alone. These two strategies are particularly interesting to investigate in Natural Questions because it's unique from other open-domain QA dataset such that all answers are grounded in one gold passage.

In this section, we describe our two approaches to training DPR, even though we only present DPR trained using gold passages in the main results.

E.1 Distantly-Supervised DPR

In distant supervision, we first retrieve the top 100 passages from the corpus using an BM25 index. We use the Pyserini[12] implementation of BM25. The input to the BM25 search is the question in each example, and we use the default BM25 hyperparameters also used by DPR (Karpukhin et al., 2020). Specifically, the parameters we use are: $b = 0.4$ (document length normalization) and $k1 = 0.9$ (term frequency scaling). Then, for each question-answer pair, we choose the positive passages by checking if the answer exists within the retrieved passage.

Another interesting aspect to consider is which answer we use for selecting the positive passage. Namely, we can use either short or long answers for short questions, and medium or long answers for medium questions. From preliminary experiments, we found that using the long answers for choosing the positive passages for short questions performed better on the development set while using the medium answers for choosing the positive passages for medium questions. This is likely due to long answer filtering reduces the number of false positives, and it is often likely to get the short answer string in irrelevant passages, and even though the training set size is reduced significantly, the higher quality of data makes up for the smaller dataset. However, using medium answers for filtering already obtain high enough quality of positive passages such that the harsher filtering with long answers will cut down on the training set size enough that it hurts retrieval performance.

When using long answer for filtering, we use a fuzzy matching where the positive passages are those that obtain a BLEU score of at least 0.5 with the long answer. When using short/medium answers for filtering, we check for exact match within the passage. All passages that were filtered out are used as hard negative passages.

For DPR$_{\text{all-DS}}$, we use the strategy that worked the best for each individual types. Specifically, we use long answer filtering for short, long, and yes/no

[11]https://github.com/facebookresearch/DPR

[12]https://github.com/castorini/pyserini

Retriever	A@1	A@5	A@20	MRR@20	
Short					
DPR$_{\text{short-DS}}$	20k	**35.5**	58.4	**73.1**	45.6
DPR$_{\text{medium-DS}}$	8k	23.6	42.6	58.0	32.5
DPR$_{\text{long-DS}}$	8k	27.3	46.9	62.5	36.4
DPR$_{\text{yesno-DS}}$	1k	16.7	31.4	43.6	23.4
DPR$_{\text{all-DS}}$	36k	35.4	**58.9**	**73.1**	**45.8**
Medium					
DPR$_{\text{short-DS}}$	20k	42.4	67.7	**85.0**	53.7
DPR$_{\text{medium-DS}}$	8k	38.7	64.5	75.6	49.5
DPR$_{\text{long-DS}}$	8k	37.9	66.0	79.1	50.2
DPR$_{\text{yesno-DS}}$	1k	28.1	43.1	56.2	34.7
DPR$_{\text{all-DS}}$	36k	**44.3**	**69.7**	83.5	**55.7**
Long					
DPR$_{\text{short-DS}}$	20k	30.4	52.2	67.2	40.0
DPR$_{\text{medium-DS}}$	8k	26.9	45.3	57.2	35.1
DPR$_{\text{long-DS}}$	8k	**34.8**	**59.2**	70.7	**45.6**
DPR$_{\text{yesno-DS}}$	1k	22.9	33.8	45.8	28.5
DPR$_{\text{all-DS}}$	36k	33.8	55.7	**71.6**	43.8
Yes/No					
DPR$_{\text{short-DS}}$	20k	**31.5**	54.8	71.2	43.1
DPR$_{\text{medium-DS}}$	8k	26.0	52.1	65.8	38.2
DPR$_{\text{long-DS}}$	8k	**31.5**	57.5	76.7	44.4
DPR$_{\text{yesno-DS}}$	1k	27.4	52.1	65.8	37.8
DPR$_{\text{all-DS}}$	36k	28.8	**65.8**	**82.2**	**45.0**

Table 9: Passage retrieval results on the MoQA test set using distantly-supervised DPR models. We retrieve top k passages from each model and evaluate them based on the presence of the gold long answer in the passages. We report top-k retrieval accuracy (A@k), and mean reciprocal rank at k (MRR@k).

Retriever		A@1	A@5	A@20	MRR@20
Short					
$\text{DPR}_{\text{short-gold}}$	56k	33.6	59.7	75.1	45.0
$\text{DPR}_{\text{medium-gold}}$	11k	27.0	50.4	67.0	37.4
$\text{DPR}_{\text{long-gold}}$	20k	23.8	48.7	65.1	34.7
$\text{DPR}_{\text{yesno-gold}}$	2k	17.7	34.4	48.5	25.2
$\text{DPR}_{\text{all-gold}}$	89k	**36.0**	**62.8**	**77.0**	**47.6**
Medium					
$\text{DPR}_{\text{short-gold}}$	56k	30.3	62.8	81.0	44.5
$\text{DPR}_{\text{medium-gold}}$	11k	**45.8**	**71.9**	**86.7**	**57.9**
$\text{DPR}_{\text{long-gold}}$	20k	32.3	64.5	81.0	46.1
$\text{DPR}_{\text{yesno-gold}}$	2k	27.8	50.2	63.3	37.3
$\text{DPR}_{\text{all-gold}}$	89k	41.4	69.5	83.3	53.7
Long					
$\text{DPR}_{\text{short-gold}}$	56k	24.4	51.7	69.7	36.9
$\text{DPR}_{\text{medium-gold}}$	11k	28.9	52.2	65.7	39.0
$\text{DPR}_{\text{long-gold}}$	20k	34.8	**65.2**	78.1	47.4
$\text{DPR}_{\text{yesno-gold}}$	2k	20.4	42.3	54.2	29.7
$\text{DPR}_{\text{all-gold}}$	89k	**37.8**	64.7	**80.6**	**49.2**
Yes/No					
$\text{DPR}_{\text{short-gold}}$	56k	24.7	43.8	75.3	35.2
$\text{DPR}_{\text{medium-gold}}$	11k	24.7	53.4	69.9	36.6
$\text{DPR}_{\text{long-gold}}$	20k	21.9	54.8	**79.5**	38.3
$\text{DPR}_{\text{yesno-gold}}$	2k	35.6	57.5	72.6	45.9
$\text{DPR}_{\text{all-gold}}$	89k	**37.0**	**64.4**	**79.5**	**49.7**

Table 10: Passage retrieval results on the MoQA test set using gold passage supervised DPR models. We retrieve top k passages from each model and evaluate them based on the presence of the gold long answer in the passages. We report top-k retrieval accuracy (A@k), and mean reciprocal rank at k (MRR@k).

questions and medium answer filtering for medium questions.

E.2 Gold Passage Supervised DPR

Our main results use the gold passage supervised DPR. We follow the BM25 retrieval steps previously described, but we choose our positive passage differently. That is, we denote the gold passage as the positive passage for every question, and we choose all other retrieved passages as the hard negative passages, except for the gold passage if it were retrieved. Our final model DPR_{all} uses all questions and their gold passages.

F Reader

F.1 Extractive Reader

For the reader model, we employ a similar architecture to the reader model from Karpukhin et al. (2020). However, one additional change we make is prepending every passage with two special tokens: `[YES]` and `[NO]`. This is a necessary addition in order to always give the reader model the choice of outputting `YES/NO`. We separate these two special tokens from the rest of the passage with a separator token </s>.

Before training the reader, we first run inference on the retriever and obtain the top 100 passages for each question. We train the reader model on 8 RTX-3090 GPU. We train $\text{RoBERTa}_{\text{all}}$ for 5 epochs, $\text{RoBERTa}_{\text{short}}$ and $\text{RoBERTa}_{\text{medium}}$ for 10 epochs, $\text{RoBERTa}_{\text{long}}$ for 20 epochs, $\text{RoBERTa}_{\text{yesno}}$ for 40 epochs. We use a learning rate of 2×10^{-5} and a batch size of 32 questions with 24 passages each; specifically, we use a batch size of 1 question with 24 passages per GPU and a gradient accumulation of 4. However, we use a total batch size of 16 for $\text{RoBERTa}_{\text{yesno}}$ due to its small training set by reducing the gradient accumulation to 2.

We first did a hyperparameter sweep over batch size $= \{16, 32\}$ and learning rate $= \{1 \times 10^{-5}, 2 \times 10^{-5}\}$ for each question type, and select our final model based on the development set performance.

For each question, we use 1 positive passage and 23 negative passages. The positive passages for short-type, medium-type, and long-type questions are passages that contain the gold answer, and the negative passages are any passages that do not contain the gold answer. We annotate the positive passage with the starting and ending position of all answers in the passage. The positive passages for yes/no-type questions are the retrieved passages with the highest F1 score with the long answer, and all other passages can serve as negative passages. In practice, we use the passages with the lowest F1 score with the long answer as negative passages. We annotate these positive passages with the correct answer span as the special tokens `[YES]` or `[NO]` accordingly to the answer.

For each question, we maximize the marginal log-likelihood of all correct spans in the positive passage combined with the log-likelihood of the correct passage being selected. We refer reader to Karpukhin et al. (2020) for more details.

During evaluation, we input the top 50 retrieved passages and select the span with the highest combined span score and passage rank score. We follow the computation in Karpukhin et al. (2020). We chose to include the top 50 passages by first sweeping over the hyperparameter $k = \{10, 25, 50, 100\}$, and chose the best k on the development set.

F.2 Fusion-in-Decoder

We follow (Izacard and Grave, 2021) and use their code repo[13] for training our FiD models, which uses T5-base. We follow the hyperparameters described in the original paper: the top 100 retrieved passages and their title are included in the input during training and evaluation, learning rate is 1×10^{-4}, 10k total steps with 1k warm up steps, and a batch size of 64. We train on 8 RTX-3090 GPUs and a gradient accumulation of 8. We evaluate the model every 500 steps and chose the model with the best development set performance for our final model.

G Classifier

We train our classifier similar to sentence classification tasks. Specifically, we use the pre-trained RoBERTa-base (Liu et al., 2019) as our base model, and finetune it for 10 epochs over our entire dataset. The input is the question, and we use the last hidden state of the `[CLS]` token followed by a linear layer and softmax to predict the probabilities of four question types. We use Huggingface[14]'s implementation of RoBERTaForSequenceClassification to train our classifier; we use Cross Entropy Loss to maximum the log probability of the correct question type.

For our hyperparameters, we use a batch size of 8 and a learning rate of 1×10^{-5}. We performed hyperparameter search over batch size $= \{8, 16, 32\}$ and learning rate $= \{1 \times 10^{-5}, 2 \times 10^{-5}, 5 \times 10^{-5}\}$, and chose the model with the highest accuracy on the development set. We also evaluate the model after every epoch and choose the model with the best development accuracy.

H Closed-Book QA

H.1 Supervised models

For supervised closed-book QA, we use T5-large (Raffel et al., 2019) as our base model. T5-large$_{\text{all}}$ is trained on all question types together. We follow (Roberts et al., 2020) for training with a constant learning rate of 0.001. We use a batch size per GPU of 8 and 8 32GB GPUs for a total batch size of 64. We train for 20k steps, and evaluate using beam search with a beam size of 4. We evaluate our model on the development set every 1k steps and choose the model with the highest performance on the development set for our final model.

[13]`https://github.com/facebookresearch/FiD`

[14]`https://huggingface.co`

H.2 Unsupervised Large Language Models

We use the following large language models in our experiments: GPT-3 (`davinci`; (Brown et al., 2020)), Codex (`code-davinci-002`; (Chen et al., 2021)), and InstructGPT (`text-davinci-003`; Ouyang et al., 2022).

The prompt used for the two-shot experiments with only two demonstration from one question type is shown in 5. We follow the same prompting strategy for the experiments with two demonstrations from each question type. Furthermore, we balance the in-context examples such that the first four demonstrations contain one example from each question type and that the last four demonstrations also contain one example from each question type. We also use one yes/no question with `YES` as the answer and another question with `NO` as the answer with the yes/no-type questions are used in the demonstrations.

For the experiments with GENREAD, we use the two-step prompting strategy shown in 6, but other experimental setups are identical to the experiments without GENREAD.

I Human Evaluation

We describe our procedure for assigning the correctness score and the explanation in further detail here. We also show examples of the annotation in 11.

We use the following guidelines when assigning the correctness score:

1. We assign an output o_i with $\texttt{correct}(o_i) =$ correct if it is factually correct and supported by A_i even if the word/phrasing is not exact. For instance, the question "Who is the 44th President of the United States" has multiple valid outputs: "Obama", "Barack Obama", and "Barack Hussein Obama" even though only "Barack Obama" is annotated as the old answer.

2. We assign an output o_i with $\texttt{correct}(o_i) =$ relevant if it does not correctly answer the question q_i according to A_i, but include some relevant information. For instance, an example of such output to the question "Who is the 44th President of the United States" include "Donald Trump" (who is the 45th President

Context	→	Q: What two products are produced in the dehydration synthesis of two amino acids? A: a molecule of water (H2O) and two amino acids joined by a peptide bond Q: When does it change from bc to ad? A: conception or birth of Jesus of Nazareth Q: What purpose did seasonal monsoon winds have on trade?
Completion	→	A:

Figure 5: Example of two-shot in-context learning used for large pretrained language models. We prompt the model with Context + A: and take the generation as the final output.

Context	→	Q: What purpose did seasonal monsoon winds have on trade?
Completion 1	→	Passage: The seasonal monsoon winds were an important factor in the development of trade in the Indian Ocean region. The monsoons were used to transport goods and people from the Arabian Peninsula to India, and from India to East Africa and Southeast Asia. The monsoons also allowed traders to travel from the Persian Gulf to the Bay of Bengal and the Malay Peninsula. The monsoons were also used to transport goods from India to China, and from China to the Middle East. The monsoons allowed traders to travel from the Persian Gulf to the Bay of Bengal and the Malay Peninsula.
Completion 2	→	A: The seasonal monsoon winds were an important factor in the development of trade in the Indian Ocean region, allowing traders to travel from the Persian Gulf to the Bay of Bengal and the Malay Peninsula.

Figure 6: Example of zero-shot in-context learning with GENREAD used for large pretrained language models. We first prompt the model with Context + Passage: to generate Completion 1. Then, we prompt the model again with the Context + Completion 1 + A: to generate the answer. We take the generation from the second step as the final output.

of the United States) and "Joe Biden" (who was Obama's Vice President as well as the 46th President of the United States). In practice, this is the most common mistake that models make, where if the ground truth answer is a politician, artist, or date, the model would typically output something in the same category. Furthermore, outputs are also put into this category if only parts of the output is factually correct but also contain unsupported information (e.g. "Obama and Biden" in this example).

3. We assign an output o_i with $\texttt{correct}(o_i) =$ wrong if it does not correctly answer the question q_i according to A_i and does not include any relevant information. For instance, an example of such output to the question "Who is the 44th President of the United States" could be "turtle eggs". In practice, this mistake rarely occurs, and we only assign this score when there is no obvious connection between the output and the question topic.

In general, the procedure for determining the explanation score involves first reading the question and the ground truth answers to decide the minimal amount of information that is needed to answer the entire question. For instance, if the question asks "what are Poseidon's symbols and what do they mean?", then an appropriate answer should include all of his symbols in Greek mythology (e.g. the trident, the horse, the bull, etc.) as well as the meaning of each symbol. If the output only include one symbol or multiple symbols without their meaning, then we would consider the output to be not sufficient, yielding a score of lacking. If the output includes things beyond the symbols but also the stories from Greek mythology about Poseidon, then we will consider the output to be too long, yielding a score of extra.

J Prediction Samples

We show example output for selected models for each question type in Figures 12, 13, 15, and 14. It is interesting to note that while both models are capable of outputting the correct answers and the appropriate granularity for some question, they still have much room for improvement. For example, both models can generate a short answer where a long answer would be more appropriate, while

Question Type	Question	Model	Output	Correctness Score	Sufficency Score
Short	who plays the woodsman in over the garden wall	FiD$_{all}$	Christopher Lloyd	Correct	Good
		GPT-3$_{all}$	Tom Kenny	Relevant	Good
Medium	what is the meaning of the greek word metanoia	RoBERTa$_{all}$	a transformative change of heart; especially: a spiritual conversion	Correct	Good
		GPT-3$_{all}$	metanoia is a Greek word meaning "change of mind" or "change of heart". It is used in the New Testament to describe a change of mind or heart in regards to one's relationship with God.	Correct	Extra
Long	where does the expression go commando come from	RoBERTa$_{all}$	The origins of the phrase "go commando" are uncertain, with some speculating that it may refer to being "out in the open" or "ready for action". "Slate" magazineś Daniel Engber dates the modern usage to United States college campuses circa 1974, where it was perhaps associated with soldiers in the Vietnam War, who were reputed to go without underwear to "increase ventilation and reduce moisture". However, more recently, Graeme Donald has pointed out that the US forces are "Rangers" rather than "Commandos"	Correct	Good
		GPT-3$_{all}$	The term commando is derived from the Spanish word comando, meaning a "detachment" or "body of troops". In English, "commando" was originally a term for a type of soldier, but in the United States military it has come to mean a member of certain special forces units.	Relevant	Good
		InstructGPT$_{all}$	The phrase "go commando" is believed to have originated in the British military during World War II.	Correct	Lacking
		FiD-all$_{all}$	unknown	Wrong	Lacking
Yes/No	do irish passport holders need visa for thailand	GPT-3$_{all}$	No, Irish citizens do not require a visa to enter Thailand.	Correct	Extra
		InstructGPT$_{all}$	No	Correct	Good

Table 11: Prediction samples from the test set with the correctness and sufficency scores.

they can also generate some short answer where a yes/no answer would be correct.

It is also worth noting that questions that may appear to require short answers may actually require a much more length explanation. In other words, even though "who", "when", and "where" questions may seem to only require short answers, they can actually sometimes require much longer explanation. For example, both "Who is responsible for redrawing congressional and legislative districts?" and "Who is covered under payment of gratuity act 1972?" may appear to be simple and straight forward at first, but there is actually greater complexity behind the question that cannot be answered by just a few words, and it only becomes clear that they require length explanations given extensive knowledge on the topic. It is worth noting that our classifier model classifies both of those questions as short questions, which motivates future work into question classification.

Other questions that require long answers even though they appear to be short questions include:

- "When is a system said to be reproducible?"
- "Where does the word christ come from and what does it mean?"
- "What makes miranda a central character in the tempest?"
- "Where does the term spelling bee come from?"

In summary, question type classification is not as simple and straight forward as it may appear, and it actually requires extensive knowledge on the related background.

Short - *answers up to 5 tokens*

Q: Who plays the woodsman in over the garden wall?
A: Christopher Lloyd
DPR$_{all}$+ RoBERTa$_{all}$: Christopher Lloyd
DPR$_{all}$+ FiD$_{all}$: Christopher Lloyd
GPT-3: Tom Kenny
GenRead+ InstructGPT: Christopher Lloyd

Q: Who has a ring of power in lotr?
A: Sauron
DPR$_{all}$+ RoBERTa$_{all}$: Frodo
DPR$_{all}$+ FiD$_{all}$: Sauron
GPT-3: Sauron
GenRead+ InstructGPT: Sauron

Q: the witch and the hundred knight 2 us release
A: 'March 2018' *or* 'March 27, 2018'
DPR$_{all}$+ RoBERTa$_{all}$: March 2018
DPR$_{all}$+ FiD$_{all}$: March 2018
GPT-3: The Witch and the Hundred Knight 2 is a Japanese action role-playing game developed by Nippon Ichi Software and published by NIS America. It is the sequel to The Witch and the Hundred Knight, and was released in Japan on March 24, 2017, and in North America and Europe on August 29, 2017.
GenRead+ InstructGPT: March 27, 2018

Table 12: Prediction samples on a short-type question from the test set.

Medium - *answers more than 5 tokens*

Q: What is the meaning of the greek word metanoia?
A: a transformative change of heart; especially: a spiritual conversion
DPR$_{all}$+ RoBERTa$_{all}$: a transformative change of heart; especially: a spiritual conversion
DPR$_{all}$+ FiD$_{all}$: a transformative change of heart
GPT-3: metanoia is a Greek word meaning "change of mind" or "change of heart". It is used in the New Testament to describe a change of mind or heart in regards to one's relationship with God.
GenRead+ InstructGPT: change of heart, mind, and outlook

Q: Where do you get male pattern baldness from?
A: combination of genetics and the male hormone dihydrotestosterone
DPR$_{all}$+ RoBERTa$_{all}$: genetics
DPR$_{all}$+ FiD$_{all}$: genetics
GPT-3: The most common cause of male pattern baldness is a genetic predisposition. Male pattern baldness is an inherited trait that is passed down from your parents.
GenRead+ InstructGPT: a combination of genetics and hormones

Q: the stonewall riot in new york city in 1969 involved a protest by
A: 'members of the gay (LGBT) community' *or* 'the gay (LGBT) community'
DPR$_{all}$+ RoBERTa$_{all}$: members of the gay (LGBT) community
DPR$_{all}$+ FiD$_{all}$: members of the gay (LGBT) community
GPT-3: gay men and lesbians
GenRead+ InstructGPT: members of the gay community

Table 13: Prediction samples on a medium-type question from the test set.

Yes/no - *answers yes/no*
Q: Do Irish passport holders need visa for Thailand? **A**: NO **DPR$_{all}$+ RoBERTa$_{all}$**: YES **DPR$_{all}$+ FiD$_{all}$**: YES **GPT-3**: No, Irish citizens do not a visa to enter Thailand. **GENREAD+ InstructGPT**: NO
Q: Does any country still fly the f4 phantom? **A**: YES **DPR$_{all}$+ RoBERTa$_{all}$**: YES **DPR$_{all}$+ FiD$_{all}$**: Iran GPT-3: Yes, the United States Air Force still flies the F-4 Phantom II. The F-4 was retired from the U.S. Navy in the 1990s, but the U.S. Marine Corps continues to operate the F-4. The F-4 is also operated by the militaries of Egypt, Greece, Iran, Israel, Japan, South Korea, Turkey, and Taiwan. **GENREAD+ InstructGPT**: YES, Iran
Q: Is there going to be another season of degrassi next class? **A**: YES **DPR$_{all}$+ RoBERTa$_{all}$**: YES **DPR$_{all}$+ FiD$_{all}$**: YES **GPT-3**: Yes, there will be a fifth season of Degrassi: Next Class. **GENREAD+ InstructGPT**: NO

Table 14: Prediction samples on a yes/no-type question from the test set.

Long - *answers in paragraph*
Q: Where does the expression go commando come from? **A**: The origins of the phrase "go commando" are uncertain, with some speculating that it may refer to being "out in the open" or "ready for action". "Slate" magazineś Daniel Engber dates the modern usage to United States college campuses circa 1974, where it was perhaps associated with soldiers in the Vietnam War, who were reputed to go without underwear to "increase ventilation and reduce moisture". However, more recently, Graeme Donald has pointed out that the US forces are "Rangers" rather than "Commandos" **DPR$_{all}$+ RoBERTa$_{all}$**: The origins of the phrase "go commando" are uncertain, with some speculating that it may refer to being "out in the open" or "ready for action". "Slate" magazine's Daniel Engber dates the modern usage to United States college campuses circa 1974, where it was perhaps associated with soldiers in the Vietnam War, who were reputed to go without underwear to "increase ventilation and reduce moisture". However, more recently, Graeme Donald has pointed out that the US forces are "Rangers" rather than "Commandos", and **DPR$_{all}$+ FiD$_{all}$**: unknown **GPT-3**: The term commando is derived from the Spanish word comando, meaning a "detachment" or "body of troops". In English, "commando" was originally a term for a type of soldier, but in the United States military it has come to mean a member of certain special forces units. **GENREAD+ InstructGPT**: The phrase "go commando" is believed to have originated in the British military during World War II.
Q: bankruptcy abuse prevention and consumer protection act of 2005 summary **A**: Bankruptcy Abuse Prevention and Consumer Protection Act of 2005 (BAPCPA) (), is a legislative act that made several significant changes to the United States Bankruptcy Code. Referred to colloquially as the "New Bankruptcy Law", the Act of Congress attempts to, among other things, make it more difficult for some consumers to file bankruptcy under Chapter 7; some of these consumers may instead utilize Chapter 13. Voting record of S. 256. **DPR$_{all}$+ RoBERTa$_{all}$**: The Bankruptcy Abuse Prevention and Consumer Protection Act of 2005 (BAPCPA) (), is a legislative act that made several significant changes to the United States Bankruptcy Code. Referred to colloquially as the "New Bankruptcy Law", the Act of Congress attempts to, among other things, make it more difficult for some consumers to file bankruptcy under Chapter 7; some of these consumers may instead utilize Chapter 13 **DPR$_{all}$+ FiD$_{all}$**: YES **GPT-3**: The Bankruptcy Abuse Prevention and Consumer Protection Act of 2005 (BAPCPA) is a United States federal law that made major changes in the United States Bankruptcy Code. The Act was passed by the 109th United States Congress and signed into law by President George W. Bush on April 20, 2005. The Act was the first major overhaul of the United States Bankruptcy Code since 1978. **GENREAD+ InstructGPT**: The Bankruptcy Abuse Prevention and Consumer Protection Act of 2005 (BAPCPA) is a federal law that made it more difficult for individuals to file for bankruptcy under Chapter 7. The law requires debtors to pass a means test to determine if they are eligible to file for Chapter 7 bankruptcy. It also requires debtors to complete a credit counseling course before filing for bankruptcy. Additionally, the law makes it more difficult for debtors to discharge certain types of debts, such as student loans and domestic support obligations.
Q: What are poseidon's symbols and what do they mean? **A**: In Greek myth, Poseidon used his trident to create water sources in Greece and the horse. Poseidon, as well as being god of the sea, was also known as the "Earth Shaker" because when he struck the earth in anger he caused mighty earthquakes and he used his trident to stir up tidal waves, tsunamis and sea storms. In relation to its fishing origins, the trident is associated with Poseidon, the god of the sea in Greek mythology **DPR$_{all}$+ RoBERTa$_{all}$**:love interest of the Cyclops Polyphemus.They symbolized everything that is beautiful and kind about the sea **DPR$_{all}$+ FiD$_{all}$**: the god of the sea **GPT-3**: Poseidon's symbols are a trident and a dolphin. The trident is a three-pronged spear, and the dolphin is a creature that is half fish and half mammal. **GENREAD+ InstructGPT**: The trident symbolizes his power over the sea, the horse symbolizes his power over horses, the bull symbolizes his power over earthquakes, and the dolphin symbolizes his power over the sea creatures. He was also associated with the colors blue and green, which symbolize the sea and the land, respectively.

Table 15: Prediction samples on a long-type question from the test set.

Exploration of multilingual prompts in document-grounded dialogue

Xiaocheng Zhang[1], **Xuelin Fu**[2], **Yongqing Huang**[3], **Xiaohong Su**[†]
[1,†]Harbin Institute of Technology, Harbin, Heilongjiang, China
[2]Guilin University of Technology, Guilin, Guangxi, China
[3]Guangdong University of Technology, Guangzhou, Guangdong, China
22s136029@stu.hit.edu.cn 1735573894@qq.com 1486590231@qq.com
sxh@hit.edu.cn

Abstract

Transferring DGD models from high-resource languages to low-resource languages is a meaningful but challenging task. Being able to provide multilingual responses to multilingual documents further complicates the task. This paper describes our method at DialDoc23 Shared Task (Document-Grounded Dialogue and Conversational Question Answering) for generate responses based on the most relevant passage retrieved. We divide it into three steps of retrieval, re-ranking and generation. Our methods include negative sample augmentation, prompt learning, pseudo-labeling and ensemble. On the submission page, we rank 2nd based on the sum of token-level F1, SacreBleu and Rouge-L scores used for the final evaluation, and get the total score of 210.25.

1 Introduction

Our team fanjuanju participates in the Third DialDoc Workshop Shared Task co-located with ACL 2023. The goal of this task is to query document knowledge through a multilingual dialogue system. The dataset contains 797 dialogues in Vietnamese (3,446 turns), 816 dialogues in French (3,510 turns), and a corpus of 17272 paragraphs, that each dialogue turn is grounded in a paragraph from the corpus. We need to use the dialogue history and the current query to retrieval the paragraph that supports the answer to the current question, and generate corresponding responses based on the knowledge in the paragraph. The score is calculated based on the sum of token-level F1(Rajpurkar et al., 2016), SacreBleu(Post, 2018) and Rouge-L metrics, hereinafter referred to as F1, Bleu, Rouge respectively.

2 Related Work

2.1 Document-grounded Dialogue (DGD)

When we have a conversation, we usually refer to the document information we know. DGD refers to the technology that uses the document as a reference in the conversation to support the conversation interaction. In practical applications, such as customer service conversation system, smart home control, etc, the document can be a product description, user manual or an article, in this case, documentation is external knowledge provided to the model, and document-based conversations can help people find answers and solve problems faster. Doc2dial(Feng et al., 2020), a doc-based dialogue data set, consists of two tasks: 1. Seeking sentences related to questions from documents (information-seeking); 2. Use the results of the previous step to generate a reasonable response; In Chinese, there are movie-chats published by Tsinghua University, in which both parties are chatting about one or more movies in a dataset; Existing document dialogue data sets mainly focus on the plain text content in documents, while ignoring the importance of common structural information such as title, serial number and table in documents to machine understanding of document content. Therefore, Doc2Bot(Fu et al., 2022), a large-scale multi-domain document dialogue data set in Chinese, was proposed by Fu et al.

2.2 Pre-trained language models

The representation of natural language is to represent human language in a way that is easier for computer to understand. Methods such as word2vec(Mikolov et al., 2013) and glove(Pennington et al., 2014) based on deep learning can represent words with similar semantics, but they can't solve the polysemy problem well. The subsequent Elmo(Peters et al., 2018), which takes into account contextual information, can better solve the polysemy representation problem. And Elmo started the pre-training and fine-tuning paradigm. Since Elmo, transformer(Vaswani et al., 2017), as a more powerful feature extractor than lstm, has been applied to various subsequent pre-

Proceedings of the Third DialDoc Workshop on Document-grounded Dialogue and Conversational Question Answering, pages 30–35
July 13, 2023 ©2023 Association for Computational Linguistics

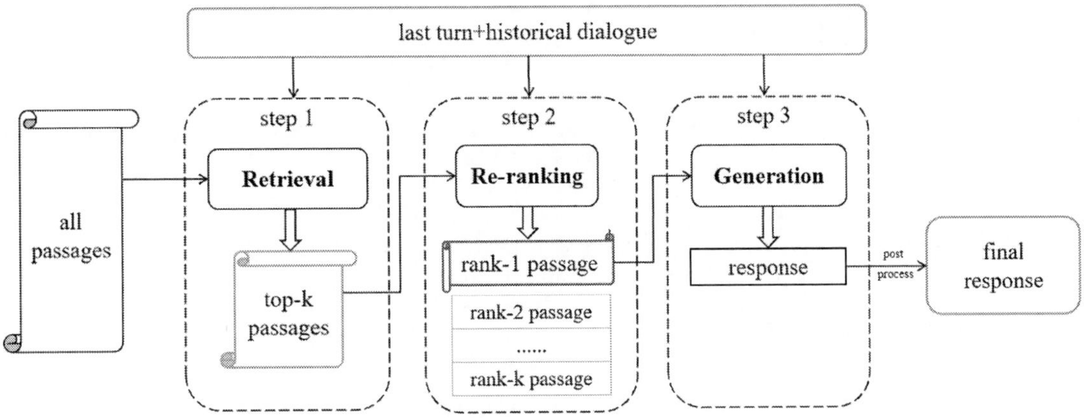

Figure 1: The framework we used in this competition.

training language models (such as GPT(Radford et al., 2018) and BERT(Devlin et al., 2019)), constantly updating the existing optimal results in various tasks of natural language processing. The most classic pre-training language model is BERT, which designed two pre-training tasks to dynamically learn word vectors. There are many subsequent improved versions of BERT, such as roberta dynamic masking(Liu et al., 2021), Bert-wwm(Cui et al., 2021) implementation of full word masking in Chinese, and ernie(Zhang et al., 2019) introducing entity information, etc. GPT series models are more representative of autoregressive models, which learn word vectors by predicting the next word by the current statement. These pre-training models pretrain and learn on large-scale corpus, and then fine-tune downstream tasks to fit the current data. For this competition, we also relied on the "shoulders of giants" of the pre-training language model, and since the data set was geared towards French and Vietnamese, we used a multi-language version of the pre-training language model for this competition.

3 Method

According to baseline(Zhang et al., 2023), we divide the tasks into three steps: retrieval, re-ranking and generation. Firstly, we use the method of contrast learning to train the retrieval model, and expand the negative example in the training process to improve the performance of the retrieval model. In the re-ranking step, we fine-tune the XLM-RoBERTa(Conneau et al., 2020) and InfoXLM(Chi et al., 2021) models, then ensemble the two models to predict the scores of the retrieved paragraphs. In the generation step, we use the prompt learning method to fine-tune MT5(Xue et al., 2021) to generate the corresponding language response, and finally add the pseudo-tag retraining to get the final response. The framework we used in this competition is illustrated in Figure 1.

3.1 Retrieval

Based on the conventional comparative learning training method, the original data set is divided into n small batches of data, and the n mini-batches of data are stored in advance. When training begins, each training batch is constructed with a normal In-Batch(IB) negative sample. At the same time, for n mini-batches of data stored in advance, if i >= 1, the previous batch of data is taken to construct incremental negative samples. We use e_{Query} and $e_{Passage}$ to represent the vectors of query and passage respectively, and use the cosine similarity function to calculate the correlation score between them.

$$cos(e_{Query}, e_{Passage}) = \frac{e_{Query} \cdot e_{Passage}}{\| e_{Query} \| \| e_{Passage} \|} \quad (1)$$

When prescribed to Addictive Margin InfoNCE Loss(Chen et al., 2020)(Yang et al., 2019) and a learnable temperature parameter τ, it's the following:

$$\mathcal{L} = -log\frac{e^{(\varphi(h,r,t)-\gamma)/\tau}}{e^{(\varphi(h,r,t)-\gamma)/\tau} + \sum_{i=1}^{|N|} e^{(\varphi(h,r,t_i))/\tau}} \quad (2)$$

Margin $\gamma > 0$, usually 1.0. is the score of the triplet, which is in the range of -1 to 1. The temperature t is adjustable and $\tau = log\frac{1}{\tau}$ is defined as a learnable parameter(Wang et al., 2022).

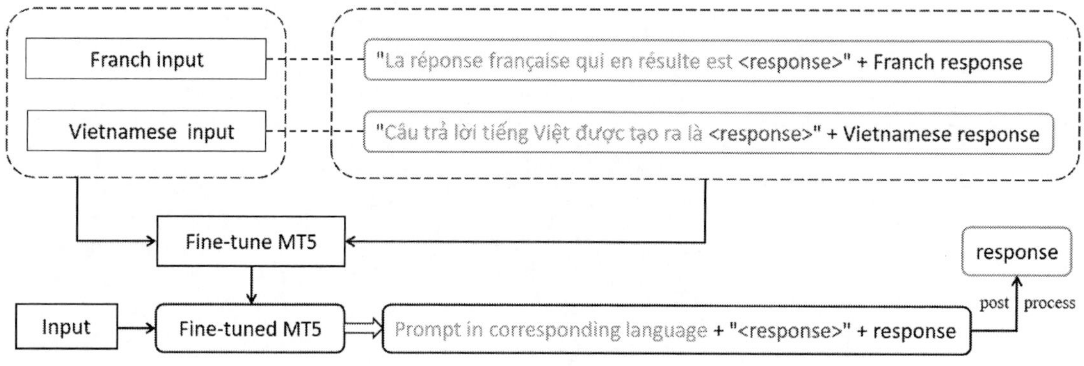

Figure 2: Concrete example of adding a prompt to a response.

3.2 Re-ranking

We fine-tune the XLM-RoBERTa and InfoXLM models on the FrDoc2BotRerank and ViDoc2BotRerank datasets. In the training process, FGM is used for adversarial training to increase the generalization performance of the model. We load the fine-tuned XLM-RoBERTa and InfoXLM models for inference. The query and the passages retrieved from the previous step are spliced separately as the input of the model, and the logits output by the model are weighted average. We use the softmax function to get the probability, and sort according to the probability to get the final result of the re-ranking model.

3.3 Response Generation

We fine-tune MT5 on the FrDoc2BotGeneration and ViDoc2BotGeneration datasets. The input of the model is a simple concatenation of the query and the passage most relevant to the query, and the output is a response. Given the input $x = \{x_i\}_{i=1}^{M}$ and its response $y = \{y_i\}_{i=1}^{N}$, we minimize the following negative log likelihood (NLL) loss:

$$\mathcal{L}_{NLL} = -\sum_{i=1}^{N} logp_\theta(y_i|x, y_{<i}) \qquad (3)$$

We add prompt and pseudo-labels to increase model performance, we also add FGM(Miyato et al., 2017) and AWP(Wu et al., 2020) for confrontation training to improve the generalization ability of the model.

3.3.1 Multilingual prompts

We employ a simple but effective prompt strategy: Add the prefix of the corresponding language to the label to guide the model to generate the response of the corresponding language. The biggest challenge in multilingual generation tasks is the problem of multilingual performance degradation(Zhu et al., 2021), the essence of its performance degradation is the interference between languages. Most of today's multilingual translation models tell the model which language to translate to by adding language tags. Inspired by this, we add corresponding prefixes to French response and Vietnamese response as prompt when fine-tuning MT5. This guides the model to generate responses for the corresponding languages. Then we use post-processing to remove the corresponding prompt in the generated text. See the Figure 2 for specific practices.

3.3.2 Pseudo label

Because the competition does not restrict pseudo-label, we use the fine-tuned model to infer the test set to obtain pseudo-label. We add it to the training set to fine-tune the model again, and load this model for inference to get the result of final test set.

4 Experiments

4.1 Experimental Settings

Our implementations of XLM-RoBERTa, InfoXLM and MT5 are based on the public Pytorch implementation from Transformers[1]. The query encoder and context encoder of the retrieval model both use XLM-RoBERTa-base, and other models are in large size. In the search task, we set the maximum input length of both query and context to 512 tokens, and set to top-48 on the dev-test set and top-100 on the final-test set. The input to both the re-ranking model and the generation model is a concatenation of query and passage. When fine-tuning the re-ranking model and generate model,

[1] https://github.com/huggingface/transformers

Table 1: The results of comparative experiments on retrieval model. "pre-batch-neg" means "use the data of the previous batch to expand the negative example" and "top-48" means "the number of retrieval model recalls is set to 48".

Methods	On dev-test set		
	F1	Bleu	Rouge
Baseline	58.39	40.12	55.64
pre-batch-neg	**59.54**	**46.56**	**57.37**
pre-batch-neg/top-48	59.06	46.29	56.79

we truncate the length of the query to 195 tokens and maximum input length to 512 tokens. We fine-tune these models on a single Tesla A100s GPU with 80gb memory, and the three steps of retrieval, re-ranking, and generation take about 10 hours, 24 hours, and 8 hours respectively.

4.2 Experimental Results and Analysis

Since the organizer is not provide the labels of the final-test set, we only did comparative experiments on the dev-test set. We conduct experiments on retrieval, reranking, and generation in sequence, and the current experiment is based on the results of the previous step. Table 1 shows the retrieval contrast experimental results on dev-test set of our method. We fine-tune baseline on the three steps corresponding data sets and get the F1 of 58.39, Bleu of 40.12 and Rouge of 55.64 on the dev-test set. We extend the negative example when fine-tuning the retrieval model, and get the F1 of 59.54, Bleu of 46.56 and Rouge of 57.37. This result proves that the expansion of negative examples in training can improve the performance of retrieval. The top-k of baseline is set to 20. When we expand it to 48 (our setting of the best score on the dev-test set submission page), the performance will slight drop. This is because the re-ranking model at this time is underperforming, and wrong predictions cause the generation model to receive mismatched input.

Table 2 shows the contrast experimental results on dev-test set of re-ranking step. Experiment under top-48, we replace the initial pre-training weight of the re-rank model with XLM-RoBERTa and InfoXLM, both of which are large size(baseline use base size). We get the F1 of 63.14, Bleu of 49.23 and Rouge of 60.78 on XLM-RoBERTa. By comparing top-48 and top-20, it can be seen that after the performance of the re-ranking model is improved, increasing the number of recalls of the

Table 2: The results of comparative experiments on re-ranking model. "top-20" means "the number of retrieval model recalls is set to 20" and "Adv" means “adversarial”.

Methods	On dev-test set		
	F1	Bleu	Rouge
RoBERTa(top-20)	62.74	48.76	60.35
RoBERTa	63.14	49.23	60.78
InfoXLM	62.83	48.75	59.46
RoBERTa(Adv)	63.59	**50.47**	**61.43**
InfoXLM(Adv)	62.77	49.21	60.38
RoBETA(adv)+ InfoXLM(adv)	**63.62**	50.41	61.40

Table 3: The results of comparative experiments on generation model. "GS/Adv/Prompt/PL" in the table respectively represents "greedy search/adversarial/prompt learning/pseudo label".

Methods	On dev-test set		
	F1	Bleu	Rouge
GS	65.76	50.58	64.44
GS/Adv	67.83	58.42	66.59
GS/Adv/prompt	69.56	60.23	67.51
GS/Adv/prompt/PL	**70.14**	**60.98**	**68.26**

retrieval model can improve the score. We add adversarial perturbations during training, and performance has been improved on both models. Our ensemble of the two models shows a slight drop in performance on the dev-test set, but a 2.05-point improvement on the final-test set.

Table 3 shows the contrast experimental results of generation on dev-test set. We conduct experiments on the improvement of the generation model under the highest score combination of the current retrieval model and the re-ranking model. We replace the generation strategy from beam search to greedy search and get the F1 of 65.76, Bleu of 50.58 and Rouge of 64.44. During training, we add adversarial perturbations using fgm and awp. The F1, Bleu and Rouge increase to 67.83, 58.42 and 66.59. Then we add a prompt to the response and get the F1 of 69.56, Bleu of 60.23 and Rouge of 67.51. It proves that prompt-learning on task data can further improve performance. At last, we add pseudo-labeled data for training and achieve 70.14 F1, 60.98 Bleu and 68.26 Rouge on the dev-test set. The last method(use ensemble on re-ranking step)achieves 210.25 score on the final-test set.

5 Conclusion

We have introduced our submission for the Third DialDoc Workshop Shared Task. Our team ranks 2nd on the final submission page. We have made improvements on the baseline and tried programs such as negative sample augmentation, ensemble, prompt learning, adversarial training, and pseudo-tagging. There are other methods that could further improve the performance of our model. Try to translate the official Chinese and English data into Vietnamese and French, and then use all available Vietnamese and French data for pre-training. You can try to combine the retrieved top k with the re-ordered relevancy for weighted ranking. Try combining a reorder task with a build task for training. You can try training a dichotomous model to score the generated statements to pick out the responses with the highest scores. Because of time and equipment constraints, we didn't try everything during the competition. We hope the above methods can be helpful to future contestants.

Acknowledgements

We thank the thoughtful suggestions from the reviewers. This work is supported by the National Natural Science Foundation of China (Grant Nos.62272132).

References

Ting Chen, Simon Kornblith, Mohammad Norouzi, and Geoffrey E. Hinton. 2020. A simple framework for contrastive learning of visual representations. In *Proceedings of the 37th International Conference on Machine Learning, ICML 2020, 13-18 July 2020, Virtual Event*, volume 119 of *Proceedings of Machine Learning Research*, pages 1597–1607. PMLR.

Zewen Chi, Li Dong, Furu Wei, Nan Yang, Saksham Singhal, Wenhui Wang, Xia Song, Xian-Ling Mao, Heyan Huang, and Ming Zhou. 2021. Infoxlm: An information-theoretic framework for cross-lingual language model pre-training. In *Proceedings of the 2021 Conference of the North American Chapter of the Association for Computational Linguistics: Human Language Technologies, NAACL-HLT 2021, Online, June 6-11, 2021*, pages 3576–3588. Association for Computational Linguistics.

Alexis Conneau, Kartikay Khandelwal, Naman Goyal, Vishrav Chaudhary, Guillaume Wenzek, Francisco Guzmán, Edouard Grave, Myle Ott, Luke Zettlemoyer, and Veselin Stoyanov. 2020. Unsupervised cross-lingual representation learning at scale. In *Proceedings of the 58th Annual Meeting of the Association for Computational Linguistics, ACL 2020, Online, July 5-10, 2020*, pages 8440–8451. Association for Computational Linguistics.

Yiming Cui, Wanxiang Che, Ting Liu, Bing Qin, and Ziqing Yang. 2021. Pre-training with whole word masking for chinese BERT. *IEEE ACM Trans. Audio Speech Lang. Process.*, 29:3504–3514.

Jacob Devlin, Ming-Wei Chang, Kenton Lee, and Kristina Toutanova. 2019. BERT: pre-training of deep bidirectional transformers for language understanding. In *Proceedings of the 2019 Conference of the North American Chapter of the Association for Computational Linguistics: Human Language Technologies, NAACL-HLT 2019, Minneapolis, MN, USA, June 2-7, 2019, Volume 1 (Long and Short Papers)*, pages 4171–4186. Association for Computational Linguistics.

Song Feng, Hui Wan, R. Chulaka Gunasekara, Siva Sankalp Patel, Sachindra Joshi, and Luis A. Lastras. 2020. doc2dial: A goal-oriented document-grounded dialogue dataset. In *Proceedings of the 2020 Conference on Empirical Methods in Natural Language Processing, EMNLP 2020, Online, November 16-20, 2020*, pages 8118–8128. Association for Computational Linguistics.

Haomin Fu, Yeqin Zhang, Haiyang Yu, Jian Sun, Fei Huang, Luo Si, Yongbin Li, and Cam-Tu Nguyen. 2022. Doc2bot: Accessing heterogeneous documents via conversational bots. In *Findings of the Association for Computational Linguistics: EMNLP 2022, Abu Dhabi, United Arab Emirates, December 7-11, 2022*, pages 1820–1836. Association for Computational Linguistics.

Zhuang Liu, Wayne Lin, Ya Shi, and Jun Zhao. 2021. A robustly optimized BERT pre-training approach with post-training. In *Chinese Computational Linguistics - 20th China National Conference, CCL 2021, Hohhot, China, August 13-15, 2021, Proceedings*, volume 12869 of *Lecture Notes in Computer Science*, pages 471–484. Springer.

Tomás Mikolov, Kai Chen, Greg Corrado, and Jeffrey Dean. 2013. Efficient estimation of word representations in vector space. In *1st International Conference on Learning Representations, ICLR 2013, Scottsdale, Arizona, USA, May 2-4, 2013, Workshop Track Proceedings*.

Takeru Miyato, Andrew M. Dai, and Ian J. Goodfellow. 2017. Adversarial training methods for semi-supervised text classification. In *5th International Conference on Learning Representations, ICLR 2017, Toulon, France, April 24-26, 2017, Conference Track Proceedings*. OpenReview.net.

Jeffrey Pennington, Richard Socher, and Christopher D. Manning. 2014. Glove: Global vectors for word representation. In *Proceedings of the 2014 Conference on Empirical Methods in Natural Language Processing, EMNLP 2014, October 25-29, 2014, Doha, Qatar, A meeting of SIGDAT, a Special Interest Group of the ACL*, pages 1532–1543. ACL.

Matthew E. Peters, Mark Neumann, Mohit Iyyer, Matt Gardner, Christopher Clark, Kenton Lee, and Luke Zettlemoyer. 2018. Deep contextualized word representations. In *Proceedings of the 2018 Conference of the North American Chapter of the Association for Computational Linguistics: Human Language Technologies, NAACL-HLT 2018, New Orleans, Louisiana, USA, June 1-6, 2018, Volume 1 (Long Papers)*, pages 2227–2237. Association for Computational Linguistics.

Matt Post. 2018. A call for clarity in reporting BLEU scores. In *Proceedings of the Third Conference on Machine Translation: Research Papers, WMT 2018, Belgium, Brussels, October 31 - November 1, 2018*, pages 186–191. Association for Computational Linguistics.

Alec Radford, Karthik Narasimhan, Tim Salimans, Ilya Sutskever, et al. 2018. Improving language understanding by generative pre-training.

Pranav Rajpurkar, Jian Zhang, Konstantin Lopyrev, and Percy Liang. 2016. Squad: 100, 000+ questions for machine comprehension of text. In *Proceedings of the 2016 Conference on Empirical Methods in Natural Language Processing, EMNLP 2016, Austin, Texas, USA, November 1-4, 2016*, pages 2383–2392. The Association for Computational Linguistics.

Ashish Vaswani, Noam Shazeer, Niki Parmar, Jakob Uszkoreit, Llion Jones, Aidan N. Gomez, Lukasz Kaiser, and Illia Polosukhin. 2017. Attention is all you need. In *Advances in Neural Information Processing Systems 30: Annual Conference on Neural Information Processing Systems 2017, December 4-9, 2017, Long Beach, CA, USA*, pages 5998–6008.

Liang Wang, Wei Zhao, Zhuoyu Wei, and Jingming Liu. 2022. Simkgc: Simple contrastive knowledge graph completion with pre-trained language models. In *Proceedings of the 60th Annual Meeting of the Association for Computational Linguistics (Volume 1: Long Papers), ACL 2022, Dublin, Ireland, May 22-27, 2022*, pages 4281–4294. Association for Computational Linguistics.

Dongxian Wu, Shu-Tao Xia, and Yisen Wang. 2020. Adversarial weight perturbation helps robust generalization. In *Advances in Neural Information Processing Systems 33: Annual Conference on Neural Information Processing Systems 2020, NeurIPS 2020, December 6-12, 2020, virtual.*

Linting Xue, Noah Constant, Adam Roberts, Mihir Kale, Rami Al-Rfou, Aditya Siddhant, Aditya Barua, and Colin Raffel. 2021. mt5: A massively multilingual pre-trained text-to-text transformer. In *Proceedings of the 2021 Conference of the North American Chapter of the Association for Computational Linguistics: Human Language Technologies, NAACL-HLT 2021, Online, June 6-11, 2021*, pages 483–498. Association for Computational Linguistics.

Yinfei Yang, Gustavo Hernández Ábrego, Steve Yuan, Mandy Guo, Qinlan Shen, Daniel Cer, Yun-Hsuan Sung, Brian Strope, and Ray Kurzweil. 2019. Improving multilingual sentence embedding using bidirectional dual encoder with additive margin softmax. In *Proceedings of the Twenty-Eighth International Joint Conference on Artificial Intelligence, IJCAI 2019, Macao, China, August 10-16, 2019*, pages 5370–5378. ijcai.org.

Yeqin Zhang, Haomin Fu, Cheng Fu, Haiyang Yu, Yongbin Li, and Cam-Tu Nguyen. 2023. Coarse-to-fine knowledge selection for document grounded dialogs. In *2023 IEEE International Conference on Acoustics, Speech and Signal Processing (ICASSP)*. IEEE.

Zhengyan Zhang, Xu Han, Zhiyuan Liu, Xin Jiang, Maosong Sun, and Qun Liu. 2019. ERNIE: enhanced language representation with informative entities. In *Proceedings of the 57th Conference of the Association for Computational Linguistics, ACL 2019, Florence, Italy, July 28- August 2, 2019, Volume 1: Long Papers*, pages 1441–1451. Association for Computational Linguistics.

Yaoming Zhu, Jiangtao Feng, Chengqi Zhao, Mingxuan Wang, and Lei Li. 2021. Counter-interference adapter for multilingual machine translation. In *Findings of the Association for Computational Linguistics: EMNLP 2021, Virtual Event / Punta Cana, Dominican Republic, 16-20 November, 2021*, pages 2812–2823. Association for Computational Linguistics.

Position Matters! Empirical Study of Order Effect in Knowledge-grounded Dialogue

Hsuan Su[⋆◇∗] **Shachi H Kumar**[◇] **Sahisnu Mazumder**[◇] **Wenda Chen**[◇]
Ramesh Manuvinakurike[◇] **Eda Okur**[◇] **Saurav Sahay**[◇] **Lama Nachman**[◇] **Shang-Tse Chen**[⋆] **Hung-yi Lee**[⋆]
National Taiwan University[⋆] Intel Labs[◇]
hsuansu.96@gmail.com

Abstract

With the power of large pretrained language models, various research works have integrated knowledge into dialogue systems. The traditional techniques treat knowledge as part of the input sequence for the dialogue system, prepending a set of knowledge statements in front of dialogue history. However, such a mechanism forces knowledge sets to be concatenated in an ordered manner, making models implicitly pay imbalanced attention to the sets during training. In this paper, we first investigate how the order of the knowledge set can influence autoregressive dialogue systems' responses. We conduct experiments on two commonly used dialogue datasets with two types of transformer-based models and find that models view the input knowledge unequally. To this end, we propose a simple and novel technique to alleviate the order effect by modifying the position embeddings of knowledge input in these models. With the proposed position embedding method, the experimental results show that each knowledge statement is uniformly considered to generate responses.

1 Introduction

Transformer-based (Vaswani et al., 2017) pretrained language models are widely used to build dialogue systems (Zhang et al., 2020; Xu et al., 2021; Komeili et al., 2021; Roller et al., 2020; Thoppilan et al., 2022; Rae et al., 2021; Chen et al., 2021; Ham et al., 2020; Hosseini-Asl et al., 2020; Bao et al., 2021). In addition to general-purpose dialogue systems, many specialized dialogue systems have been proposed. Representative examples include personalized dialogue systems (Wolf et al., 2019; Zhang et al., 2018; Wu et al., 2021; Cao et al., 2022; Song et al., 2020), knowledge-grounded dialogue systems (Dinan et al., 2019; Kim et al., 2021; Tao et al., 2021; Cai et al., 2020; Liu et al., 2021), and prompting dialogue systems (Su et al., 2022).

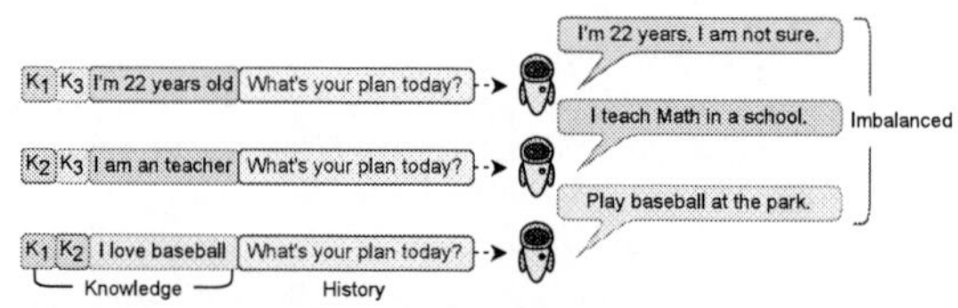

Figure 1: The order effect illustration. Models' responses are influenced by the order of the input knowledge set.

To build specialized dialogue systems, integrating additional information into the input sequence is necessary. Wolf et al. (2019) prepend persona sentences to personalize the history; while Su et al. (2022); Dinan et al. (2020); Keskar et al. (2019); Xu et al. (2020a) prepending task-specific signals to prompt and control the model.

These methods prepend additional information in front of the history as a sequence for models' input. Furthermore, the approach generates an unnecessary order among equal knowledge sets since the knowledge is connected in the sequence. Thus models might be influenced by the order and generate imbalanced responses.

Previous works focus on how perturbations in dialog history affect models' responses (Sankar et al., 2019; O'Connor and Andreas, 2021; Sinha et al., 2021; Lampinen et al., 2022; Webson and Pavlick, 2021; Xu et al., 2020b; Khandelwal et al., 2018). They conduct many experiments and measure the effect of perturbations from the aspect of response quality and information theory to show that these language models are robust and not sensitive to the perturbations in input history. However, dialog history and knowledge are inherently different aspects of a conversation. Dialog history has a temporal property, i.e., the topic and specificity of conversation change as the dialog progresses, whereas knowledge facts are information referenced to generate a response. Although the perturbation in history does not influence the

[∗]Work done when interning at Intel Labs.

Proceedings of the Third DialDoc Workshop on Document-grounded Dialogue and Conversational Question Answering, pages 36–43
July 13, 2023 ©2023 Association for Computational Linguistics

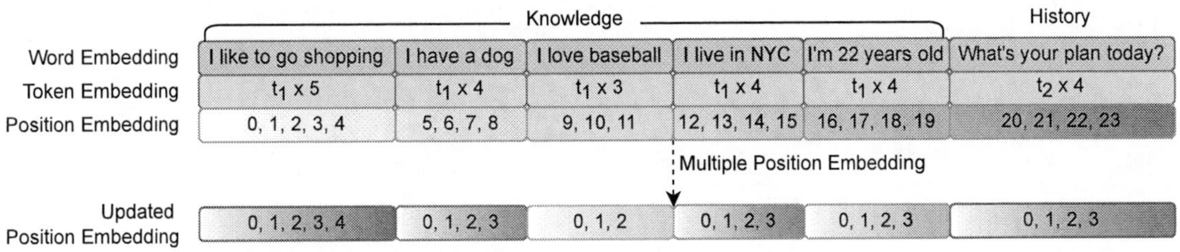

Figure 2: Input format for GPT-series models. The position ids do not treat knowledge equally but as a sequence. The updated position embeddings show our proposed method, where each knowledge statement is encoded with its own position embeddings, hence, models can treat each input sentence equally during training. The same color of blocks indicates using the same layer to generate embeddings.

results generated by the model (Sankar et al., 2019; O'Connor and Andreas, 2021), in our early observation, we found that prepending knowledge influences models' responses. For example, Figure 1 demonstrates an example where the model exhibits imbalanced attention to input knowledge, and the order of knowledge influences the generated responses. This might cause the model to generate inappropriate responses since it attends to knowledge that might not be relevant to a dialog context. The contributions of this work are as follows:

- We conduct experiments across two typical methods and two models on multiple datasets to show that the order of knowledge sentences does affect generated responses.
- We propose a simple approach to alleviate this sentence-level order effect by manipulating the position embedding layers.

2 Knowledge-grounded Dialogue Methods

In this work, we study the order effect in TransferTransfo (Wolf et al., 2019), which is a state-of-the-art knowledge-grounded method. We train TransferTransfo on two datasets and measure the sentence-level order effect on the test datasets.

2.1 TransferTransfo

The TransferTransfo architecture is built on top of GPT-series models, which simply concatenates the knowledge sets and context in a single sequence, putting the reply at the end. To help models distinguish speakers and position of input tokens, it builds three parallel input sequences for word, position, and segments, and fuses them into a single sequence. For the loss function, in addition to a language modeling loss, a next sentence prediction loss is added. The total loss is the weighted sum of the 1) language modeling loss, which is computed as the cross-entropy loss between the predicted logits and the ground truth response and 2) the next-sentence prediction loss, which is a classification loss to distinguish the ground truth response from distractors that are randomly sampled from the dataset.

In the original TransferTransfo implementation, the authors have already pointed out that the order of the knowledge set influences the model's performance. To this end, they augment training data by permuting the knowledge sets several times.

2.2 Experimental Setups

We conduct experiments on two datasets:
Persona-Chat (Zhang et al., 2018): This persona-grounded dialogue dataset consists of crowd-sourced dialogues between a pair of annotators provided with 4-5 persona statements each.
Topical-Chat (Gopalakrishnan et al., 2019): This is a knowledge-grounded dialogue dataset, where the dialogs are constructed by a pair of annotators conversing about specific topics. The annotators are provided with wiki data with 4-5 facts as knowledge sources.

In our experimental setup, we shuffle the knowledge set's order 50 times during testing and implement TransferTransfo on GPT (Radford et al., 2018) and GPT-2 (Radford et al., 2019) models.

3 The Order Effect of the Knowledge Set

Models are said to have an order effect of input if the generated responses are sensitive and influenced by order of input sequence. Previous works (Sankar et al., 2019; O'Connor and Andreas, 2021; Sinha et al., 2021; Lampinen et al., 2022; Webson

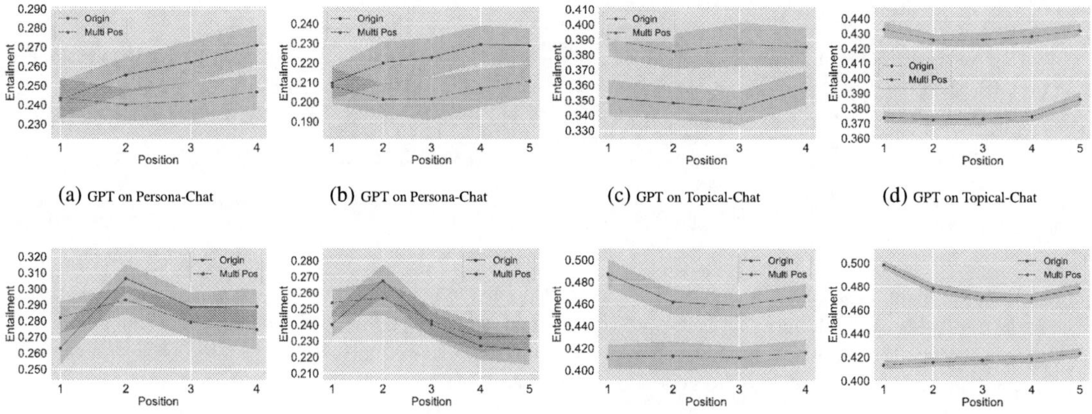

(a) GPT on Persona-Chat (b) GPT on Persona-Chat (c) GPT on Topical-Chat (d) GPT on Topical-Chat

(e) GPT-2 on Persona-Chat (f) GPT-2 on Persona-Chat (g) GPT-2 on Topical-Chat (h) GPT-2 on Topical-Chat

Figure 3: Experimental results under TransferTransfo method, the lines indicate the average of 50 times shuffling results with standard deviation represented in the area. The data with 4 and 5 knowledge sets are displayed separately.

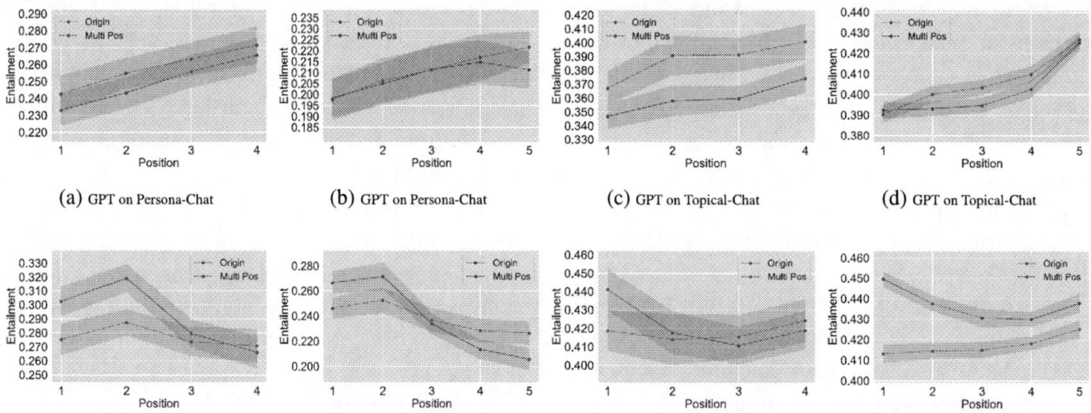

(a) GPT on Persona-Chat (b) GPT on Persona-Chat (c) GPT on Topical-Chat (d) GPT on Topical-Chat

(e) GPT-2 on Persona-Chat (f) GPT-2 on Persona-Chat (g) GPT-2 on Topical-Chat (h) GPT-2 on Topical-Chat

Figure 4: Experimental results under LM loss only method, the lines indicate the average of 50 times shuffling results with standard deviation represented in the area. The data with 4 and 5 knowledge sets are displayed separately.

and Pavlick, 2021; Xu et al., 2020b; Khandelwal et al., 2018) focus on whether perturbation in dialogue history affect models' responses. In this work, to be more specific, we investigate if sentence level change in the order of input knowledge sets will result in substantial semantic differences in the generated responses.

3.1 The Order Effect Measurement

To address the sentence-level order effect of the input knowledge set in models, we aim to measure the semantic difference given different orders of knowledge sentences. It is intuitive to measure if the response content is influenced by knowledge sets order. In other words, we measure the distribution of response-knowledge relationship in different positions. We build a Natural Language Inference (NLI) classifier to evaluate the degree of entailment between responses and each knowledge in the set.

The Natural Language Inference Classifier is built with BERT model (Devlin et al., 2019), trained on the Dialogue NLI dataset (Welleck et al., 2019), which is built on top of Persona-Chat dataset (Zhang et al., 2018). The annotators label the relationship between persona and response in Persona-Chat with entail, neutral, and contradict classes.

3.2 Results and Discussions for Order Effect

Figures 3 and 4 show the entailment scores of the response with each position of knowledge. Figure 3 presents the experiments of TransferTransfo with GPT and GPT-2 models across Persona-Chat and Topical-Chat datasets. Figure 4 shows the re-

Model	Method	Persona		Topical	
		TT.	LM.	TT.	LM.
		Entailment Max - Min			
GPT	Origin	.048 / .037	.052 / .035	.037 / .022	.046 / .041
	Multi Pos	**.023 / .028**	.051 / .041	**.031 / .016**	.058 / .044
GPT-2	Origin	.062 / .062	.075 / .085	.052 / .036	.052 / .027
	Multi Pos	**.039 / .044**	**.038 / .045**	**.027 / .018**	**.035 / .021**
		Perplexity ↓			
GPT	Origin	52.29	54.31	39.31	36.80
	Multi Pos	55.47	58.43	42.37	42.98
GPT-2	Origin	61.69	61.80	20.50	18.84
	Multi Pos	60.18	58.91	17.40	17.30
		Coherence			
GPT	Origin	0.633	0.636	0.793	0.770
	Multi Pos	0.644	0.621	0.732	0.744
GPT-2	Origin	0.661	0.667	0.840	0.843
	Multi Pos	0.648	0.662	0.830	0.831
		Diverstiy ↓			
GPT	Origin	0.815	0.822	0.844	0.846
	Multi Pos	0.821	0.833	0.870	0.862
GPT-2	Origin	0.808	0.811	0.833	0.833
	Multi Pos	0.816	0.817	0.843	0.845

Table 1: The results of measurements. The Max-Min of entailment are reported in 4 knowledge / 5 knowledge. The mean of quality across 50 runs are reported and standard deviation are reported in Appendix A.3.

sults with "LM Loss only Method", which refers to TransferTransfo without the next sentence prediction. We observe that the distribution of data containing only four knowledge statements is very different compared to data containing five knowledge statements. Hence we show them separately.

The NLI classification results are shown with BLUE lines. We can see that the distribution of entailment scores on different positions are imbalanced. In the experiments on the GPT model, (figures 3a, 3b, 3c, 3d, 4a, 4b, 4c, and 4d), it can be observed under both TransferTransfo and LM loss only methods, the entailment score on the last position is always the highest. In fact, there is a huge gap between the entailment scores with the first knowledge and the last knowledge statements. This indicates that GPT model focuses more on the last position of knowledge.

However, the behavior of GPT-2 is very different from GPT model. From Figures 3e, 3f, 3g, 3h, 4e, 4f, 4g, and 4h, we can see that GPT-2 models focus more on the earlier knowledge statements in the sequence rather than the later ones.

These results show that the order effect exists across GPT and GPT-2 models (although different) and is influencing models' responses and this needs to be solved.

4 Alleviate the Order Effect

In this section, we analyse the reason for the order effect in the GPT-series models and propose a method to alleviate the phenomenon. Figure 2 shows the input format of the classic GPT-series. There are three types of embeddings in the model: word embedding to capture the semantic meaning of each word, token embedding to represent the speaker and absolute position embedding that encodes position information of input sequence.

Figure 2 shows that the position ids for each knowledge start from zero with different positional embedding layers. In this naive setting, knowledge of the set are treated equally and not input with the order during training.

4.1 Results and Discussion

In the same Figures 3 and 4, the RED lines demonstrate the entailment result after applying multiple position embedding. We observe that all the red lines, which are the GPT-series applied multiple position embeddings, are much smoother compared to BLUE lines in both figures. Furthermore, we report the difference between maximum and minimum entailment across the positions in Table 1. It shows that the difference is negligible after applying multiple position embeddings. This indicates that we can alleviate the order effect under models trained with with multiple position embedding. However, we also observed that on Figure 4 some red lines are still as steep as before, which means the order effect still exists. We think that the model trained only with LM loss treats knowledge like history and does not ground models on knowledge sets. Under this scenario, the multiple position embedding doesn't work well.

For the measurement of quality, Table 1 shows the perplexity, coherence, and diversity. The details are included in Appendix A.2. We found tiny drops between origin and multiple position embedding. More specifically, our proposed method does not crash the models and can still make models generate plausible responses.

5 Conclusions

In this paper, we investigate whether the order of knowledge set will influence dialogue models' responses. Our experiments across several datasets show that the GPT-series models unfairly pay attention to the knowledge set and are influenced by order of knowledge. To solve this problem, we study the reason for the phenomenon and propose simple method to alleviate the order effect in models. The experimental results show that our approach reduces the order effect and makes the model select the knowledge uniformly.

Limitations

This work has potential limitations:

- We found that on the Figure 3 and 4, The entailment of the methods after applying multiple position embedding (RED lines) are sometimes lower than origin methods(BLUE lines). This is not meet our expectations since we don't want our method to decrease performance. In our opinion, we think the reason might be the embedding method has never been seen before during the pretraining of models, which requires the model's additional efforts to adapt the embedding, thus hurts the performance.. We leave it as future work to be improved.

- We also found that the multiple position embedding does not work very well to alleviate the order effect in the LM loss-only settings4. We have discussed this in previous sections. Since LM loss only does not help the model distinguish which parts in the input sequence are knowledge set and thus treat them the same as history. The multiple position embedding will not be trained finely to help the model distinguish. We also left this as a future work to be improved.

References

Siqi Bao, Bingjin Chen, H. He, Xin Tian, Hanxu Zhou, Fan Wang, Hua Wu, Haifeng Wang, Wenquan Wu, and Yingzhan Lin. 2021. A unified pre-training framework for conversational ai. *ArXiv*, abs/2105.02482.

Yuanyuan Cai, Min Zuo, Qingchuan Zhang, Haitao Xiong, and Ke Li. 2020. A bichannel transformer with context encoding for document-driven conversation generation in social media. *Complex.*, 2020:3710104:1–3710104:13.

Yu Cao, Wei Bi, Meng Fang, Shuming Shi, and Dacheng Tao. 2022. A model-agnostic data manipulation method for persona-based dialogue generation. In *ACL*.

Moya Chen, Paul A. Crook, and Stephen Roller. 2021. Teaching models new apis: Domain-agnostic simulators for task oriented dialogue.

Stanley F Chen, Douglas Beeferman, and Roni Rosenfeld. 1998. Evaluation metrics for language models.

Jacob Devlin, Ming-Wei Chang, Kenton Lee, and Kristina Toutanova. 2019. BERT: Pre-training of deep bidirectional transformers for language understanding. In *Proceedings of the 2019 Conference of the North American Chapter of the Association for Computational Linguistics: Human Language Technologies, Volume 1 (Long and Short Papers)*, pages 4171–4186, Minneapolis, Minnesota. Association for Computational Linguistics.

Emily Dinan, Angela Fan, Adina Williams, Jack Urbanek, Douwe Kiela, and Jason Weston. 2020. Queens are powerful too: Mitigating gender bias in dialogue generation. In *Proceedings of the 2020 Conference on Empirical Methods in Natural Language Processing (EMNLP)*, pages 8173–8188, Online. Association for Computational Linguistics.

Emily Dinan, Stephen Roller, Kurt Shuster, Angela Fan, Michael Auli, and Jason Weston. 2019. Wizard of wikipedia: Knowledge-powered conversational agents. *ArXiv*, abs/1811.01241.

Xiang Gao, Yizhe Zhang, Michel Galley, Chris Brockett, and Bill Dolan. 2020. Dialogue response ranking-training with large-scale human feedback data. In *EMNLP*.

Karthik Gopalakrishnan, Behnam Hedayatnia, Qinlang Chen, Anna Gottardi, Sanjeev Kwatra, Anu Venkatesh, Raefer Gabriel, and Dilek Hakkani-Tür. 2019. Topical-Chat: Towards Knowledge-Grounded Open-Domain Conversations. In *Proc. Interspeech 2019*, pages 1891–1895.

Donghoon Ham, Jeong-Gwan Lee, Youngsoo Jang, and Kee-Eung Kim. 2020. End-to-end neural pipeline for goal-oriented dialogue systems using GPT-2. In *Proceedings of the 58th Annual Meeting of the Association for Computational Linguistics*, pages 583–592, Online. Association for Computational Linguistics.

Ehsan Hosseini-Asl, Bryan McCann, Chien-Sheng Wu, Semih Yavuz, and Richard Socher. 2020. A simple language model for task-oriented dialogue. *arXiv preprint arXiv:2005.00796*.

Nitish Shirish Keskar, Bryan McCann, Lav R. Varshney, Caiming Xiong, and Richard Socher. 2019. Ctrl: A conditional transformer language model for controllable generation.

Urvashi Khandelwal, He He, Peng Qi, and Dan Jurafsky. 2018. Sharp nearby, fuzzy far away: How neural language models use context. In *ACL*.

San Kim, Jin Yea Jang, Minyoung Jung, and Saim Shin. 2021. A model of cross-lingual knowledge-grounded response generation for open-domain dialogue systems. In *EMNLP*.

Mojtaba Komeili, Kurt Shuster, and Jason Weston. 2021. Internet-augmented dialogue generation.

Andrew Kyle Lampinen, Ishita Dasgupta, Stephanie C. Y. Chan, Kory Matthewson, Michael Henry Tessler, Antonia Creswell, James L. McClelland, Jane X. Wang, and Felix Hill. 2022. Can language models learn from explanations in context? *ArXiv*, abs/2204.02329.

Shilei Liu, Xiaofeng Zhao, Bochao Li, Feiliang Ren, Longhui Zhang, and Shujuan Yin. 2021. A three-stage learning framework for low-resource knowledge-grounded dialogue generation. In *EMNLP*.

Joe O'Connor and Jacob Andreas. 2021. What context features can transformer language models use? In *Proceedings of the 59th Annual Meeting of the Association for Computational Linguistics and the 11th International Joint Conference on Natural Language Processing (Volume 1: Long Papers)*, pages 851–864, Online. Association for Computational Linguistics.

Kishore Papineni, Salim Roukos, Todd Ward, and Wei-Jing Zhu. 2002. Bleu: a method for automatic evaluation of machine translation. In *Proceedings of the 40th annual meeting of the Association for Computational Linguistics*, pages 311–318.

Alec Radford, Karthik Narasimhan, Tim Salimans, and Ilya Sutskever. 2018. Improving language understanding by generative pre-training.

Alec Radford, Jeff Wu, Rewon Child, David Luan, Dario Amodei, and Ilya Sutskever. 2019. Language models are unsupervised multitask learners.

Jack W. Rae, Sebastian Borgeaud, Trevor Cai, Katie Millican, Jordan Hoffmann, Francis Song, John Aslanides, Sarah Henderson, Roman Ring, Susannah Young, Eliza Rutherford, Tom Hennigan, Jacob Menick, Albin Cassirer, Richard Powell, George van den Driessche, Lisa Anne Hendricks, Maribeth Rauh, Po-Sen Huang, Amelia Glaese, Johannes Welbl, Sumanth Dathathri, Saffron Huang, Jonathan Uesato, John Mellor, Irina Higgins, Antonia Creswell, Nat McAleese, Amy Wu, Erich Elsen, Siddhant Jayakumar, Elena Buchatskaya, David Budden, Esme Sutherland, Karen Simonyan, Michela Paganini, Laurent Sifre, Lena Martens, Xiang Lorraine Li, Adhiguna Kuncoro, Aida Nematzadeh, Elena Gribovskaya, Domenic Donato, Angeliki Lazaridou, Arthur Mensch, Jean-Baptiste Lespiau, Maria Tsimpoukelli, Nikolai Grigorev, Doug Fritz, Thibault Sottiaux, Mantas Pajarskas, Toby Pohlen, Zhitao Gong, Daniel Toyama, Cyprien de Masson d'Autume, Yujia Li, Tayfun Terzi, Vladimir Mikulik, Igor Babuschkin, Aidan Clark, Diego de Las Casas, Aurelia Guy, Chris Jones, James Bradbury, Matthew Johnson, Blake Hechtman, Laura Weidinger, Iason Gabriel, William Isaac, Ed Lockhart, Simon Osindero, Laura Rimell, Chris Dyer, Oriol Vinyals, Kareem Ayoub, Jeff Stanway, Lorrayne Bennett, Demis Hassabis, Koray Kavukcuoglu, and Geoffrey Irving. 2021. Scaling language models: Methods, analysis & insights from training gopher.

Stephen Roller, Emily Dinan, Naman Goyal, Da Ju, Mary Williamson, Yinhan Liu, Jing Xu, Myle Ott, Kurt Shuster, Eric M. Smith, Y-Lan Boureau, and Jason Weston. 2020. Recipes for building an open-domain chatbot.

Chinnadhurai Sankar, Sandeep Subramanian, Chris Pal, Sarath Chandar, and Yoshua Bengio. 2019. Do neural dialog systems use the conversation history effectively? an empirical study. In *Proceedings of the 57th Annual Meeting of the Association for Computational Linguistics*, pages 32–37, Florence, Italy. Association for Computational Linguistics.

Koustuv Sinha, Robin Jia, Dieuwke Hupkes, Joelle Pineau, Adina Williams, and Douwe Kiela. 2021. Masked language modeling and the distributional hypothesis: Order word matters pre-training for little. In *Proceedings of the 2021 Conference on Empirical Methods in Natural Language Processing*, pages 2888–2913, Online and Punta Cana, Dominican Republic. Association for Computational Linguistics.

Haoyu Song, Yan Wang, Weinan Zhang, Xiaojiang Liu, and Ting Liu. 2020. Generate, delete and rewrite: A three-stage framework for improving persona consistency of dialogue generation. *ArXiv*, abs/2004.07672.

Hsuan Su, Pohan Chi, Shih-Cheng Huang, Chung Ho Lam, Saurav Sahay, Shang-Tse Chen, and Hung yi Lee. 2022. Few-shot prompting towards controllable response generation.

Chongyang Tao, Changyu Chen, Jiazhan Feng, Ji rong Wen, and Rui Yan. 2021. A pre-training strategy for zero-resource response selection in knowledge-grounded conversations. In *ACL*.

Romal Thoppilan, Daniel De Freitas, Jamie Hall, Noam Shazeer, Apoorv Kulshreshtha, Heng-Tze Cheng, Alicia Jin, Taylor Bos, Leslie Baker, Yu Du, YaGuang Li, Hongrae Lee, Huaixiu Steven Zheng, Amin Ghafouri, Marcelo Menegali, Yanping Huang, Maxim Krikun, Dmitry Lepikhin, James Qin, Dehao Chen, Yuanzhong Xu, Zhifeng Chen, Adam Roberts, Maarten Bosma, Vincent Zhao, Yanqi Zhou, Chung-Ching Chang, Igor Krivokon, Will Rusch, Marc Pickett, Pranesh Srinivasan, Laichee Man, Kathleen Meier-Hellstern, Meredith Ringel Morris, Tulsee Doshi, Renelito Delos Santos, Toju Duke, Johnny Soraker, Ben Zevenbergen, Vinodkumar Prabhakaran, Mark Diaz, Ben Hutchinson, Kristen Olson, Alejandra Molina, Erin Hoffman-John, Josh Lee, Lora Aroyo, Ravi Rajakumar, Alena Butryna, Matthew Lamm, Viktoriya Kuzmina, Joe Fenton, Aaron Cohen, Rachel Bernstein, Ray Kurzweil, Blaise Aguera-Arcas, Claire Cui, Marian Croak, Ed Chi, and Quoc Le. 2022. Lamda: Language models for dialog applications.

Ashish Vaswani, Noam Shazeer, Niki Parmar, Jakob Uszkoreit, Llion Jones, Aidan N Gomez, Ł ukasz

Kaiser, and Illia Polosukhin. 2017. Attention is all you need. In *Advances in Neural Information Processing Systems*, volume 30. Curran Associates, Inc.

Albert Webson and Ellie Pavlick. 2021. Do prompt-based models really understand the meaning of their prompts? *ArXiv*, abs/2109.01247.

Sean Welleck, Jason Weston, Arthur Szlam, and Kyunghyun Cho. 2019. Dialogue natural language inference. In *Proceedings of the 57th Annual Meeting of the Association for Computational Linguistics*, pages 3731–3741, Florence, Italy. Association for Computational Linguistics.

Thomas Wolf, Victor Sanh, Julien Chaumond, and Clement Delangue. 2019. Transfertransfo: A transfer learning approach for neural network based conversational agents. *CoRR*, abs/1901.08149.

Chen Henry Wu, Yinhe Zheng, Xiaoxi Mao, and Minlie Huang. 2021. Transferable persona-grounded dialogues via grounded minimal edits. In *Proceedings of the 2021 Conference on Empirical Methods in Natural Language Processing*, pages 2368–2382, Online and Punta Cana, Dominican Republic. Association for Computational Linguistics.

Jing Xu, Arthur Szlam, and Jason Weston. 2021. Beyond goldfish memory: Long-term open-domain conversation.

Peng Xu, Mostofa Patwary, Mohammad Shoeybi, Raul Puri, Pascale Fung, Anima Anandkumar, and Bryan Catanzaro. 2020a. MEGATRON-CNTRL: Controllable story generation with external knowledge using large-scale language models. In *Proceedings of the 2020 Conference on Empirical Methods in Natural Language Processing (EMNLP)*, pages 2831–2845, Online. Association for Computational Linguistics.

Yilun Xu, Shengjia Zhao, Jiaming Song, Russell Stewart, and Stefano Ermon. 2020b. A theory of usable information under computational constraints. *ArXiv*, abs/2002.10689.

Saizheng Zhang, Emily Dinan, Jack Urbanek, Arthur Szlam, Douwe Kiela, and Jason Weston. 2018. Personalizing dialogue agents: I have a dog, do you have pets too? In *Proceedings of the 56th Annual Meeting of the Association for Computational Linguistics (Volume 1: Long Papers)*, pages 2204–2213, Melbourne, Australia. Association for Computational Linguistics.

Yizhe Zhang, Siqi Sun, Michel Galley, Yen-Chun Chen, Chris Brockett, Xiang Gao, Jianfeng Gao, Jingjing Liu, and Bill Dolan. 2020. Dialogpt: Large-scale generative pre-training for conversational response generation. In *ACL, system demonstration*.

Yaoming Zhu, Sidi Lu, Lei Zheng, Jiaxian Guo, Weinan Zhang, Jun Wang, and Yong Yu. 2018. Texygen: A benchmarking platform for text generation models. In *The 41st International ACM SIGIR Conference on Research & Development in Information Retrieval*, pages 1097–1100.

A Appendix

A.1 Experimental Details

- **Hyperparameters**: For the Hyperparameters we use to conduct experiments, we follow TransferTransfo link `https://github.com/huggingface/transfer-learning-conv-ai`. They obtain these Hyperparameters by grid searching. More specifically, They finetuned the model with a batch size of 32 sequences , and finetune the models approximately 2 epochs over training dataset. They used Adam with a learning rate of 6.25e-5, and a coefficient of 2 on the LM loss when summing with the next-sentence prediction loss . The learning rate was linearly decayed to zero over the course of the training.

- **Datasets**: The link to download Persona-Chat `https://parl.ai/docs/tasks.html#persona-chat` and the train/valid/test split is 9907/1000/968 dialogues.. For the link to download Topical-Chat `https://github.com/alexa/Topical-Chat` and the train/valid/test split is 8628/1078/1078 dialogues.

- **Pretrained Models**: For GPT model we use gpt-medium as our pretrain model and use microsoft/DialoGPT-medium as initial checkpoint for GPT-2 model.

A.2 Evaluation Metrics

In addition to entailment, we aimed to employ other metrics that are also important to measure a dialogue system.

Perplexity (Chen et al., 1998): Here we employed the pretrained GPT-2 language model GPT to judge if the output sentence $C(x)$ was an acceptable sentence. The computation of Perplexity (Chen et al., 1998) is shown below.

$$PPL = \prod_{i=1}^{T} \frac{1}{(GPT(C(x,D)_i|x))^{1/T}} \quad (1)$$

Coherence: We employed the DialogRPT (Gao et al., 2020) to calculate the coherence between conversation model's output and the input context. DialogRPT (Gao et al., 2020) is a GPT2-based ranker that finetuned on 133M human feedback data. With the contrastive learning approach that

DialogRPT used. The ranker has better understanding on how relevant the response is for the given context. In our evaluation, we take the the probability that output by DialogRPT coherence model (*human_vs_rand*) as our coherence metric.

Diversity: BLEU score (Papineni et al., 2002) is a commonly used metric for automatically evaluating machine translation. However, the Self-BLEU (Zhu et al., 2018) score here was applied to measure the diversity of chatbot responses. Regarding one sentence as the prediction and the others as the reference, we can calculate BLEU score for every sentence, and the average is the Self-BLEU score. A lower Self-BLEU score implies more diversity of the chatbot responses.

A.3 Standard Deviation of Quality Metrics

Model	Method	Persona		Topical	
		TT.	LM.	TT.	LM.
		Perplexity			
GPT	Origin	0.23	0.27	0.20	0.25
	Multi Pos	0.22	0.26	0.27	0.22
GPT-2	Origin	0.31	0.29	0.120	0.09
	Multi Pos	0.28	0.23	0.10	0.110
		Coherence			
GPT	Origin	0.001	0.001	0.002	0.002
	Multi Pos	0.001	0.001	0.002	0.002
GPT-2	Origin	0.002	0.001	0.001	0.001
	Multi Pos	0.001	0.001	0.001	0.001
		Diverstiy			
GPT	Origin	0.002	0.002	0.002	0.002
	Multi Pos	0.002	0.002	0.002	0.002
GPT-2	Origin	0.002	0.002	0.002	0.002
	Multi Pos	0.002	0.002	0.002	0.001

Table 2: The results of quality measurements. The standard deviation across 50 runs are reported.

Enhancing Multilingual Document-Grounded Dialogue Using Cascaded Prompt-Based Post-Training Models

Jun Liu[1,2,3,*] **Shuang Cheng**[1,2,3,*] **Zineng Zhou**[1,2,3,*]
Yang Gu[1,2,3†] **Jian Ye**[1,2,3] **Haiyong Luo**[1,2,3]
[1]Institute of Computing Technology, Chinese Academy of Sciences, Beijing, China
[2]University of Chinese Academy of Sciences
[3]Beijing Key Laboratory of Mobile Computing and Pervasive Device
{liujun22s, chengshuang22s, zhouzineng22s, guyang, jye, yhluo}@ict.ac.cn

Abstract

The Dialdoc23 shared task presents a Multilingual Document-Grounded Dialogue Systems (MDGDS) challenge, where system responses are generated in multiple languages using user's queries, historical dialogue records and relevant passages. A major challenge for this task is the limited training data available in low-resource languages such as French and Vietnamese. In this paper, we propose Cascaded Prompt-based Post-training Models, dividing the task into three subtasks: Retrieval, Reranking and Generation. We conduct post-training on high-resource language such as English and Chinese to enhance performance of low-resource languages by using the similarities of languages. Additionally, we utilize the prompt method to activate model's ability on diverse languages within the dialogue domain and explore which prompt is a good prompt. Our comprehensive experiments demonstrate the effectiveness of our proposed methods, which achieved the first place on the leaderboard with a total score of 215.40 in token-level F1, SacreBleu, and Rouge-L metrics.

1 Introduction

Document-Grounded Dialogue Systems (DGDS) have emerged as a research focus in the natural language processing field. They leverage documents to provide targeted information for specialized tasks such as question answering and recommendations (Chen et al., 2019; Rashkin et al., 2021). These systems ensure accuracy and reliability by leveraging comprehensive knowledge bases while enhancing real-time responsiveness and information retrieval efficiency (Gao et al., 2022). Additionally, they can accommodate the expanding scalability of new documents and knowledge sources (Rashkin et al., 2021). Nonetheless, these systems encounter challenges when operating with low-resource languages, including limited training data (Dabre et al., 2019; Gritta et al., 2022), and significant disparities in grammar, vocabulary, and semantics across languages (Artetxe et al., 2017). To address these challenges, researchers are developing multilingual approaches to improve the performance of low-resource languages in DGDS.

The DialDoc23 shared task introduces training and evaluation datasets for MDGDS in Vietnamese and French. The training dataset comprises three distinct components: query, passage, and response. Additionally, the dataset includes a set of documents for retrieval. The query combines the historical dialogue with the current inquiry. During inference, the intelligent agent retrieves the most relevant document from the document set based on the query and generates a response. Notably, this task focuses on low-resource languages, setting it apart from previous tasks.

In this paper, we propose cascaded prompt-based post-training models to solve MDGDS challenge. As inspried by Re2G (Glass et al., 2022) framework, our approach tackles the overall task by dividing it into three subtasks: Retrieval, Reranking, and Generation, with parallel training and sequential inference. As illustrated in Figure 1, the retrieval step identifies top k relevant passages, followed by reranking to select the most relevant passage, and in generation step the query and passage information are incorporated to generate the final response. To enhance the performance of retrieval and generation in low-resource languages such as French and Vietnamese, we conduct post-training on high-resource languages such as English and Chinese to learn language similarities. Additionally, we activate the models' capabilities in diverse languages within the dialogue domain by employing the prompt method. Besides, We employ domain loss function to align the domain of the query and passage during retrieval training. We conducted comprehensive experiments on the

*Equal contribution.
†Corresponding author.

Proceedings of the Third DialDoc Workshop on Document-grounded Dialogue and Conversational Question Answering, pages 44–51
July 13, 2023

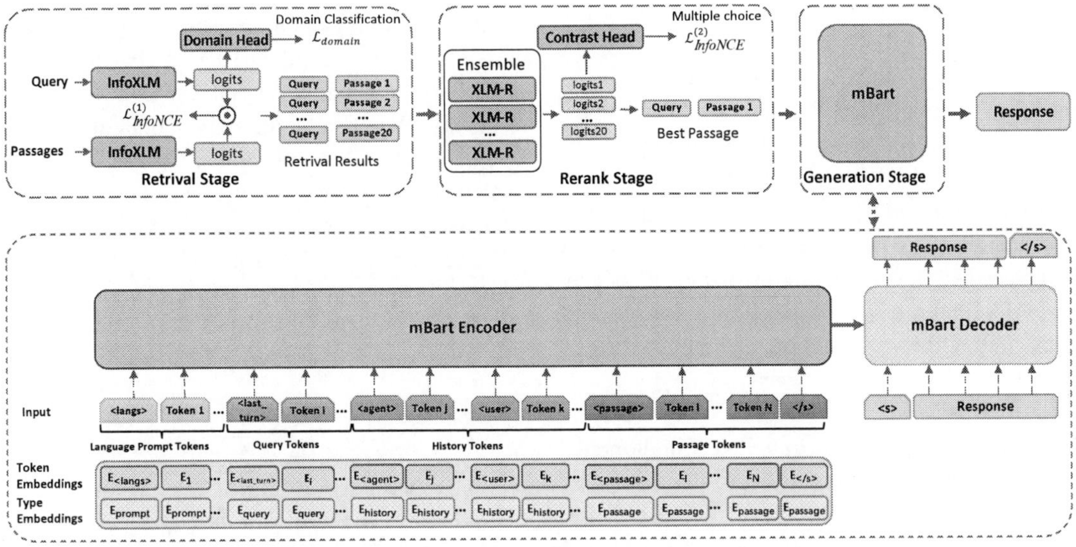

Figure 1: The framework comprises three main stages: (1) Retrieval Stage, which retrieves the top k relevant passages based on a dialogue context. (2) Reranking Stage, which reranks the top k retrieved passages to find the candidate passage. (3) Generation Stage, which generates a system response using user's query, historical dialogue, selected passage, and language prompts.

DialDoc23 shared task, which demonstrated the effectiveness of our proposed methods and resulted in the first place position in the competition.

2 Related Works

2.1 Document Grounded Dialogue Systems

In recent years, substantial advances have been made in DGDS, facilitated by high-quality annotated datasets like SQuAD 2.0 (Rajpurkar et al., 2018), CoQA (Reddy et al., 2019), and MultiDoc2Dial (Feng et al., 2021). Retrieval-and-Generation is a typical framework for implementing DGDS. The framework comprises two sequential stages: (i) retrieving relevant passages from knowledge bases, and (ii) generating responses based on the retrieved passages and users' input. To improve knowledge retrieval, scholars have proposed a variety of approaches such as learning sentence embeddings from dialogue (Liu et al., 2022, 2021a), adding a reranker after retriever retrieval (Re2G) (Glass et al., 2022), and using priori and posteriori knowledge selection (Chen et al., 2020). As for generation, recent studies have also introduced new techniques, such as improving dialogue generation via proactively querying grounded knowledge (Zhao et al., 2022) and leveraging fusion-in-decoder (FiD) (Izacard and Grave, 2021).

2.2 Multilingual Dialogue Generation

Multilingual dialogue is a new research topic in DGDS, aiming for high-quality and fluent communication across different languages. Pre-trained language models have the benefit of automatically learning similarities between languages and enabling unsupervised learning to improve performance in conversations across different languages. Models such as XLM-RoBERTa (Conneau et al., 2019), InfoXLM (Chi et al., 2020), mT5 (Xue et al., 2020), and mBART (Tang et al., 2020), can assist in implementing multilingual transfer learning to improve the performance and fluency of multilingual conversations. However, despite recent technological advancements(Ma et al., 2022), multilingual dialogues continue to face challenges. In particular, the lack of training data for many of the world's languages, especially those with limited resources and research, has significantly impeded the development of multilingual dialogue generation(Majewska et al., 2023). In order to combat the aforementioned challenges, our model leverages the similarities between language structures to augment post-training data, while incorporating prompt techniques to enhance language comprehension.

3 Method

The proposed method consists of three main stages: retrieval, reranking, and generation, as depicted Figure 1. Using contrast learning techniques, the retrieval step efficiently identifies top k relevant passages, followed by reranking to select the most pertinent passage. In the generation step, the query and passage information are incorporated to generate the final response. Each step is described in detail in the following section.

3.1 Passage Retrieval

Passage retrieval constitutes a fundamental component of MDGDS. Given the historical dialogue records $\{u_1, u_2..., u_{T-1}\}$ and the user turn u_T, the passage retrieval identify the top-k relevant passages from a given document set $P = \{p_1, p_2, ..., p_M\}$.

Retriever For efficient passage retrieval, we implement a Bi-encoder architecture to encode the dialogue context and passages independently, as described in Zhang et al. (2023). Further, we leverage two InfoXLM cross-lingual models to derive semantic representations. During the inference phase, we regard the input dialogue context C as the search query and retrieve the top-k passages from the document set based on dot product similarity. In the training stage, each training sample consist of three attributes: the dialogue context, relevant passage, and non-relevant passage. In a training batch, the positive passage refers to the relevant passage, while the negative passage includes the non-relevant passage and the other passages in the batch. The objective function $\mathcal{L}_{InfoNCE}$ for the constrastive learning is formulated as:

$$\mathcal{L}^{(1)}_{InfoNCE} = -\log \frac{\exp\left(\boldsymbol{q} \cdot \boldsymbol{p}^{+}/\tau\right)}{\sum_{\boldsymbol{p} \in \boldsymbol{P}^{\pm}} \exp\left(\boldsymbol{q} \cdot \boldsymbol{p}/\tau\right)} \quad (1)$$

where $\boldsymbol{q}$ and $\boldsymbol{p}$ represent the semantic features of dialogue context and passage extracted by multilingual models, respectively.

Domain classification The Bi-encoder architecture has exhibited efficacy in text retrieval. Nonetheless, the absence of fine-grained supervision signals might hinder the alignment of semantic features between queries and passages. To surmount this constraint, we suggest incorporating domain classification information to guide the representation learning of queries and to align the encoding information of both queries and passages, without compromising the Bi-encoder architecture's efficiency. Technically, for a given dialogue context C, we derive its domain label y from the associated golden passage and employ a linear layer to classify the dialogue context's semantic feature accordingly. We subsequently train the model by minimizing the cross-entropy loss function $\mathcal{L}_{domain}$.

$$\mathcal{L}_{domain} = -\sum_{i=1}^{d} y_i \cdot log(p_i) \quad (2)$$

$$\mathcal{L} = \mathcal{L}_{InfoNCE} + \alpha \mathcal{L}_{domain} \quad (3)$$

where d represent the number of domain set $\mathcal{D}$, and p_i denote the probability of a given category i, α is a hyper-parameter weighting the domain classification loss.

Retrieval Post-training To further address the low-resource target language problem while leveraging the cross-lingual pretraining model's capabilities, we conducted a post-training on English and Chinese dialogue datasets for the same task. Techinically, we utilized the golden passage of the dialogue as the positive samples and retrieved the most relevant documents using the BM25 algorithm from the remaining document set as negative samples.

3.2 Passage Reranking

Passage reranking is the process of reordering the top-k highest-scoring passages C_p retrieved in the previous step, with the aim of improving the probability of the most relevant passages being retrieved correctly. To perform the reranking, We employ XLM-RoBERTa$_{large}$ as the encoder of the reranker, following the pipeline developed by (Zhang et al., 2023). The reranker concatenated the dialogue context C with the candidate passages $p \in P^{\pm}$, inserting a "<passage>" token between them as a separator. The reranker then utilized a contrastive loss function, known as the InfoNCE loss, to recalculate the scores of the passages. The highest-scoring passage is thereafter selected as an input for generation. The objective function $\mathcal{L}_{InfoNCE}$ is formulated as:

$$S\left(C|p\right) = \text{Sigmoid}\left\{\text{linear}\left[XLM\text{-}R\left(\left[C, p\right]\right)\right]\right\} \tag{4}$$

$$\mathcal{L}_{InfoNCE}^{(2)} = -\log \frac{\exp\left(S\left(C, p^{+}\right)/\tau\right)}{\sum_{p \in P^{\pm}} \exp\left(S\left(C, p^{+}\right)/\tau\right)} \tag{5}$$

where $S\left(C|p\right)$ represents the similarity between the dialogue context and passage, which is obtained by applying a Sigmoid activation function and a linear layer to the output of XLM-RoBERTa$_{large}$ model, τ is a temperature factor which is set to 1 in our experiment. To enhance the model's generalization ability, we apply an ensemble method in which multiple models receive the input, and the most relevant passages are voted on separately. Subsequently, the passage with the most votes is used as input for the generation stage.

Although both retrieval and reranking are methods used to evaluate the relevance of passage and dialogue context, they differ in the way they understand and score relevance. Retrieval method employs two encoders to encode the passage and dialogue and then calculates the similarity between them. In contrast, reranking methods prioritize sequence structure and semantic information, enabling a more profound comprehension of the content. Due to reranking requires greater computational resources, it is implemented after retrieval.

3.3 Response Generation

The main objective of response generation is to present the user with a system response u_{T+1} that is constructed using the historical dialogue records $\{u_1, u_2, ..., u_{T-1}\}$, a user turn u_T, and the selected passage p, while ensuring that it blends skillfully into the ongoing discourse.

We leverage the large pre-trained model mBART$_{large}$ (Liu et al., 2020) to deal with multilingual generation task. Our dataset contains a significantly greater amount of data in English and Chinese languages compared to French and Vietnamese. In order to improve the performance of low-resource languages utilizing data-rich languages, we employ prompt-based and post-training techniques.

3.3.1 Input Representation

Language Prompts The prompt method that aims to make better use of pre-trained knowledge has recently been successful in transferring pre-trained language models (PLMs) to downstream tasks (Liu et al., 2021b). Some researchers also find prompts can be effective in multilingual scenarios (Fu et al., 2022b; Huang et al., 2022). We leverage prompt techniques to activate model's capability of different languages. As inspired by Fu et al. (2022b), we design both in-lingual prompts(IP) and cross-lingual prompts(CP). In-lingual prompts refer to the prompts where the language used is identical to the target language. The prompts for the different languages are listed in Table 1. While cross-lingual prompts are the prompts templates which involve using the same language across various languages. We use Vietnamese prompts as the unified prompts for all languages.

Language	Prompts
En	Answer user questions based on document content and historical conversations.
Zh	根据文档内容和历史对话回答用户问题。
Fr	Répondre aux questions des utilisateurs sur la base du contenu des documents et de l'historique des conversations.
Vi	Trả lời câu hỏi của người dùng dựa trên nội dung tài liệu và các cuộc hội thoại lịch sử.

Table 1: In-lingual prompts in different languages

Input Setting For the input of generation model, we define our input to a concatenation:

$$x := [prompt; u_T; u_{T-1}...u_1; p] \tag{6}$$

where $prompt, u_t, p$ is the prompt corresponding to the target language, the utterance of turn t, the chosen passage respectively.

Separator tokens We define several separator tokens to delimit different components of the input, as illustrated in Figure 1. We utilize the token $<Langs>\in S$ to correspond with the target language, where the set S is defined as S=$\{<En>,<Zh>,<Fr>,<Vi>\}$. We add $<last\_turn>$ before u_T to identify the last query, we utilize $<agent>$ and $<user>$ tokens to specify historical system responses and user's utterance, respectively. $<passage>$ token is added to specify the selected passage. $<s>$ and $</s>$ tokens are used to specify the start and the end of generation tokens.

Type Embedding We use type embedding to distinguish prompt, query, history and passage as illustrated in Figure 1. This embedding comprises of four distinct values.

3.3.2 Training

Training objective Our approach use a sequence-to-sequence language model to achieve multilingual generation training. The objective function is to maximize the log-likelihood of the output text and is defined as follows:

$$\mathcal{L} = -\sum_{i=1}^{|y|} \log P\left(y_i \mid y_{<i}, x; \theta\right) \quad (7)$$

Where $|y|$ is the number of tokens in the decoded text, y_i is the i_{th} token and $y_{<i}$ is the tokens before the time step i. Here, x denotes the input of the model specified by the Equation 6. The symbol θ represents the set of training parameters.

Generation Post-training The post-training method is used to transfer knowledge from high-resource languages to low-resource languages. To begin with, the model is post-trained on English, Chinese, French, and Vietnamese with a response generation task. Here, the French and Vietnamese data undergo translation from the English language. The model is then fine-tuned on our target languages, French and Vietnamese.

R-drop Regularization methods like the dropout technique are crucial in training a deep neural network as they prevent overfitting and enhance the generalization ability of deep models. However, dropout results in a unnegligible inconsistency between the training and inference stages (Ma et al., 2016). R-drop (Wu et al., 2021), which allows each data sample to go through the forward pass twice, is an effective measure to mitigate this inconsistency. R-Drop forces the two forward pass distributions for the same data sample outputted by the different dropout model to be consistent with each other, through minimizing the bidirectional Kullback-Leibler(KL) divergence between the two distributions.

4 Experiments

4.1 Dataset and Evaluation Metrics

We conduct our experiments on DialDoc23 shared task, which introduces multilingual document-grounded dialogue dataset in Vietnamese and French[1]. This dataset contains 797 dialogues in Vietnamese (3,446 turns), 816 dialogues in French (3,510 turns), and a corpus of 17272 paragraphs. Each turn utterance is annotated with a number of grounding passages and a corresponding response. And we incorporate additional English and Chinese datasets for post-training. Vietnamese language has a significant number of words derived from Chinese while English and French both belong to the Indo-European language family. We utilize the Doc2Bot dataset (Fu et al., 2022a), which comprises 5760 turns of dialogue in Chinese, and MultiDoc2Dial (Feng et al., 2021), containing 26,506 turns of dialogue in English.

The leaderboard evaluation method employs the token-level F1 score (F1), SacreBLEU (S-BLEU), and ROUGE-L metrics (Feng et al., 2021).

4.2 Experiment Detail

For the retrieval training stage, we utilized a batch size of 128 and a learning rate of 1e-4 and 2e-5 for post-training and fine-tuning, respectively. And retrieval passage number top-k is 20. In the reranking training stage, we set the batch size to 20 and the learning rate to 2e-5. During the generation stage, we used a batch size of 32 with a learning rate of 1e-4 and 1e-5 for post-training and fine-tuning, respectively. For R-drop, we set the dropout rate to 0.1, and the KL-divergence loss weight α 0.02 (Wu et al., 2021). For post-training, we post-train the model on English, Chinese, French, and Vietnamese with a response generation task. Here, the French and Vietnamese data undergo translation from the English language. During each training session, AdamW is utilized as our optimizer with a 10% linear warmup technique. All experiments are conducted on an NVIDIA A100 GPU. To select the best model, we separated 200 French and 200 Vietnamese samples as our validation set. For testing, we utilize two test sets, referred to as DevTest and Test, obtained from the Leaderboard platform, each consisting of 194 dialogues. Since the Test dataset is not accessible to the public now and only the Score-all is visible on the leaderboard, we opted to present only the Score-all result. And due to the limit on the number of submissions for the Test dataset and the closure of the leaderboard, we only have the results of a relatively good performance.

4.3 Experimental Results and Analysis

Retrivel Results Table 3 presents the experimental results on the validation set for different

[1]https://modelscope.cn/datasets/DAMO_ConvAI/FrViDoc2Bot

Method	TestDev				Test
	F1	**S-BLEU**	**ROUGE-L**	**Score-all**	**Score-all**
Re2G(Baseline)	58.55	42.03	55.83	156.42	-
mBart$_{large}$	67.26	56.94	65.06	189.26	-
+FID	63.54	54.92	62.39	180.85	-
+CP	67.42	57.25	65.39	190.06	-
+CP+Post	69.27	58.39	66.39	194.05	-
+CP+Post+R-drop	69.19	59.13	66.85	195.17	214.46
+IP	68.09	57.56	66.06	191.71	-
+IP+Post	69.95	58.95	67.36	196.26	-
+IP+Post+R-drop	**70.25**	**59.73**	**68.48**	**198.46**	**215.40**

Table 2: Results of generation method on Leaderboard of MDGDS. The "+Fid" method denotes the application of the Fusion-in-Decoder model, while the "+Post" method refers to fine-tuning the model on the post-training model. "+IP" and "+CP" represent the usage of in-lingual prompts and cross-lingual prompts, respectively. Besides, the "+R-drop" method utilizes the R-drop technique.

Model	$R@1$	$R@5$	$R@10$	$R@20$
XLM-R$_{base}$	48.75	68.25	76.25	81.25
XLM-R$_{large}$	55.75	73.25	80.25	88.00
InfoXLM$_{large}$	57.75	76.75	81.75	89.00
+Post	62.25	80.25	85.75	90.50
+Post+DomainCls	**64.50**	**82.50**	**87.00**	**91.25**

Table 3: Retrieval results on the development set. The "+Post" method refers to the use of the InfoXLM$_{large}$ multilingual pre-training model, followed by post-training with Chinese and English languages, and finally fine-tuning on the target language dataset. "DomainCls" represents the adoption of topic category optimization for sentence representations within dialogue records.

Model	$R@1$	$R@2$	$R@3$	$R@5$
XLM-R$_{base}$	80.50	86.25	86.25	94.50
XLM-R$_{large}$	92.50	97.00	98.25	99.00
+Ensemble	**93.75**	-	-	-

Table 4: Reranking results on the development set. The "+Ensemble" method involves the integration of 10 XLM-Roberta-large models created in the same training, and subsequently making the final selection through a voting process to identify the best passages.

multilingual models, with post-training and domain classification.

In the experimental setup, we evaluated the capabilities of XLM-R$_{base}$, XLM-R$_{large}$, and InfoXLM$_{large}$ multilingual models to identify the most suitable cross-lingual model. Furthermore, we conducted post-training on the InfoXLM$_{large}$ model using Chinese and English, and then fine-tuned it on the target language. Moreover, we assessed the effectiveness of optimizing dialogue content representation using topic category information based on the previous two steps.

Experimental results indicate that the performance of InfoXLM$_{large}$ surpasses that of XLM-R$_{large}$. Furthermore, post-training of the pre-trained model has improved the $R@20$ score by 1.50. Additionally, introducing domain-specific supervision signals in the representation learning of dialogue content can enhance the semantic feature representation, which has improved the $R@20$ score by 0.75.

Reranking Results Table 4 presents the experimental results on the validation set for different multilingual models. The results illustrate that employing a model ensemble in the reranking stage yields an improvement of 1.25 in $R@1$ score.

Generation Results Tabel 2 presents the results of different methods. Our generation methods employ the passage selected through the best retrieval and reranking models. Our method outperforms the baseline by a significant margin. This improvement can be attributed to both the generative model's design and the retrieval of the most relevant passages by the first two tasks.

To determine which type of prompt is more effective, we conducted experiments using both in-lingual and cross-lingual prompts. It is shown that in-lingual prompts outperform cross-lingual prompts in all settings. We think that the model's ability in various languages is triggered by distinct language prompts. This makes it easier to recall knowledge from the pre-training stage using in-lingual prompts.

To leverage the retrieval of multiple passages by the first two stages, we conducted an experiment using Fusion-in-Decoder (FiD) (Izacard and Grave, 2021). The FiD model employs the seq2seq framework to encode each passage independently with a query and subsequently decode all the encoded features to generate responses. Specifically, we configured the encoder to accept two passages as input. The results indicate that the FiD model does not perform well in our generation task. We think this is due to the fact that the gold response is highly relevant to the retrieved passage, whereas FiD considers the top 2 passages, introducing noise to the model.

The results indicate that the method of post-training on datasets of English, Chinese, French, and Vietnamese followed by fine-tuning on the target languages, French and Vietnamese, enhances the performance a lot. The post-training method improves the performance of both cross-lingual prompts and in-lingual prompts considerably, yielding scores of 3.99 and 4.55 respectively. This suggests that using high-resource languages to enhance low-resource languages, by leveraging the similarities between the languages, can be an effective approach. Additionally, when combined with R-drop, it further enhances the performance of cross-lingual prompts and in-lingual prompts by 1.12 and 2.20, respectively, offering an effective solution to mitigate the inconsistency between training and inference.

5 Conclusion

In this paper, we propose a cascaded prompt-based post-training framework comprising Retrieval, Reranking, and Generation three-stage, to solve the MDGD challenge. To enhance the retrieval and generation performance in low-resource languages such as French and Vietnamese, we exploit the similarities between these and high-resource languages such as Chinese and English by applying post-training techniques. Prompt method are used to activate model's ability in a specific language and dialogue domain, and in-lingual prompts show superior results. Furthermore, we employ DomainCls loss function in retrieval, emsemble method in Rerank, and R-drop method to attain the best results in the Dialdoc23 shared task.

6 Acknowledge

The research work is supported by National Key Research and Development Program of China (No.2020YFC2007104), Beijing Municipal Science & Technology Commission(No.Z221100002722009), Youth Innovation Promotion Association CAS (No.2021101), National Key R&D Program of China (No.2022YFB3904700), Key Research and Development Program of in Shandong Province (2019JZZY020102), Key Research and Development Program of Jiangsu Province (No.BE2018084), Industrial Internet Innovation and Development Project in 2021 (TC210A02M, TC210804D), Opening Project of Beijing Key Laboratory of Mobile Computing and Pervasive Device.

References

Mikel Artetxe, Gorka Labaka, and Eneko Agirre. 2017. Learning bilingual word embeddings with (almost) no bilingual data. In *Proceedings of the 55th Annual Meeting of the Association for Computational Linguistics (Volume 1: Long Papers)*, pages 451–462.

Qibin Chen, Junyang Lin, Yichang Zhang, Ming Ding, Yukuo Cen, Hongxia Yang, and Jie Tang. 2019. Towards knowledge-based recommender dialog system. *arXiv preprint arXiv:1908.05391*.

Xiuyi Chen, Fandong Meng, Peng Li, Feilong Chen, Shuang Xu, Bo Xu, and Jie Zhou. 2020. Bridging the gap between prior and posterior knowledge selection for knowledge-grounded dialogue generation. In *Proceedings of the 2020 conference on empirical methods in natural language processing (EMNLP)*, pages 3426–3437.

Zewen Chi, Li Dong, Furu Wei, Nan Yang, Saksham Singhal, Wenhui Wang, Xia Song, Xian-Ling Mao, Heyan Huang, and Ming Zhou. 2020. Infoxlm: An information-theoretic framework for cross-lingual language model pre-training. *arXiv preprint arXiv:2007.07834*.

Alexis Conneau, Kartikay Khandelwal, Naman Goyal, Vishrav Chaudhary, Guillaume Wenzek, Francisco Guzmán, Edouard Grave, Myle Ott, Luke Zettlemoyer, and Veselin Stoyanov. 2019. Unsupervised cross-lingual representation learning at scale. *arXiv preprint arXiv:1911.02116*.

Raj Dabre, Atsushi Fujita, and Chenhui Chu. 2019. Exploiting multilingualism through multistage fine-tuning for low-resource neural machine translation. In *Proceedings of the 2019 Conference on Empirical Methods in Natural Language Processing and the 9th International Joint Conference on Natural Language Processing (EMNLP-IJCNLP)*, pages 1410–1416.

Song Feng, Siva Sankalp Patel, Hui Wan, and Sachindra Joshi. 2021. Multidoc2dial: Modeling dialogues grounded in multiple documents. *arXiv preprint arXiv:2109.12595*.

Haomin Fu, Yeqin Zhang, Haiyang Yu, Jian Sun, Fei Huang, Luo Si, Yongbin Li, and Cam Tu Nguyen. 2022a. Doc2Bot: Accessing heterogeneous documents via conversational bots. In *Findings of the Association for Computational Linguistics: EMNLP 2022*, pages 1820–1836, Abu Dhabi, United Arab Emirates. Association for Computational Linguistics.

Jinlan Fu, See-Kiong Ng, and Pengfei Liu. 2022b. Polyglot prompt: Multilingual multitask promptraining. *arXiv preprint arXiv:2204.14264*.

Chang Gao, Wenxuan Zhang, and Wai Lam. 2022. Unigdd: A unified generative framework for goal-oriented document-grounded dialogue. *arXiv preprint arXiv:2204.07770*.

Michael Glass, Gaetano Rossiello, Md Faisal Mahbub Chowdhury, Ankita Rajaram Naik, Pengshan Cai, and Alfio Gliozzo. 2022. Re2g: Retrieve, rerank, generate. *arXiv preprint arXiv:2207.06300*.

Milan Gritta, Ruoyu Hu, and Ignacio Iacobacci. 2022. Crossaligner & co: Zero-shot transfer methods for task-oriented cross-lingual natural language understanding. *arXiv preprint arXiv:2203.09982*.

Lianzhe Huang, Shuming Ma, Dongdong Zhang, Furu Wei, and Houfeng Wang. 2022. Zero-shot cross-lingual transfer of prompt-based tuning with a unified multilingual prompt. *arXiv preprint arXiv:2202.11451*.

Gautier Izacard and Edouard Grave. 2021. Leveraging passage retrieval with generative models for open domain question answering. In *Proceedings of the 16th Conference of the European Chapter of the Association for Computational Linguistics: Main Volume*, pages 874–880, Online. Association for Computational Linguistics.

Che Liu, Rui Wang, Junfeng Jiang, Yongbin Li, and Fei Huang. 2022. Dial2vec: Self-guided contrastive learning of unsupervised dialogue embeddings. *arXiv preprint arXiv:2210.15332*.

Che Liu, Rui Wang, Jinghua Liu, Jian Sun, Fei Huang, and Luo Si. 2021a. Dialoguecse: Dialogue-based contrastive learning of sentence embeddings. *arXiv preprint arXiv:2109.12599*.

Pengfei Liu, Weizhe Yuan, Jinlan Fu, Zhengbao Jiang, Hiroaki Hayashi, and Graham Neubig. 2021b. Pre-train, prompt, and predict: A systematic survey of prompting methods in natural language processing.

Yinhan Liu, Jiatao Gu, Naman Goyal, Xian Li, Sergey Edunov, Marjan Ghazvininejad, Mike Lewis, and Luke Zettlemoyer. 2020. Multilingual denoising pre-training for neural machine translation. *Transactions of the Association for Computational Linguistics*, 8:726–742.

Xuezhe Ma, Yingkai Gao, Zhiting Hu, Yaoliang Yu, Yuntian Deng, and Eduard Hovy. 2016. Dropout with expectation-linear regularization. *arXiv preprint arXiv:1609.08017*.

Zhanyu Ma, Jian Ye, Xurui Yang, and Jianfeng Liu. 2022. Hcld: A hierarchical framework for zero-shot cross-lingual dialogue system. In *Proceedings of the 29th International Conference on Computational Linguistics*, pages 4492–4498.

Olga Majewska, Evgeniia Razumovskaia, Edoardo M Ponti, Ivan Vulić, and Anna Korhonen. 2023. Cross-lingual dialogue dataset creation via outline-based generation. *Transactions of the Association for Computational Linguistics*, 11:139–156.

Pranav Rajpurkar, Robin Jia, and Percy Liang. 2018. Know what you don't know: Unanswerable questions for squad. *arXiv preprint arXiv:1806.03822*.

Hannah Rashkin, David Reitter, Gaurav Singh Tomar, and Dipanjan Das. 2021. Increasing faithfulness in knowledge-grounded dialogue with controllable features. *arXiv preprint arXiv:2107.06963*.

Siva Reddy, Danqi Chen, and Christopher D Manning. 2019. Coqa: A conversational question answering challenge. *Transactions of the Association for Computational Linguistics*, 7:249–266.

Yuqing Tang, Chau Tran, Xian Li, Peng-Jen Chen, Naman Goyal, Vishrav Chaudhary, Jiatao Gu, and Angela Fan. 2020. Multilingual translation with extensible multilingual pretraining and finetuning. *arXiv preprint arXiv:2008.00401*.

Lijun Wu, Juntao Li, Yue Wang, Qi Meng, Tao Qin, Wei Chen, Min Zhang, Tie-Yan Liu, et al. 2021. R-drop: Regularized dropout for neural networks. *Advances in Neural Information Processing Systems*, 34:10890–10905.

Linting Xue, Noah Constant, Adam Roberts, Mihir Kale, Rami Al-Rfou, Aditya Siddhant, Aditya Barua, and Colin Raffel. 2020. mt5: A massively multilingual pre-trained text-to-text transformer. *arXiv preprint arXiv:2010.11934*.

Yeqin Zhang, Haomin Fu, Cheng Fu, Haiyang Yu, Yongbin Li, and Cam-Tu Nguyen. 2023. Coarse-to-fine knowledge selection for document grounded dialogs.

Xiangyu Zhao, Longbiao Wang, and Jianwu Dang. 2022. Improving dialogue generation via proactively querying grounded knowledge. In *ICASSP 2022-2022 IEEE International Conference on Acoustics, Speech and Signal Processing (ICASSP)*, pages 6577–6581. IEEE.

Enhanced Training Methods for Multiple Languages

Anonymous ACL submission

Abstract

Document-grounded dialogue generation based on multilingual is a challenging and realistic task. Unlike previous tasks, it need to tackle with multiple high-resource languages facilitating low-resource languages. This paper summarizes our research based on a three-stage pipeline that includes retrieval, re-rank and generation where each component is individually optimized. In different languages with limited data scenarios, we mainly improve the robustness of the pipeline through data augmentation and embedding perturbation with purpose of improving the performance designing three training methods: cross-language enhancement training, weighted training with neighborhood distribution augmentation, and ensemble adversarial training, all of that can be used as plug and play modules. Through experiments with different settings, it has been shown that our methods can effectively improve the generalization performance of pipeline with score ranking 6th among the public submissions on leaderboards.

1 Introduction

Question Answering (QA) system has received extensive attention in recent researches. The QA system aims to provide precise answers in response to the user's questions in natural language. An essential task in the QA system is conversational question answering and document-grounded dialogue modeling. Lack of data is one of the main challenges (Zhang et al., 2020).

Retrieval-augmented Generation (RAG) (Lewis et al., 2020) proposes a two-stage generation method with retriever extracting multiple documents related to the query and feeding them into answer generator. A survey of document-grounded dialogue systems (Ma et al., 2020) points that it is a mainstream method to indirectly search for key text before directly generating replies. There have been various works for knowledge-grounded dialogue systems (Zhan et al., 2021; Wen et al., 2022; Ma et al., 2020) to address this problem. A new framework UniGDD (Gao et al., 2022) use prompt learning for context guidance and design multitask learning. PPTOD (Su et al., 2022) proposes a dialogue pre-trained model that implements the current SOTA.

As a more realistic task, MultiDoc2Dial (Feng et al., 2021) faces challenges of identifying useful pieces of text from documents and generating response simultaneously which is goal-oriented dialogues generation based on multiple documents. Unlike former task, Doc2dial (Zhang et al., 2023) upgrades the difficulty level by introducing multiple languages.

To alleviate the problem of limited datasets in low-resource languages, on the one hand, it is necessary to effectively utilize datasets in the other high-resource languages. On the other hand, we design three training methods. These designs are all aimed at enhancing the generalization ability of the model. Our model is based on a three-stage framework: retriever, re-ranker and generator, the aims of first and second step are obtaining the most relevant paragraphs to the question, and then generating answer text. The first stage is responsible for the coverage of relevant texts that is the comprehensiveness of input texts; in the second stage, it is necessary to filter out the most relevant text that is the accuracy of the input text; the third stage generates answers based on the input text, which is clearly the most important part. Our contributions are as follows:

- a cross language enhancement training method is designed which can effectively improve generalization ability by replacing the high-frequency tokens of

Proceedings of the Third DialDoc Workshop on Document-grounded Dialogue and Conversational Question Answering, pages 52–56
July 13, 2023 ©2023 Association for Computational Linguistics

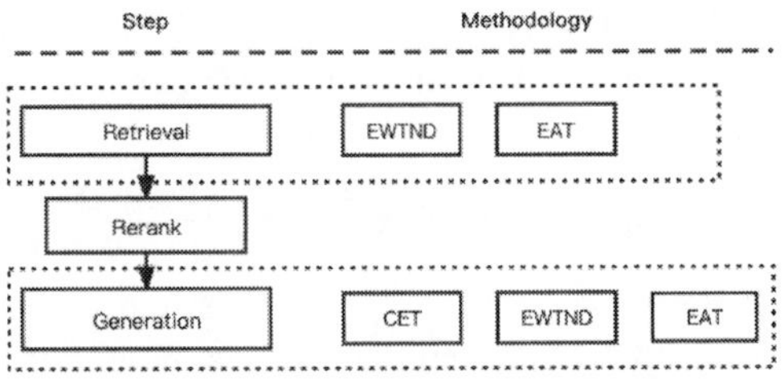

Figure 1: Training process of our pipeline.

high-resource languages with that of low-resource languages in pre-trained model.

- enhanced weighted training approach based on neighborhood distribution is presented, the diversity of input texts can be increased through data augmentation, and the problem of semantic inaccuracy can be alleviated through weight.
- ensemble adversarial training method is proposed including two classic adversarial training methods to improve the model's anti-interference ability and reduce text generation bias.

The above three enhancement training methods can be easily applied to other languages models as plug and play modules. Based on the published dataset, sufficient experiments are conducted confirming the method can effectively improve the generalization performance of the model.

2 Task Definition

Given dialogue history $\{q_1, \cdots, q_{t-1}\}$ and current user's query q_t, DialDoc task need to produce the response based on knowledge from a set of relevant documents $D_0 \subseteq D$, where D denotes all knowledge documents. Besides, the task provides similar format dataset of four languages including two high-resource languages (English and Chinese and two low-resource languages (French and Vietnamese), and the latter one is evaluated.

3 Methodology

To start with design, our pipeline is based on the three-stage baseline (Zhang et al., 2023). The three training augmentation methods that we propose can be applied to retrieval and generation. The specific framework process is as Figure 1.

3.1 Cross-Language Enhancement Training (CET)

From perspective of tokenizer, we designed a enhancement training method with token exchange between various languages. In different languages pairs, words with high frequency may have similar semantics, so that transfer learning can be used to facilitate low-resource languages training with embedding layers of high-resource languages. The basic idea is that as for pre-training model's tokenizer , replace high-resource languages' tokens with that of low-resource languages according to the rank of tokens' frequency which should follow four principles: (i) the total number of tokens of the high-resource languages need to be larger than that of the low-resource languages. (ii) select every similar language pairs, replace the high-resource tokens with low-resource tokens according to the rank order of frequency separately. In this paper, it should replace Chinese with Vietnamese and English with French. (iii) if the tokens of a language pair are insufficient, they can be mapped to the remaining unaligned tokens of another language. In this paper, there does not need to do it as the number of tokens in English higher than that of French, so do Chinese and Vietnamese. (iv) punctuation marks, [UNK] and other special marks remain unchanged.

After obtaining the mapping relationship of the tokenizer, we replace low-resource languages' datasets into high-resource languages' datasets as additional data, setting training weight w for the new one.

3.2 Enhanced Weighted Training of Neighborhood Distribution (EWTND)

To alleviate the limited datasets about low-resource languages, we propose enhanced weighted training of neighborhood distribution method. By enhancing the texts from semantic neighbor-hood distribution, the diversity of input text increases, and the problem of semantic inaccuracy of neighborhood distribution is alleviated through weighted training. The steps of the method are as follows: (i) in top n words $\{w_1, \cdots, w_n\}$ with the highest frequency, using the last layer of pre-trained mT5 (Xue et al., 2021; Raffel et al., 2020; Zhang et al., 2020) encoder to produce 512 dimensional vectors $\{v_1, \cdots, v_n\}$ for each token (except for punctuation mark). (ii) for every v, find the k words with the largest similarity through vector retrieval by Faiss (Johnson et al., 2019) vector retrieval library, and record their similarities. So we get the text neighborhood

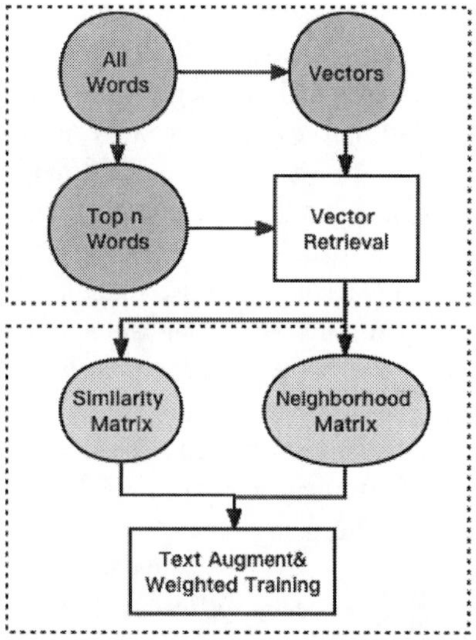

Figure 2: The key parts of EWTND.

matrix t_{ij} and similarity matrix s_{ij}, where $1 \leq i \leq n, 1 \leq j \leq k$. (iii) during training, each sentence has a $p\%$ probability to apply replacing that is words in w are replaced by one of its neighborhood from t with equal probability, and the calculation weight of sample loss is updated to the mean of similarity from s in every sentence.

3.3 Ensemble Adversarial Training (EAT)

As a regularization method, adversarial training can improve the robustness of the model by introducing perturbations in embedding (Tramèr et al., 2020; Miyato et al., 2021). We propose an ensemble adversarial training method that blend two classic adversarial training methods to improve the model's anti-interference ability and reduce text generation bias. Adversarial training can be described by a general formula as follows: (Madry et al., 2019)

$$\min_{\theta} \mathbb{E}_{(x,y)\sim D}[\max_{\Delta x \in \Omega} L(x + \Delta x, y; \theta)]$$

where D is training dataset, x is input, y is target, θ is model parameter, $L(x + \Delta x, y; \theta)$ is loss of single sample, Ω is disturbance space, Δx is perturbation. What's more, the main changes in different adversarial training methods are Δx and Ω. FGM method (Ian et al., 2015; Wong et al., 2020) raise the gradient with parameter ϵ and standardize it getting new Δx:

$$\Delta x = \epsilon \frac{\nabla L(x, y; \theta)}{\|\nabla L(x, y; \theta)\|}$$

While PGD method (Madry et al., 2019) split Δx into multiple steps, set the constraint space to a sphere:

$$\Delta x_{t+1} = \prod_{x+S} (\Delta x_t + \alpha \frac{\nabla L(x_t, y; \theta)}{\|\nabla L(x_t, y; \theta)\|})$$

where $S = r \in \mathbb{R}^d, \|r\|_2 < \epsilon$, α is step size.

We add the FGM and PGD into training. For each batch in training process, we set the probabilities of the different training methods, there is $p_1\%$ probability of PGD, $p_2\%$ probability of FGM, and $p_3\%$ probability of not changing. The proportion can be determined by the ordinal of the model's convergence effect. In this paper, the rank of PGD, FGM, and non enhancement are 3:2:1 respectively, which means the probabilities are 50%, 33%, 17%. After multiple experiments, we believe that there is a correlation between the final convergence loss of the method and the dataset, so the all possibilities should cannot be directly set and need to be determined based on the training results.

4 Experiments

We evaluate our methods using datasets provided by shared task which include four languages. As for generator, EWTND uses French and Vietnamese dialogue generation dataset, while CET also requires English and Chinese dialogue dataset. Besides, the score is calculated based on the sum of token-level F1, SacreBleu and Rouge-L metrics.

The experiments are mainly conducted on fine-tuning the retriever and generator based on the open-source baseline in three-stage framework. All the performances of methods can be evaluated by score of generator.

w	F1	Sarcebleu	Rouge-L	Score
0	58.55	42.03	55.83	156.42
0.2	60.74	43.30	57.92	161.96
0.25	61.85	43.72	59.21	164.78
0.3	61.97	44.38	59.31	**165.66**
0.35	61.71	43.63	59.08	164.42
$0^{\text{half bz}}$	61.13	43.36	58.18	162.67

Table 1: The results of CET on Doc2dial validation dataset.

Implementation As for CET and EWTND, when they are used in generator, we change the "passages" and "re-rank" corresponding text in dataset; when they are used in retriever, we change the "positive" and "negative" corresponding text in dataset; while "query" text and "target" text won't be changed. As for EWTND, we use the cosine similarity. Faiss vector retrieval use product quantization to divide vector into 8 sub vectors, with 100 k-means clustering for each sub vector. There is no threshold set to limit the number of synonyms k which facilitates parallelization acceleration. We also set no limit to training epochs with early stopping epochs as 5, as EAT will need at least double training time.

Results Table 1 reports the performance of generator by using CET. When the weight is small, there can be a significant improvement. As weight increases to a certain extent, there will be score jitter. It proves that the CET can utilize the embedding of high-resource languages to improve low-resource languages. Meanwhile, this may also be due to more training batches. By reducing the batch size to half, it can be observed that score still improves, but under nearly equal training time, CET still achieves better results.

n	k	p	Score
500	1	0.2	170.23
500	2	0.2	**172.45**
500	3	0.2	166.38
500	2	0.3	171.81
1000	2	0.2	170.75

Table 2: The results of EWTND on Doc2dial validation dataset.

Table 2 shows the effect of generator by using EWTND, it still use CET and EWTND but only strengthen the origin data. When $\boldsymbol{k}$ increases from 2 to 3, the reason why score drops might be uncertainty of the neighborhood's semantic meaning, the same reason can explain the time when $\boldsymbol{n}$ increases.

p_1	p_2	p_3	Score
100%	0%	0%	175.05
0%	100%	0%	172.45
50%	33%	17%	**175.39**
60%	25%	15%	174.48
45%	35%	20%	173.60

Table 3: The results of EAT on Doc2dial validation dataset.

Table 3 shows the ensemble effect of adversarial training, it proves that such training method will provide stable improving although not much.

Method	EWTND	EAT	CET	Score
Retriever	✓			181.57
Retriever	✓	✓		181.60
mT5				173.42
mT5			✓	183.05
mT5	✓		✓	186.71
mT5	✓	✓	✓	188.62

Table 4: The results of adding training methods into other models on Doc2dial validation dataset.

Table 4 shows effectiveness of three training methods as plug and play modules. By enhancing the retriever, the generator still improves but disadvantage is that it increases training time around 1.5 times. Besides, the improved performance is not as good as methods applied to the generator. With the best retriever and origin re-ranker, we replace the generator with origin mT5 (Xue et al., 2021) model which shows that it is better than generator in baseline. Finally, we achieve best performance by adding three enhanced training methods into mT5.

The above experiments have shown that our methods have significant advantages: (i) three training methods can effectively increase model's performance without affecting prediction speed. (ii) almost all language models with token as input can apply these methods. (iii) the methods can have more potentials in future work, especially in cross language scenarios, EWTND can be extended to more similar language pairs; EAT can use more complex sampling methods based on the neighborhood distribution of different languages.

5 Conclusion

In this paper, we propose three training methods to improve model's performance from perspective of embedding enhancement and data augmentation. CET Introduces cross language learning through high-frequency words; EWTND use weighted augmentation from the neighborhood distribution of high-frequency words; EAT strengthen the robustness of the model through embedding perturbation. Compared to the baseline mode, our methods achieve the stable rise in score.

References

Song Feng, Siva Sankalp Patel, Hui Wan, and Sachindra Joshi. 2021. Multidoc2dial: Modeling dialogues grounded in multiple documents. *In EMNLP.*

Zhang, Yeqin and Fu, Haomin and Fu, Cheng and Yu, Haiyang and Li, Yongbin and Nguyen, Cam-Tu. 2023. Coarse-to-Fine Knowledge Selection for Document Grounded Dialogs. *2023 IEEE International Conference on Acoustics, Speech and Signal Processing.*

Patrick S. H. Lewis, Ethan Perez, Aleksandra Pik- tus, Fabio Petroni, Vladimir Karpukhin, Naman Goyal, Heinrich Küttler, Mike Lewis, Wen-tau Yih, Tim Rocktäschel, Sebastian Riedel, and Douwe Kiela. 2020. Retrieval-augmented generation for knowledge-intensive NLP tasks. *In Advances in Neu- ral Information Processing Systems 33: Annual Conference on Neural Information Processing Systems 2020, NeurIPS 2020, December 6-12, 2020, virtual.*

Haolan Zhan, Lei Shen, Hongshen Chen, and Hainan Zhang. 2021. CoLV: A collaborative latent variable model for knowledge-grounded dialogue generation. *In Proceedings of the 2021 Conference on Empiri- cal Methods in Natural Language Processing, pages 2250–2261, Online and Punta Cana, Dominican Re- public. Association for Computational Linguistics.*

Xiaofei Wen, Wei Wei and Xian-Ling Mao. 2022. Sequential Topic Selection Model with Latent Variable for Topic-Grounded Dialogue. *In Proceedings of the 2022 Conference on Empirical Methods in Natural Language Processing (Findings of EMNLP'2022), Abu Dhabi.*

Ian J. Goodfellow, Jonathon Shlens and Christian Szegedy. 2015. Explaining and Harnessing Adversarial Examples. *arXiv preprint arXiv: 1412.6572.*

Aleksander Madry, Aleksandar Makelov, Ludwig Schmidt, Dimitris Tsipras and Adrian Vladu. 2019. Towards Deep Learning Models Resistant to Adversarial Attacks. *arXiv preprint arXiv: 1706.06083.*

Linting Xue, Noah Constant, Adam Roberts, Mihir Kale, Rami Al-Rfou, Aditya Siddhant, Aditya Barua and Colin Raffel. 2021. mT5: A massively multilingual pre-trained text-to-text transformer. *arXiv preprint arXiv: 2010.11934.*

Johnson, Jeff Douze, Matthijs Jegou, Herve. 2019. Billion-scale similarity search with {GPUs}. *IEEE Transactions on Big Data.*

Chang Gao, Wenxuan Zhang and Wai Lam. 2022. UniGDD: A Unified Generative Framework for Goal-Oriented Document-Grounded Dialogue. *arXiv preprint arXiv: 2204.07770.*

Longxuan Ma, Wei-Nan Zhang,Mingda Li and Ting Liu. 2020. A Survey of Document Grounded Dialogue Systems (DGDS). *arXiv preprint arXiv: 2004.13818.*

Colin Raffel, Noam Shazeer, Adam Roberts, Katherine Lee, Sharan Narang, Michael Matena, Yanqi Zhou, Wei Li, Peter J. Liu. 2020. Exploring the Limits of Transfer Learning with a Unified Text-to-Text Transformer. *arXiv preprint arXiv: 1910.10683.*

Florian Tramèr, Alexey Kurakin, Nicolas Papernot, Ian Goodfellow, Dan Boneh and Patrick McDaniel. 2020. Ensemble Adversarial Training: Attacks and Defenses. *arXiv preprint arXiv: 1705.07204.*

Takeru Miyato, Andrew M. Dai, Ian Goodfellow. 2021. Adversarial Training Methods for Semi-Supervised Text Classification. *arXiv preprint arXiv: 1605.07725.*

Longxuan Ma, Weinan Zhang, Runxin Sun, Ting Liu. 2020. A Compare Aggregate Transformer for Understanding Document-grounded Dialogue. *arXiv preprint arXiv: 2010.00190.*

Zheng Zhang, Ryuichi Takanobu, Qi Zhu, Minlie Huang and Xiaoyan Zhu. 2020. Recent Advances and Challenges in Task-oriented Dialog System. *arXiv preprint arXiv: 2003.07490.*

Jingqing Zhang, Yao Zhao, Mohammad Saleh, Peter J. Liu. 2020. PEGASUS: Pre-training with Extracted Gap-sentences for Abstractive Summarization. *arXiv preprint arXiv: 1912.08777.*

Eric Wong, Leslie Rice, J. Zico Kolter. 2020. Fast is better than free: Revisiting adversarial training. *ICLR 2020.*

Yixuan Su, Lei Shu, Elman Mansimov, Arshit Gupta, Deng Cai, YiAn Lai, Yi Zhang. 2022. Multi-Task Pre-Training for Plug-and-Play Task-Oriented Dialogue System. *Proceedings of the 60th Annual Meeting of the Association for Computational Linguistics.*

SLDT: Sequential Latent Document Transformer for Multilingual Document-based Dialogue

Zhanyu Ma[1,2,4] **Zeming Liu**[3] **Jian Ye**[1,2,4*]
Institute of Computing Technology, Chinese Academy of Sciences, Beijing, China[1]
University of Chinese Academy of Sciences[2]
Research Center for Social Computing and Information Retrieval,
Harbin Institute of Technology, Harbin, China[3]
Beijing Key Laboratory of Mobile Computing and Pervasive Device[4]
mazhanyu21s@ict.ac.cn zmliu@ir.hit.edu.cn jye@ict.ac.cn

Abstract

Multilingual document-grounded dialogue, where the system is required to generate responses based on both the conversation multilingual context and external knowledge sources. Traditional pipeline methods for knowledge identification and response generation, while effective in certain scenarios, suffer from error propagation issues and fail to capture the interdependence between these two sub-tasks. To overcome these challenges, we propose the application of the SLDT method, which treats passage-knowledge selection as a sequential decision process rather than a single-step decision process. We achieved the winner 3rd in dialdoc 2023 and we also validated the effectiveness of our method on other datasets. The ablation experiment also shows that our method significantly improves the basic model compared to other methods.

1 Introduction

The advancements in neural models and the development of large-scale dialogue datasets have significantly propelled dialog generation research (Huang et al., 2020; Liu et al., 2022a; Ma et al., 2022). Open-domain dialogue systems strive to produce more informative and fluent responses (Ke et al., 2018; Zhang et al., 2020; Liu et al., 2021; Meng et al., 2021), finding applications in a wide array of areas such as emotional companionship, mental health support, and social chatbots.

Despite demonstrating promising results, most existing dialogue generation systems (Liu et al., 2022b; Bao et al., 2020; Li et al., 2020) depend on substantial data resources. In real-world scenarios, dialogue corpora for many languages are not readily available, thereby restricting the applicability of dialogue systems for low-resource or even zero-resource languages. Consequently, it is crucial to develop methods capable of effectively transferring knowledge from a source language with ample resources to a target language.

One such task is multilingual document-grounded dialogue (Sannigrahi et al., 2023), where the system is required to generate responses based on both the conversation multilingual context and external knowledge sources, such as documents or databases (Glass et al., 2022; Qi et al., 2022). While various methods have been proposed to address the challenges of knowledge selection and response generation in this task (Kim et al., 2020; Lai et al., 2023), including sequential latent knowledge selection for document-grounded dialogue. There is a need for a novel approach that combines the advantages of these methods (Zhang et al., 2022b). In this paper, we propose a new method to address the problem of document dialogue by employing the Sequential Latent Document Transformer (SLDT) to select the most relevant knowledge for conversation from a multilingual document set.

The motivation behind focusing on multilingual document-grounded dialogue lies in its potential to provide more informative and engaging responses by leveraging external knowledge sources (Gao et al., 2022; Zhang et al., 2022a), thereby enabling the dialogue system to better assist users in satisfying their diverse information needs. Traditional pipeline methods for knowledge identification and response generation, while effective in certain scenarios, suffer from error propagation issues and fail to capture the interdependence between these two sub-tasks. To overcome these challenges, we propose the application of the SLDT method, which has shown promising results in knowledge-grounded dialogue, to the task of document dialogue. The use of SLDT in document conversations is expected to bring several advantages, such as better modeling the diversity in document-knowledge selection, more accurate leveraging of response information, and the ability to work even when

* Corresponding author.

Proceedings of the Third DialDoc Workshop on Document-grounded Dialogue and Conversational Question Answering, pages 57–67
July 13, 2023 ©2023 Association for Computational Linguistics

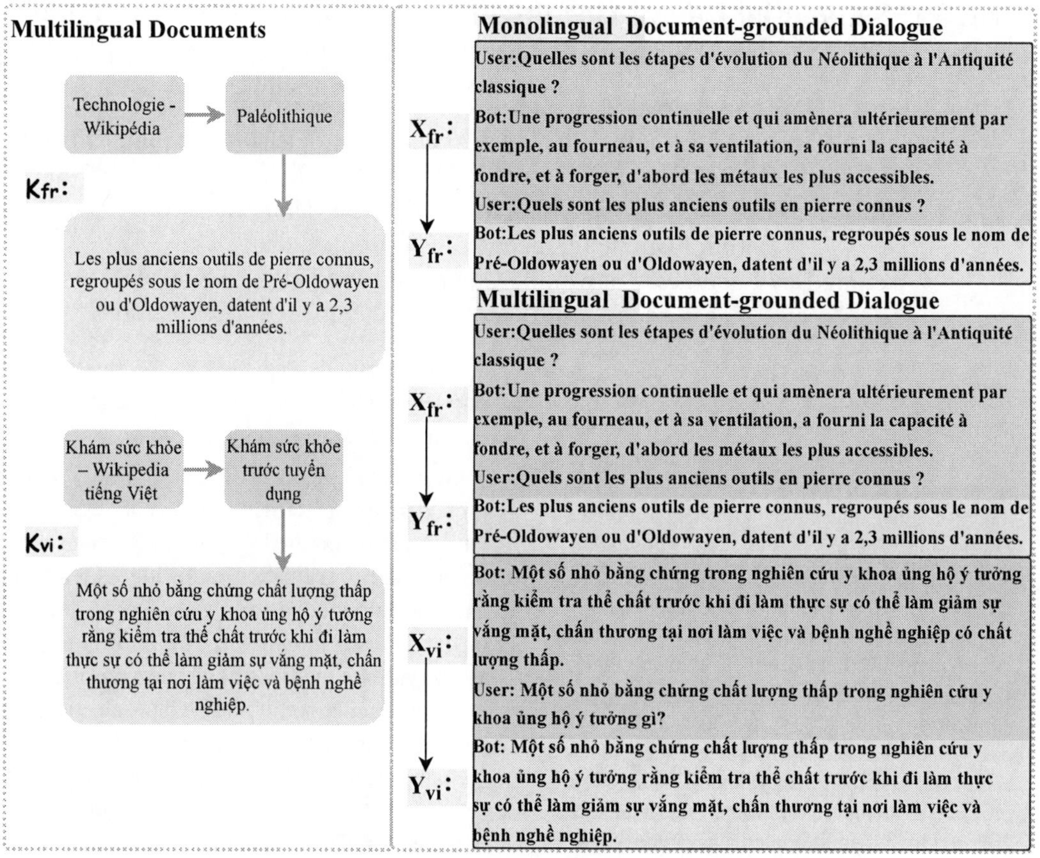

Figure 1: Introduction of Multilingual Document-grounded Dialogue.

knowledge selection labels for previous dialogues are not available . These properties of SLDT make it a suitable candidate for selecting relevant knowledge from documents to carry on the conversation. Our primary research goal is to develop an SLDT-based method for document dialogue that can effectively select the K most relevant documents from the document set based on the conversation history and input them into the generation module after concatenation.

Our method achieved excellent results on dialdoc 2023 Share Task. Obtained 208 points in online testing. We also validated the effectiveness of our method on other datasets. The ablation experiment also shows that our method significantly improves the basic model compared to other methods.

2 Related Works

Document-grounded dialogue systems (DGDS) categorize unstructured, semi-structured, and structured data in documents to facilitate the comprehension of human knowledge and interactions, thus fostering more natural human-computer interactions (HCI) (Zhou et al., 2018). The objective of DGDS is to generate conversational modes based on information (utterances, turns, context, clarification) supplied by a document or documents (Ma et al., 2020). DGDS are particularly advantageous in task-oriented and goal-oriented settings as they replicate the natural dialogue flow. A recent example of DGDS, closely related to our work, is Doc2Dial, a multi-domain DGDS dataset designed for goal-oriented dialogue that models hypothetical dialogue flows and scenes to simulate authentic interactions between a user and a machine agent in information-seeking contexts (Feng et al., 2020). In our proposed task, we adopt a similar approach, but we also permit users to pose clarification questions, the responses to which may not be directly grounded in the document. This aspect is crucial in the development of instruction-giving conversational agents, as the dialogue pipeline requires increased flexibility, as previously mentioned.

Multilingual dialogue tasks typically utilize a code-switching approach to achieve semantic alignment between various languages (Liu et al., 2020b;

Chapuis et al., 2021; Qin et al., 2021). This method of code-switching enables implicit semantic alignment without the need for parallel corpus pairs. Drawing inspiration from these studies, we apply the code-switching technique to transfer knowledge from English dialogue history to other target languages lacking training examples. In line with previous work (Chapuis et al., 2021) on multilingual representation, we implement code-switching at the utterance level, although code-switching at the word or span level is more prevalent (Banerjee et al., 2018; Bawa et al., 2020; Doğruöz et al., 2021).

3 Methodology

We utilize XLM-R (Conneau et al., 2020) as our retrieval model, employing a representation-based bi-encoder consisting of a dialogue query encoder, denoted as $q(\cdot)$, and a passage context encoder, represented by $p(\cdot)$.

For a given input query Q and a set of passages $\{P_i\}_{i=1}^{M}$, the encodings for the query and passage are computed as $q(Q)$ and $p\left(P_i\right)$, respectively. The similarity between these encodings is determined by the dot product $\langle q(Q), p\left(P_i\right)\rangle$, with the model being trained to minimize the negative log likelihood of the correct passage among L in-batch and challenging negatives.

Subsequently, we pre-calculate the representations for all passages and index them offline. During inference, the top-K passages are retrieved using Maximum Inner Product Search (MIPS) in conjunction with Faiss.

We introduce a Sequential Latent Document Transformer tailored for multilingual document-based dialogue, as illustrated in Figure 2. The objective of the model is to generate customized and informative responses by learning a probabilistic model $p(R|C,\mathcal{K},\mathcal{P})$ that leverages passage-knowledge and context flowing (Kim et al., 2020).

We proceed by iterating through dialogue turns with $1 \leq t \leq T$, iterating over words in the utterances of the apprentice and wizard using $1 \leq m \leq M$ and $1 \leq n \leq N$, and denoting knowledge sentences in the pool with $1 \leq l \leq L$. Here, T represents the dialogue length, M and N correspond to the lengths of the apprentice and wizard's utterances, and L denotes the passage-knowledge pool size.

The input to the SLDT at turn t comprises previous conversation turns, which include user utterances $\mathbf{x}^1, ..., \mathbf{x}^t$, system responses $\mathbf{y}^1, ..., \mathbf{y}^{t-1}$, and the passage pool $\mathbf{k}^1, ..., \mathbf{k}^t$, where $\mathbf{k}^t = \{\mathbf{k}^{t,l}\} = \mathbf{k}^{t,1}, ..., \mathbf{k}^{t,L}$. The model's output consists of the chosen sample passage-knowledge $\mathbf{k}_s^t$ and the response $\mathbf{y}^t$. We provide an in-depth explanation of sentence embedding, passage-knowledge selection, and utterance decoding.

First, we consider passage-knowledge selection a sequential rather than a one-step decision-making process. Due to the diversity of passage-knowledge selection in dialogue, we model it with latent variables. Therefore, we can conduct joint inference for multiple turns of passage-knowledge selection and response generation, as opposed to distinct inference on a turn-by-turn basis.

Various studies have been conducted on sequential latent variable models. For instance, some have proposed a posterior attention model that represents the attention mechanism in seq2seq models as sequential latent variables. Drawing inspiration from these works, we factorize response generation with latent document passage-knowledge selection and derive the variational lower bound as follows. The conditional probability of generating response $\mathbf{y}^t$ given dialogue context $\mathbf{x}^{\leq t}$ and $\mathbf{y}^{<t}$:

$$p(\mathbf{y}^t|\mathbf{x}^{\leq t}, \mathbf{y}^{<t}) \approx \prod_{i=1}^{t-1} \sum_{\mathbf{k}^i} q_\psi(\mathbf{k}^i)\Big(\sum_{\mathbf{k}^t} p_\gamma(\mathbf{y}^t|\mathbf{x}^{\leq t}, \mathbf{y}^{<t}, \mathbf{k}^t)\pi_\gamma(\mathbf{k}^t)\Big) \tag{1}$$

Note that $p_\gamma(\mathbf{y}^t|\cdot)$ is a decoder network, $\pi_\gamma(\mathbf{k}^t)$ is a categorical conditional distribution of knowledge given dialogue context and previously selected knowledge, and $q_\psi(\mathbf{k}^t)$ is an inference network to approximate posterior distribution $p_\gamma(\mathbf{k}^t|\mathbf{x}^{\leq t}, \mathbf{y}^{\leq t}, \mathbf{k}^{<t})$.

Eq.(1) means that we first infer from the knowledge posterior which knowledge would be used up to previous turn $t-1$, estimate the knowledge for current turn t from prior knowledge distribution and generate an utterance from the inferred knowledge. Figure 2 shows an example of this generation process at $t = 3$. We parameterize the decoder network p_γ, the prior distribution of knowledge π_γ, and the approximate posterior q_ψ with deep neural networks as will be discussed.

4 Experiments

For the retrieval training stage, we utilized a batch size of 128 and a learning rate of 1e-4 and 5e-5 for post-training and fine-tuning, respectively. And retrieval passage number top-k is 25. During the generation stage, we used a batch size of 32 with

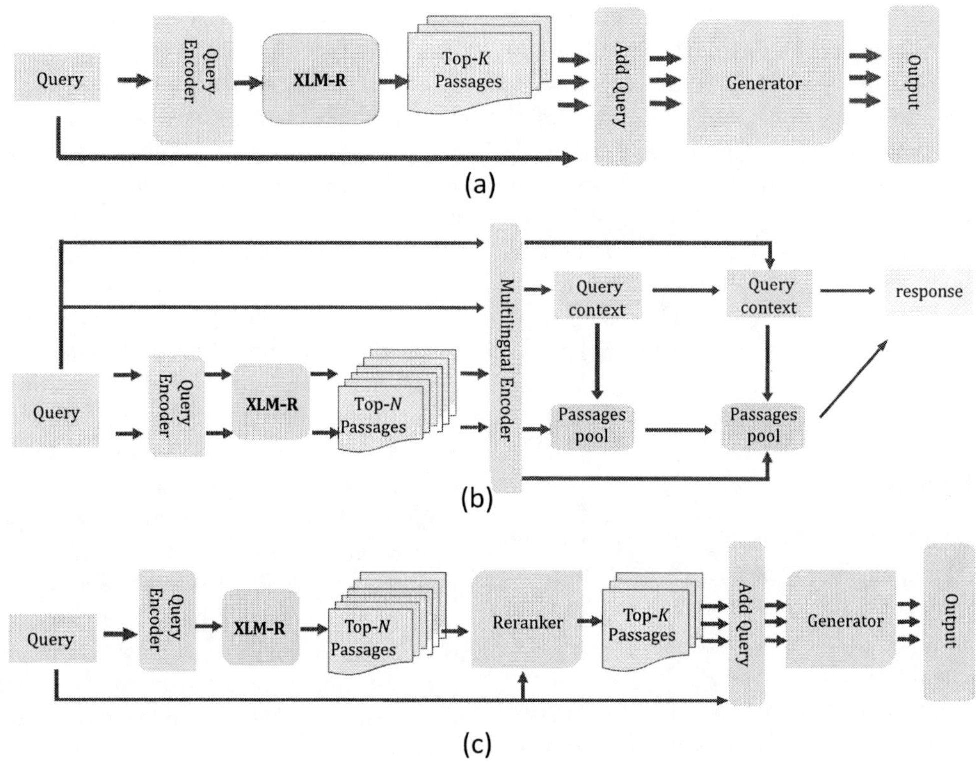

Figure 2: Subfigure (a) and (c) show the document-based dialogue in two-stage and three-stage (Glass et al., 2022), respectively, while subfigure (b) show our SLDT, a new paradigm between (a) and (c).

a learning rate of 1e-4 and 1e-5 for post-training and fine-tuning, respectively. For R-drop, we set the dropout rate to 0.1, and the KL-divergence loss weight 0.02.

4.1 Datasets

FrViDoc2Bot contains annotated Vietnamese and French document-grounded dialogue training data, the development data that the participants are required to provide the model predicts, as well as the passage corpus that the training and development data depend on (DAMO_ConvAI, 2023). Each piece of data in the training set contains three attributes: query, passages, and response. The query is a concatenation of the conversation history in reverse order, with the last turn marked as "<last_turn>" and the rest marked with "" for user input and "" for system output. The 'passages' attribute contains the passage arranged according to reply dependencies, followed by a reverse-ordered chain of titles concatenated with "/" as the delimiter. The response attribute is the desired output, beginning with "". They have provided the 'passage corpus' that all dialogues in the training, validation, and test sets rely on in passages.csv. We sampled 200 pieces of train data from it as a dev set during offline validation for Table 1 and 2.

Wizard of Wikipedia dataset is a large dataset with conversations directly grounded with knowledge retrieved from Wikipedia. It is used to train and evaluate dialogue systems for knowledgeable open dialogue with clear grounding. The dataset contains dialogues in which a bot needs to respond to user inputs in a knowledgeable way. Each response should be grounded on a sentence from Wikipedia that is relevant to the conversation topic. WoW encompasses a total of 18,430 dialogues for training, 1,948 dialogues for validation, and 1,933 dialogues for testing (Dinan et al., 2019a). The test set is divided into two subsets: *Test Seen*, containing 965 dialogues on topics overlapping with the training set, and *Test Unseen*, consisting of 968 dialogues on topics not previously encountered in the training and validation sets.

4.2 Automatic Evaluation

The F1 (Dinan et al., 2019b) value is used to evaluate the consistency between the predicted and golden responses when the golden response exists.

Model	Parameters	Response Generation									
		B-1	B-2	B-3	DIS-1	DIS-2	R-1	R-2	R-L	F1	S-BLEU
$MT5_S$ (golden kg)	300M	24.7	23.2	21.3	5.3	9.8	32.1	28.4	31.2	19.7	21.3
$MT5_S$ (no kg)		19.1	17.6	15.7	3.3	4.1	26.5	22.8	25.6	14.1	15.7
$MT5_B$ (golden kg)	580M	45.3	43.8	42.0	25.9	30.3	53.0	49.3	52.1	40.3	42.0
$MT5_B$ (no kg)		30.3	28.8	27.0	10.9	15.4	37.7	34.0	36.8	25.3	27.0
$MBART_B$ (golden kg)	170M	47.4	45.9	44.0	28.0	32.4	55.0	51.3	54.1	42.4	44.0
$MBART_B$ (no kg)		30.6	29.1	28.0	11.2	15.6	39.0	35.3	38.1	25.6	28.0
$MBART_L$ (golden kg)	680M	53.7	52.2	50.3	34.3	38.7	61.0	57.3	60.1	48.6	50.2
$MBART_L$ (no kg)		32.4	30.9	29.3	13.5	16.9	41.4	37.7	39.9	36.2	35.3

Table 1: Automatic evaluation results of different Pre-trained models on the FrViDoc2Bot dev set.

Model	Response Generation										
	B-1	B-2	B-3	DIS-1	DIS-2	R-1	R-2	R-L	F1	PPL	S-BLEU
MBART + No knowledge	31.4	27.9	19.3	10.5	12.9	21.4	20.7	19.9	16.2	-	35.3
MBART + Random knowledge	33.4	30.4	21.8	12.8	17.2	26.1	21.6	23.4	23.1	-	37.8
MBART + Repeat last utterance	35.5	32.9	23.3	15.1	18.5	31.4	22.5	26.9	26.7	103.7	40.3
MBART + Norm retrieval	47.6	45.3	39.8	27.4	25.8	46.2	38.4	38.4	37.0	88.3	42.8
MBART + XLM-R	49.6	47.6	43.3	29.8	30.0	51.0	44.3	45.8	45.4	83.5	45.3
MBART + XLM-R + SLDT	51.7	49.9	46.8	32.1	34.3	56.1	50.8	53.2	52.2	76.4	47.8
MBART + XLM-R + SLDT + Copy	53.7	52.2	50.3	34.3	38.7	61.0	57.3	60.1	58.6	64.4	50.3

Table 2: Automatic evaluation results of different models on the FrViDoc2Bot dev set.

Perplexity (PPL) (Meister and Cotterell, 2021) can determine the coherence of the predicted query to a certain extent. We additionally used BLEU (Papineni et al., 2002; Chen and Cherry, 2014; Post, 2018) to evaluate the consistency of predicted responses with standard responses, Distinct (Li et al., 2016a) to evaluate the diversity of responses in the test set (Li et al., 2016b).

4.3 Pre-training Models

XLM-R (Conneau et al., 2020) is an improved version of XLM based on the RoBERTa model (Liu et al., 2019). XLM-R is trained with a cross-lingual masked language modeling objective on data in 100 languages from Common Crawl. To improve the pre-training data quality, pages from Common Crawl were filtered by an n-gram language model trained on Wikipedia (Wenzek et al., 2020).

mBART (Liu et al., 2020a) is a multilingual encoder-decoder model that is based on BART (Lewis et al., 2020). mBART is trained with a combination of span masking and sentence shuffling objectives on a subset of 25 languages from the same data as XLM-R.

MT5 (Multilingual T5) is a massively multilingual pretrained text-to-text transformer model (Xue et al., 2021). It is trained following a similar recipe as T5. Current natural language processing (NLP) pipelines often make use of transfer learning, where a model is pre-trained on a data-rich task before being fine-tuned on a downstream task of interest.

4.4 Knowledge Access Methods

Weak correlation passage-knowledge in knowledge-based dialogue refers to the knowledge that is not directly related to the current dialogue context but is still useful for generating a response. It is called weak correlation because it is not directly related to the current dialogue context but is still useful for generating a response. For example, if you are talking about a movie and you mention that you like action movies,

Model	Response Generation (Test seen)										
	B-1	B-2	B-3	DIS-1	DIS-2	R-1	R-2	R-L	F1	PPL	S-BLEU
MBART + No knowledge	9.0	6.5	4.3	5.7	7.8	5.4	3.9	4.7	5.2	-	9.3
MBART + Random knowledge	8.9	6.1	4.0	6.8	8.5	6.9	4.2	5.8	6.6	-	9.6
MBART + Repeat last utterance	14.1	11.7	9.7	10.6	15.2	12.4	2.1	10.0	12.0	89.7	13.6
MBART + SLDT	17.3	15.3	13.4	15.4	20.9	16.9	5.4	14.4	16.4	64.4	18.6
MBART + SLDT + Copy	18.5	16.9	15.1	18.2	24.6	19.4	6.7	16.8	18.8	52.1	21.6

Table 3: Automatic evaluation results of different models on Wizard of Wikipedia test seen set.

Model	Response Generation (Test Unseen)										
	B-1	B-2	B-3	DIS-1	DIS-2	R-1	R-2	R-L	F1	PPL	S-BLEU
MBART + No knowledge	6.3	5.2	4.1	4.0	6.7	3.9	-	1.5	2.9	-	5.8
MBART + Random knowledge	6.4	5.8	5.6	4.4	7.5	7.3	-	4.6	6.3	-	6.6
MBART + Repeat last utterance	12.5	9.7	9.1	7.5	12.3	10.6	2.2	7.7	9.7	113.4	13.4
MBART + SLDT	15.6	12.6	12.6	11.6	17.1	14.9	3.7	11.8	11.0	90.5	15.2
MBART + SLDT + Copy	16.7	13.5	14.2	13.7	19.9	17.2	4.1	13.9	13.3	81.3	18.0

Table 4: Automatic evaluation results of different models on Wizard of Wikipedia test unseen set.

Model	Response Generation										
	B-1	B-2	B-3	DIS-1	DIS-2	R-1	R-2	R-L	F1	PPL	S-BLEU
Ours-FiD	43.6	51.5	58.4	32.3	36.0	58.4	53.9	56.3	46.2	73.2	46.3
Ours-R_drop	54.2	52.8	51.5	35.9	39.3	62.1	58.8	61.3	50.5	65.2	52.6
Ours-Prompt	56.6	54.0	52.2	36.4	39.6	63.2	56.0	61.8	53.2	63.8	53.1
Ours-Post_pretrain	58.9	56.2	53.9	40.5	44.3	64.6	57.2	62.1	61.8	47.3	58.6
Ours-Ensemble	60.7	58.5	55.6	43.4	48.8	67.0	61.4	66.3	66.7	38.9	60.5

Table 5: Automatic evaluation results of leaderboard submission which is based on the FrViDoc2Bot test set.

then the system can use this weak correlation passage-knowledge to recommend other action movies that you might like.

Norm retrieval means regaining the norm of the lost signal from its intensity measurements. It arises naturally from phase retrieval when one utilizes both a collection of subspaces and their orthogonal complements. Norm retrieval can be done using projections and can be used to extend certain results for frames.

4.5 Results and Analysis

4.5.1 Performance of Pre-training models

The experimental analysis presented in Table 1 aims to compare the performance of different pre-trained models on the FrViDoc2Bot dev set. The models investigated include MT5 and mBART, with small (S), base (B), and large (L) variants. The table further distinguishes between the models' performances when utilizing the golden knowledge (golden kg) and when relying solely on dialogue history information (no kg).

Upon analyzing the results, it is evident that the models' performance generally improves with the inclusion of the golden kg, as indicated by higher scores across most evaluation metrics. This implies that the utilization of external knowledge is beneficial for response generation tasks. For instance, the $MT5\_S$ model achieves a B-1 score of 24.7 with the golden kg, while the same model without the kg attains a B-1 score of 19.1. Similar improvements can be observed for other models and evaluation metrics.

Comparing the performance of MT5 and mBART models, it can be observed that mBART consistently outperforms MT5 for the same model size and knowledge condition. For example, mBART_B (golden kg) achieves a B-1 score of 47.4, while MT5_B (golden kg) scores 45.3. This trend is consistent across most of the evaluation metrics, indicating the superior performance of mBART models in this specific task.

Furthermore, it is noticeable that larger models generally yield better results than their smaller counterparts. For instance, mBART_L (golden kg) achieves a B-1 score of 53.7, outperforming both mBART_B (golden kg) and mBART_S (golden kg) with respective B-1 scores of 47.4 and 24.7. This suggests that larger model sizes can enhance the performance of response generation tasks.

4.5.2 Knowledge Access Methods

In this section, we analyze the performance of various knowledge acquisition methods on the FrViDoc2Bot dev set, as presented in Table 2. The models can be divided into several categories based on the knowledge acquisition strategy employed, and we will discuss the impact of these strategies on the performance of the knowledge dialogue system.

Performance of Basic Models The MBART + No knowledge model serves as the baseline, relying solely on the conversation history without incorporating any external knowledge. As expected, this model yields the lowest performance across all evaluation metrics. Introducing random knowledge (MBART + Random knowledge) provides some improvement, suggesting that even arbitrary knowledge can be useful in generating responses.

Incorporation of Targeted Knowledge When knowledge is specifically targeted to the conversation, such as with the MBART + Repeat last utterance model, we observe a significant improvement in performance. Repeating the last utterance as knowledge allows the model to generate more coherent responses by drawing on the context provided. However, this model's performance is still limited by its reliance on only one piece of knowledge.

Retrieval-Based Knowledge Acquisition The next category of models utilizes retrieval-based methods to acquire relevant knowledge from a knowledge base. The MBART + Norm retrieval model leverages a traditional retrieval model and exhibits a considerable performance boost compared to the previous models. This improvement underscores the importance of selecting appropriate knowledge to inform dialogue generation. The MBART + XLM-R model replaces the traditional retrieval model with XLM-R, a more advanced retrieval model. This change results in further performance gains across all metrics, highlighting the effectiveness of using powerful retrieval models to acquire relevant knowledge.

Sequential Latent Document Transformer The MBART + XLM-R + SLDT model incorporates the Sequential Latent Document Transformer (SLDT) into the knowledge selection process. This addition allows the model to perform a second stage of knowledge selection, leading to even better performance compared to the previous models. The SLDT mechanism effectively refines the retrieved knowledge, enabling the model to generate more accurate and coherent responses.

Incorporating Copy Mechanism Lastly, the MBART + XLM-R + SLDT + Copy model optimizes the decoding strategy by introducing a copy mechanism. This mechanism allows the model to copy or point to elements from the input sequence, leading to a more nuanced and accurate response generation. The introduction of the copy mechanism results in the best performance across all evaluation metrics, demonstrating the importance of a well-designed decoding strategy in knowledge dialogue systems.

Through the analysis of various knowledge acquisition methods and their impact on the knowledge dialogue system, we observe that incorporating targeted and relevant knowledge is crucial for generating coherent and accurate responses. Advanced retrieval models and techniques, such as XLM-R and SLDT, can significantly improve performance. Additionally, the incorporation of a copy mechanism in the decoding strategy leads to further enhancements. Overall, this analysis underscores the importance of effective knowledge acquisition and utilization in the development of high-performing knowledge dialogue systems.

4.5.3 Performance on the Wizard of Wikipedia

In this section, we examine the efficacy of various models on the Wizard of Wikipedia dataset, focusing on the impact of knowledge acquisition methods on knowledge dialogue systems. The performance of each model is evaluated on both seen and unseen test data.

Table 3 presents the results of the response generation for the test seen data. We observe that the MBART + SLDT + Copy model performs the best across most metrics. This demonstrates that the Sequential Latent Document Transformer model (SLDT), when combined with the copy mechanism (Li et al., 2019), significantly improves the efficacy of the knowledge dialogue system. The copy mechanism, which is inspired by the Pointer Network (Vinyals et al., 2015; Yang and Tu, 2022), allows the model to copy or point to input sequence elements, improving the generated output.

In contrast, the MBART + No knowledge and MBART + Random knowledge models exhibit lower performance in most metrics. This finding indicates that merely considering the conversation history or randomly selecting knowledge from the knowledge base is not sufficient for generating high-quality responses in a knowledge dialogue system.

Table 4 reports the results for the test unseen data. Similar to the test seen data, the MBART + SLDT + Copy model outperforms the other models across various metrics. This result confirms the robustness of the SLDT model combined with the copy mechanism, even when tested on unseen data.

The performance trends observed in this analysis are consistent with those reported in related research on the Wizard of Wikipedia dataset. For example, previous studies have shown that incorporating external knowledge and employing effective retrieval mechanisms enhance the response quality in knowledge dialogue systems.

4.5.4 Performance of Leaderboard Submission

In this section, we present a comprehensive analysis of various models' performance on the FrViDoc2Bot test set, focusing on response generation. Table 5 provides the automatic evaluation results for different models, showcasing their performance on metrics. The models in consideration are Ours-FiD, Ours-R_drop, Ours-Prompt, Ours-Post_pretrain, and Ours-Ensemble.

Ours-FiD is a model that leverages the Fusion-in-Decoder (FiD) (Izacard and Grave, 2021) mechanism, which has been demonstrated to improve knowledge integration and retrieval capabilities in large-scale language models. Despite the promise of the FiD mechanism, our implementation yields relatively modest performance in comparison to other models, suggesting that further optimization is required.

Ours-R_drop employs the R-drop (Wu et al., 2021) regularization technique, which encourages the model to generate diverse responses by minimizing the KL-divergence between two independently sampled outputs. This model exhibits improvements over Ours-FiD in various metrics, particularly DIS-1 and DIS-2, indicating that the R-drop technique contributes positively to response diversity.

Ours-Prompt focuses on utilizing prompt engineering to enhance the model's contextual understanding and control. The model's performance on most metrics surpasses that of Ours-FiD and Ours-R_drop, which highlights the effectiveness of prompt engineering in improving the model's ability to generate more contextually relevant and coherent responses.

Ours-Post_pretrain incorporates additional post-pretraining steps to fine-tune the model on the specific task of response generation in the Chinese and Englinsh of FrViDoc2Bot dataset. This model demonstrates superior performance across all metrics, especially in F1 and PPL scores, as compared to the previous models. The results support the notion that further task-specific pretraining can lead to significant performance gains.

Lastly, Ours-Ensemble combines the strengths of the aforementioned models by employing a voting-based ensemble method. This approach achieves the highest scores across all metrics, underlining the benefits of leveraging diverse model architectures and techniques in an ensemble setting.

5 Conclusion

In this paper, we present a novel SLDT method for multilingual document-grounded dialogue , with a focus on addressing the challenges of selecting the most relevant documents for conversation and generating informative responses based on the selected knowledge. We then present an extensive experimental evaluation of our method, demonstrating its effectiveness in comparison to existing approaches.

Acknowledgement

The research work is supported by National Key R&D Program of China (No.2022YFB3904700), Key Research and Development Program of in Shandong Province (2019JZZY020102), Key Research and Development Program of Jiangsu Province (No.BE2018084), Industrial Internet Innovation and Development Project in 2021 (TC210A02M, TC210804D), Opening Project of Beijing Key Laboratory of Mobile Computing and Pervasive Device.

Limitations

Our method relies on large-scale computing power and can only achieve the best results through NVIDIA-A100-80G training.

References

Suman Banerjee, Nikita Moghe, Siddhartha Arora, and Mitesh M Khapra. 2018. A dataset for building code-mixed goal oriented conversation systems. In *Proceedings of the 27th International Conference on Computational Linguistics*, pages 3766–3780.

Siqi Bao, Huang He, Fan Wang, Hua Wu, and Haifeng Wang. 2020. Plato: Pre-trained dialogue generation model with discrete latent variable. In *Proceedings of the 58th Annual Meeting of the Association for Computational Linguistics*, pages 85–96.

Anshul Bawa, Pranav Khadpe, Pratik Joshi, Kalika Bali, and Monojit Choudhury. 2020. Do multilingual users prefer chat-bots that code-mix? let's nudge and find out! *Proceedings of the ACM on Human-Computer Interaction*, 4(CSCW1):1–23.

Emile Chapuis, Pierre Colombo, Matthieu Labeau, and Chloe Clavel. 2021. Code-switched inspired losses for generic spoken dialog representations. *arXiv preprint arXiv:2108.12465*.

Boxing Chen and Colin Cherry. 2014. A systematic comparison of smoothing techniques for sentence-level bleu. In *Proceedings of the 9th Workshop on Statistical Machine Translation*, pages 362–367.

Alexis Conneau, Kartikay Khandelwal, Naman Goyal, Vishrav Chaudhary, Guillaume Wenzek, Francisco Guzmán, Edouard Grave, Myle Ott, Luke Zettlemoyer, and Veselin Stoyanov. 2020. Unsupervised cross-lingual representation learning at scale. In *Proceedings of the 58th Annual Meeting of the Association for Computational Linguistics*, pages 8440–8451, Online. Association for Computational Linguistics.

DAMO_ConvAI. 2023. French and vietnamese document-grounded dialogue data set. In *modelscope*.

Emily Dinan, Stephen Roller, Kurt Shuster, Angela Fan, Michael Auli, and Jason Weston. 2019a. Wizard of wikipedia: Knowledge-powered conversational agents. In *International Conference on Learning Representations*.

Emily Dinan, Stephen Roller, Kurt Shuster, Angela Fan, Michael Auli, and Jason Weston. 2019b. Wizard of wikipedia: Knowledge-powered conversational agents. *International Conference on Learning Representations*.

A Seza Doğruöz, Sunayana Sitaram, Barbara Bullock, and Almeida Jacqueline Toribio. 2021. A survey of code-switching: Linguistic and social perspectives for language technologies. In *Proceedings of the 59th Annual Meeting of the Association for Computational Linguistics and the 11th International Joint Conference on Natural Language Processing (Volume 1: Long Papers)*, pages 1654–1666.

Song Feng, Hui Wan, Chulaka Gunasekara, Siva Patel, Sachindra Joshi, and Luis Lastras. 2020. doc2dial: A goal-oriented document-grounded dialogue dataset. In *Proceedings of the 2020 Conference on Empirical Methods in Natural Language Processing (EMNLP)*, pages 8118–8128, Online. Association for Computational Linguistics.

Chang Gao, Wenxuan Zhang, and Wai Lam. 2022. UniGDD: A unified generative framework for goal-oriented document-grounded dialogue. In *Proceedings of the 60th Annual Meeting of the Association for Computational Linguistics (Volume 2: Short Papers)*, pages 599–605, Dublin, Ireland. Association for Computational Linguistics.

Michael Glass, Gaetano Rossiello, Md Faisal Mahbub Chowdhury, Ankita Naik, Pengshan Cai, and Alfio Gliozzo. 2022. Re2G: Retrieve, rerank, generate. In *Proceedings of the 2022 Conference of the North American Chapter of the Association for Computational Linguistics: Human Language Technologies*, pages 2701–2715, Seattle, United States. Association for Computational Linguistics.

Minlie Huang, Xiaoyan Zhu, and Jianfeng Gao. 2020. Challenges in building intelligent open-domain dialog systems. *ACM Transactions on Information Systems (TOIS)*, 38(3):1–32.

Gautier Izacard and Édouard Grave. 2021. Leveraging passage retrieval with generative models for open domain question answering. In *Proceedings of the 16th Conference of the European Chapter of the Association for Computational Linguistics: Main Volume*, pages 874–880.

Pei Ke, Jian Guan, Minlie Huang, and Xiaoyan Zhu. 2018. Generating informative responses with controlled sentence function. In *Proceedings of the 56th Annual Meeting of the Association for Computational Linguistics (Volume 1: Long Papers)*, pages 1499–1508.

Byeongchang Kim, Jaewoo Ahn, and Gunhee Kim. 2020. Sequential latent knowledge selection for knowledge-grounded dialogue. In *International Conference on Learning Representations*.

Tuan Lai, Giuseppe Castellucci, Saar Kuzi, Heng Ji, and Oleg Rokhlenko. 2023. External knowledge acquisition for end-to-end document-oriented dialog systems. In *Proceedings of the 17th Conference of the European Chapter of the Association for Computational Linguistics*, pages 3615–3629, Dubrovnik, Croatia. Association for Computational Linguistics.

Mike Lewis, Yinhan Liu, Naman Goyal, Marjan Ghazvininejad, Abdelrahman Mohamed, Omer Levy, Veselin Stoyanov, and Luke Zettlemoyer. 2020. BART: Denoising sequence-to-sequence pre-training for natural language generation, translation, and comprehension. In *Proceedings of the 58th Annual Meeting of the Association for Computational Linguistics*, pages 7871–7880, Online. Association for Computational Linguistics.

Chunyuan Li, Xiang Gao, Yuan Li, Baolin Peng, Xiujun Li, Yizhe Zhang, and Jianfeng Gao. 2020. Optimus: Organizing sentences via pre-trained modeling of a latent space. In *Proceedings of the 2020 Conference on Empirical Methods in Natural Language Processing (EMNLP)*, pages 4678–4699.

Jiwei Li, Michel Galley, Chris Brockett, Jianfeng Gao, and Bill Dolan. 2016a. A diversity-promoting objective function for neural conversation models. In *Proceedings of the 2016 Conference of the North American Chapter of the Association for Computational Linguistics: Human Language Technologies*, pages 110–119.

Jiwei Li, Michel Galley, Chris Brockett, Jianfeng Gao, and Bill Dolan. 2016b. A diversity-promoting objective function for neural conversation models. In *Proceedings of the 2016 Conference of the North American Chapter of the Association for Computational Linguistics: Human Language Technologies*, pages 110–119, San Diego, California. Association for Computational Linguistics.

Zekang Li, Cheng Niu, Fandong Meng, Yang Feng, Qian Li, and Jie Zhou. 2019. Incremental transformer with deliberation decoder for document grounded conversations. In *Proceedings of the 57th Annual Meeting of the Association for Computational Linguistics*, pages 12–21.

Yinhan Liu, Jiatao Gu, Naman Goyal, Xian Li, Sergey Edunov, Marjan Ghazvininejad, Mike Lewis, and Luke Zettlemoyer. 2020a. Multilingual denoising pre-training for neural machine translation. *arXiv preprint arXiv:2001.08210*.

Yinhan Liu, Myle Ott, Naman Goyal, Jingfei Du, Mandar Joshi, Danqi Chen, Omer Levy, Mike Lewis, Luke Zettlemoyer, and Veselin Stoyanov. 2019. RoBERTa: A robustly optimized BERT pretraining approach. *arXiv preprint arXiv:1907.11692*.

Zeming Liu, Haifeng Wang, Zheng-Yu Niu, Hua Wu, and Wanxiang Che. 2021. Durecdial 2.0: A bilingual parallel corpus for conversational recommendation. In *Proceedings of the 2021 Conference on Empirical Methods in Natural Language Processing*, pages 4335–4347.

Zeming Liu, Jun Xu, Zeyang Lei, Haifeng Wang, Zheng-Yu Niu, and Hua Wu. 2022a. Where to go for the holidays: Towards mixed-type dialogs for clarification of user goals. In *Proceedings of the 60th Annual Meeting of the Association for Computational Linguistics (Volume 1: Long Papers)*, pages 1024–1034.

Zeming Liu, Ding Zhou, Hao Liu, Haifeng Wang, Zheng-Yu Niu, Hua Wu, Wanxiang Che, Ting Liu, and Hui Xiong. 2022b. Graph-grounded goal planning for conversational recommendation. *IEEE Transactions on Knowledge and Data Engineering*.

Zihan Liu, Genta Indra Winata, Zhaojiang Lin, Peng Xu, and Pascale Fung. 2020b. Attention-informed mixed-language training for zero-shot cross-lingual task-oriented dialogue systems. In *Proceedings of the AAAI Conference on Artificial Intelligence*, volume 34, pages 8433–8440.

Longxuan Ma, Wei-Nan Zhang, Mingda Li, and Ting Liu. 2020. A survey of document grounded dialogue systems (DGDS). *CoRR*, abs/2004.13818.

Zhanyu Ma, Jian Ye, Xurui Yang, and Jianfeng Liu. 2022. Hcld: A hierarchical framework for zero-shot cross-lingual dialogue system. In *Proceedings of the 29th International Conference on Computational Linguistics*, pages 4492–4498.

Clara Isabel Meister and Ryan Cotterell. 2021. Language model evaluation beyond perplexity. In *Proceedings of the 59th Annual Meeting of the Association for Computational Linguistics and the 11th International Joint Conference on Natural Language Processing*, volume 1, pages 5328–5339. Association for Computational Linguistics.

Chuan Meng, Pengjie Ren, Zhumin Chen, Zhaochun Ren, Tengxiao Xi, and Maarten de Rijke. 2021. Initiative-aware self-supervised learning for knowledge-grounded conversations. In *Proceedings of the 44th International ACM SIGIR Conference on Research and Development in Information Retrieval*, pages 522–532.

Kishore Papineni, Salim Roukos, Todd Ward, and Wei-Jing Zhu. 2002. Bleu: a method for automatic evaluation of machine translation. In *Proceedings of the 40th Annual Meeting of the Association for Computational Linguistics*, pages 311–318, Philadelphia, Pennsylvania, USA. Association for Computational Linguistics.

Matt Post. 2018. A call for clarity in reporting BLEU scores. In *Proceedings of the Third Conference on Machine Translation: Research Papers*, pages 186–191, Brussels, Belgium. Association for Computational Linguistics.

Le Qi, Shangwen Lv, Hongyu Li, Jing Liu, Yu Zhang, Qiaoqiao She, Hua Wu, Haifeng Wang, and Ting Liu. 2022. DuReader$_{\text{vis}}$: A Chinese dataset for open-domain document visual question answering. In *Findings of the Association for Computational Linguistics: ACL 2022*, pages 1338–1351, Dublin, Ireland. Association for Computational Linguistics.

Libo Qin, Minheng Ni, Yue Zhang, and Wanxiang Che. 2021. Cosda-ml: Multi-lingual code-switching data augmentation for zero-shot cross-lingual nlp. In *Proceedings of the Twenty-Ninth International Joint Conference on Artificial Intelligence*.

Sonal Sannigrahi, Josef Van Genabith, and Cristina España-bonet. 2023. Are the best multilingual document embeddings simply based on sentence embeddings? In *Findings of the Association for Computational Linguistics: EACL 2023*, pages 2261–2271, Dubrovnik, Croatia. Association for Computational Linguistics.

Oriol Vinyals, Meire Fortunato, and Navdeep Jaitly. 2015. Pointer networks. In *Proceedings of the 28th International Conference on Neural Information Processing Systems-Volume 2*, pages 2692–2700.

Guillaume Wenzek, Marie-Anne Lachaux, Alexis Conneau, Vishrav Chaudhary, Francisco Guzmán, Armand Joulin, and Edouard Grave. 2020. CCNet: Extracting high quality monolingual datasets from web crawl data. In *Proceedings of the 12th Language Resources and Evaluation Conference*, pages 4003–4012, Marseille, France. European Language Resources Association.

Lijun Wu, Juntao Li, Yue Wang, Qi Meng, Tao Qin, Wei Chen, Min Zhang, Tie-Yan Liu, et al. 2021. R-drop: Regularized dropout for neural networks. *Advances in Neural Information Processing Systems*, 34:10890–10905.

Linting Xue, Noah Constant, Adam Roberts, Mihir Kale, Rami Al-Rfou, Aditya Siddhant, Aditya Barua, and Colin Raffel. 2021. mt5: A massively multilingual pre-trained text-to-text transformer. In *Proceedings of the 2021 Conference of the North American Chapter of the Association for Computational Linguistics: Human Language Technologies*, pages 483–498.

Songlin Yang and Kewei Tu. 2022. Bottom-up constituency parsing and nested named entity recognition with pointer networks. In *Proceedings of the 60th Annual Meeting of the Association for Computational Linguistics (Volume 1: Long Papers)*, pages 2403–2416.

Shiwei Zhang, Yiyang Du, Guanzhong Liu, Zhao Yan, and Yunbo Cao. 2022a. G4: Grounding-guided goal-oriented dialogues generation with multiple documents. In *Proceedings of the Second DialDoc Workshop on Document-grounded Dialogue and Conversational Question Answering*, pages 108–114, Dublin, Ireland. Association for Computational Linguistics.

Yizhe Zhang, Siqi Sun, Michel Galley, Yen-Chun Chen, Chris Brockett, Xiang Gao, Jianfeng Gao, Jingjing Liu, and Bill Dolan. 2020. Dialogpt: Large-scale generative pre-training for conversational response generation. In *ACL (demo)*.

Yusen Zhang, Ansong Ni, Ziming Mao, Chen Henry Wu, Chenguang Zhu, Budhaditya Deb, Ahmed Awadallah, Dragomir Radev, and Rui Zhang. 2022b. Summ^n: A multi-stage summarization framework for long input dialogues and documents. In *Proceedings of the 60th Annual Meeting of the Association for Computational Linguistics (Volume 1: Long Papers)*, pages 1592–1604, Dublin, Ireland. Association for Computational Linguistics.

Kangyan Zhou, Shrimai Prabhumoye, and Alan W Black. 2018. A dataset for document grounded conversations. In *Proceedings of the 2018 Conference on Empirical Methods in Natural Language Processing*, pages 708–713, Brussels, Belgium. Association for Computational Linguistics.

A Dialogue System for Assessing Activities of Daily Living: Improving Consistency with Grounded Knowledge

Zhecheng Sheng **Raymond Finzel** **Michael Lucke**
Sheena Dufresne **Maria Gini** **Serguei Pakhomov**
University of Minnesota. Twin Cities
{sheng136, finze006}@umn.edu

Abstract

In healthcare, the ability to care for oneself is reflected in the "Activities of Daily Living (ADL)," which serve as a measure of functional ability (functioning). A lack of functioning may lead to poor living conditions requiring personal care and assistance. To accurately identify those in need of support, assistance programs continuously evaluate participants' functioning across various domains. However, the assessment process may encounter consistency issues when multiple assessors with varying levels of expertise are involved. Novice assessors, in particular, may lack the necessary preparation for real-world interactions with participants. To address this issue, we developed a dialogue system that simulates interactions between assessors and individuals of varying functioning in a natural and reproducible way. The dialogue system consists of two major modules, one for natural language understanding (NLU) and one for natural language generation (NLG), respectively. In order to generate responses consistent with the underlying knowledge base, the dialogue system requires both an understanding of the user's query and of biographical details of an individual being simulated. To fulfill this requirement, we experimented with query classification and generated responses based on those biographical details using some recently released InstructGPT-like models.

1 Introduction

Conversational AI is expanding beyond use in general applications like virtual assistants (Sciuto et al., 2018) to use in specialized domains such as healthcare and finance where it can aid patients or customers in various scenarios. Specifically, there is interest in applications of this technology for patient care and monitoring after hospital discharge (Fadhil, 2018). Assessing functioning is crucial in clinical and non-clinical fields, such as nursing, physical and occupational therapy, geriatric medicine, neurology, rheumatology, disability, and human services. A person's ability to perform day-to-day activities independently depends on their cognitive, motor, and perceptual abilities, which are collectively referred to as Activities of Daily Living (ADL) (Edemekong et al., 2023). Impairments in these abilities often require assistive devices, external supervision, assistance, or a long-term support plan. The Minnesota Department of Human Services (MNDHS) provides significant public resources to assist individuals with impaired functioning based on their specific needs. Certified assessors conduct face-to-face interviews with individuals to determine the level of support required to meet their needs, covering a wide range of areas related to ADLs. The goal of these assessments is to determine an individual's level of independence in performing ADLs. However, ensuring consistency across numerous assessors (e.g., 1,700 in the state of Minnesota) and preparing novice assessors for diverse field interactions poses a challenge to the state's intake process.

Despite the availability of free corpora for training end-to-end neural models, most dialogue systems in healthcare are still rule-based (Laranjo et al., 2018). With the proliferation of neural models, there has been an increasing concern about the factual consistency of AI-powered applications. Factual consistency with a knowledge source, explicated in prior work as knowledge-grounding or attributability (Rashkin et al., 2022), refers to the ability of a model to generate responses that are accurate and consistent with the information present in a verified knowledge base. Knowledge grounding is particularly important in language models used for tasks that require accurate information, such as question-answering, dialogue systems, and chatbots (Honovich et al., 2022; Tam et al., 2022; Nan et al., 2021).

To tackle these challenges and facilitate the training of certified assessors in conducting ADL as-

Proceedings of the Third DialDoc Workshop on Document-grounded Dialogue and Conversational Question Answering, pages 68–79
July 13, 2023 ©2023 Association for Computational Linguistics

sessments, we propose a coaching dialogue system presented in this paper. Specifically, our contributions can be summarized as follows: 1. We created a novel dataset for developing and evaluating dialogue systems focused on ADL assessments. 2. We compared several statistical models used for natural language understanding. 3. We experimented with several approaches to grounding language generation with large language models by using knowledge contained in a manually constructed knowledge base.

2 Related Work

Relevant previous work has been conducted on dialogue systems developed for use in healthcare settings (Jaffe et al., 2015; Llanos et al., 2015; Nirenburg et al., 2008; Laleye et al., 2020). These dialogue systems simulate a virtual standardized patient to deliver healthcare education from structured encounter data and rely on matching algorithms to extract scripted answers. In contrast, the dialogue system we have created generates responses that are dependent on various synthetic profile characteristics and allows off-topic conversations, thus offering a greater degree of variability while still remaining grounded in the knowledge contained in the synthetic profile. This allows the system to simulate several possible patients with different attributes, with the goal of giving assessors a chance to practice their interview skills with simulated patients of different functioning levels and communication styles. Knowledge grounding using external knowledge graphs in combination with transformer models was previously explored (Lucke, 2023; Liu et al., 2021; Agarwal et al., 2021; Koncel-Kedziorski et al., 2019). Open domain conversational dataset and dialogue systems based on factual knowledge have also been developed (Dinan et al., 2019; Dziri et al., 2022). In this paper we focus on the fine-tuning of InstructGPT-like models, and also on the combination of these fine-tuned models with a knowledge base of pre-written natural language facts using query classification and information retrieval via similarity matching. We previously published on earlier versions of this system, referred to as Conversational Agent for Daily Living Assessment Coaching(CADLAC) (Gaydhani et al., 2020). These earlier versions as well as the current version of the system were deployed as a demonstration with a web-based interface (Finzel et al., 2021).

3 Methods

3.1 Data

3.1.1 Synthetic Dialogues

We administered a survey to approximately 1,700 certified assessors aiming to collect sample dialogues across 18 ADL domains(Appendix A). The assessors were requested to recall interactions they had with participants during past assessment interviews and provide up to 3 dialogue turns between themselves and the person being interviewed. The survey also included questions on the gender and age category of the person, the domain of the conversation, and the person's ability level within the domain. The survey results in a total of 2,885 dialogues. A labeled sample record is shown in Appendix B. The survey data was utilized to fine-tune a query classification model for our system.

3.1.2 Historical Assessment

The grounded knowledge relies on the database of 10,000 historical assessments that were conducted by experienced certified assessors and were overseen by Minnesota Department of Human Services(DHS). Each assessment includes various fields that detail each individual's ability to perform ADLs, along with basic demographic information such as age range and gender. Additionally, the assessments contain notes taken by the certified assessors during the interview, which briefly describe the person's difficulties, preferences, and any assistive devices they use, among other information organized by the ADL domains. All historical records were anonymized by removing any individually identifiable information including names and exact age. Likewise, sensitive information such as phone numbers, email and physical addresses were removed.

3.1.3 Synthetic Profiles

The de-identified historical assessment notes were utilized to create synthetic profiles of individuals that specify varying levels of independence in 18 ADL domains and their specific needs. Categorical attributes related to independence levels in the historical assessments were mapped to numerical ratings to create these profiles. Furthermore, the synthetic profiles were populated with assessor notes about intents or action types from the historical data. Since the synthetic profiles were created based on real individual data, they can convey various sources of biases. To mitigate those biases, we

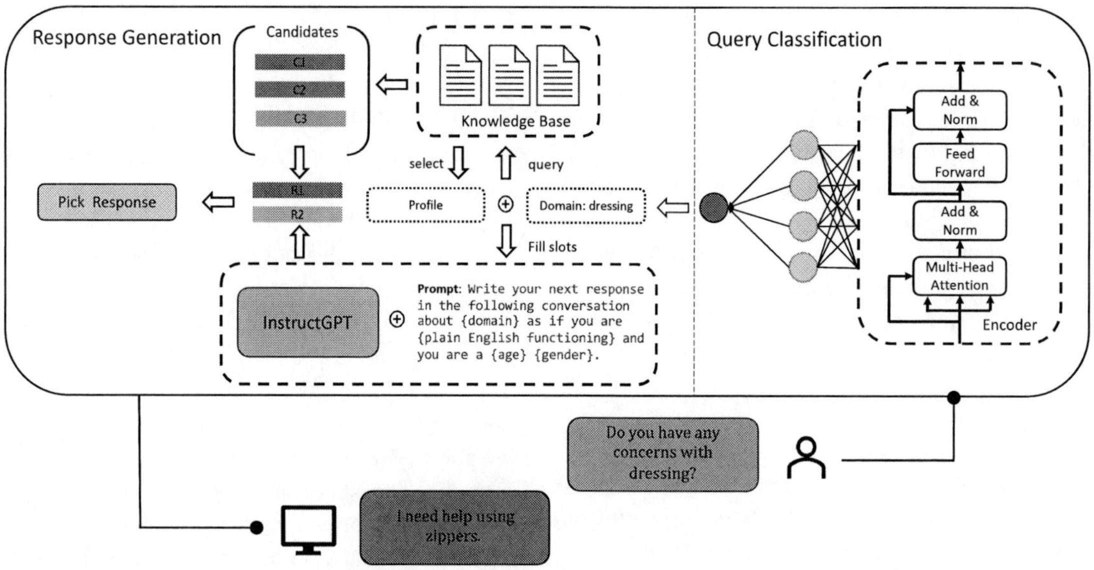

Figure 1: Workflow of the dialogue system: the user communicates with a pre-selected profile through the web interface and with typing or voice. A pre-trained classification model on the back-end dispatches the query to the correct domain. The system tries to match the query against the knowledge base through some similarity measurements. If there is no contents similar to the incoming query, it turns to a fine-tuned InstructGPT model to generate a reasonable turn of dialogue.

conducted a stratified sampling based on gender and race from the original assessment collection, and create a balanced set of profiles in terms of demographics.

3.1.4 Manual Annotation

The synthetic profiles are used as grounded documents for the dialogue system to generate responses that are tailored to the question asked by the assessor and are factual consistent with the underlying profile information. However, as the original historical assessments only represent brief descriptions of different ADL conditions for the assessed participant, they can not be directly used as materials for response generation. To overcome this challenge, we manually translated short assessor notes into natural conversations with several turns, which is correlated with the note. Specifically, our annotators, who had domain-related language expertise, wrote the responses by inferring what the person being assessed might have said during the assessment that led the assessor to jot down the particular note. To illustrate, suppose a 60-year old male was commented "Prefer shower" in the assessor's note. In that case, the annotator may deduce that during the interview, the assessed person answered *"I do not like baths, I prefer to shower."* and continue the conversation with several follow-up responses: *"I like taking long showers."*, *"It's nice to have reminders to get out of the shower when I have been in there for a while."*

This proposed annotation guideline generated two distinct types of responses, "direct" and "indirect," based on the requirements of the assessment situation. Direct responses are written in first-person narrative, while indirect responses are in third-person narrative. The responses primarily rely on the information present in the assessor note, but other fields of information are also used to formulate the response. Direct speech is generated for adults, while indirect speech is used for simulating assessments of children, in which case the assessor would be interviewing the child's parents/caregivers.

For the experiments presented in this paper, 10 annotated synthetic profiles were included and their characteristic are shown in Table 4. Given the amount of data we have collected and the efforts made to create the annotated conversations, we believe it would be a valuable novel corpus for the computational linguistics community. We plan to develop this corpus and release it in the near future.

3.2 Dialogue System

A typical dialogue system consists of distinct NLU and NLG modules that interact with a dialogue manager to maintain a conversation. For the rest of this paper we focus on the NLU and NLG modules which will be referred to as query classification and response generation, respectively, as shown in Fig 1. The back-end of the system is built upon the open conversational AI platform MindMeld [1]. The current iteration of the system is equipped with recently emerging deep transformer models, which represents a better ability to capture desired knowledge, and provides a framework in which to evaluate the capacity of the InstructGPT family of transformers.

3.2.1 Query Classification

To ensure the factual consistency of the system, the incoming user query can be mapped to a domain and intent to assist the generative model in producing reasonable responses. In the following experimental setup, we only considered performance differences in the domain classification task because a large portion of intents under the same domain share similar utterances. When we apply similarity measurements we are searching over all the intents except certain ones(e.g. *preference, equipment*). This strategy increases the system's sensitivity and makes the impact of intent classification more subtle. We used DistilBERT (Sanh et al., 2019) as the intent classifier for the sake of efficiency throughout the conversation experiments.

For domain classification we conducted experiments with 4 different models, ranging from simple multinomial logistic regression to transformer based encoders including BERT (Devlin et al., 2018), RoBERTa (Conneau et al., 2019) and DeBERTa (He et al., 2021). All the pre-trained models from Section 3.2.1 and 3.2.2 were available from the public Huggingface model hub [2]. In the deployment of the dialogue system, two additional fields *follow up* and *other* were added to existing domains to allow assessors to ask more about specific responses or to converse casually. A collection of phrases for greeting, ending the conversation, and also phrases for generic follow up questions were created and added to the labeled corpus specifically. For experiments, 20% of the resultant corpus was randomly sampled for testing and the remaining 80% was used for training. As one can observe from Figure 2, the original training corpus contains a limited number of utterances from each domain and may undermine the ability of the deep transformer models to distinguish between domains. To investigate the effect of this limited corpus, we applied the abstractive text summarization model PEGASUS (Zhang et al., 2019) to generate paraphrases of the original utterances. This model employed a self-supervised objective for pre-training transformer encoder-decoder models that involves removing several whole sentences from a document and then asking the model to recover them without extensive human annotation efforts. In our case, the model recovers and recreates utterances in the training corpus under each domain. The frequency distribution of the augmented training corpus is also shown in Figure 2.

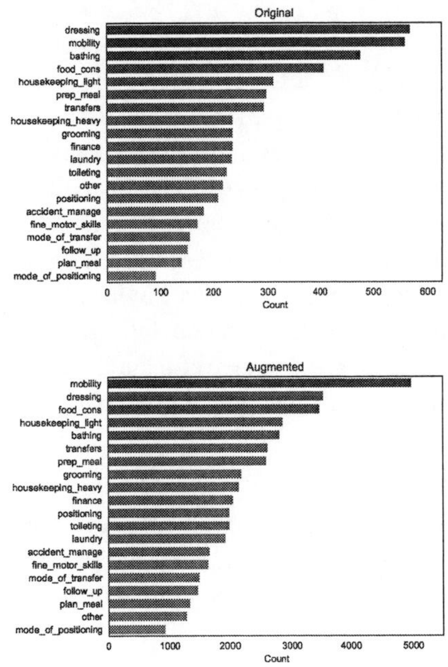

Figure 2: Counts of examples for each domain in the training data.

We fine-tuned different models with the two training corpus and repeated each experiment 10 times to get the statistics of different settings.

3.2.2 Response Generation

The primary goal of developing this dialogue system is to generate human-like responses that are consistent with factual information present in the knowledge base. This requires the generation to at least partially rely on the documents that have been collected and used to construct synthetic profiles. Even though there is plenty of evidence showing that large language models learn some factual knowledge during pre-training (Wang et al., 2020)

[1] https://github.com/cisco/mindmeld
[2] https://huggingface.co/models

and could potentially be used as sources of accurate information (Petroni et al., 2019), model adaptation is still needed for the models to represent concepts from specific domains. Model fine-tuning is a common way to ensure that a language model includes some external knowledge. This section will showcase assessments of the response generation of some InstructGPT-like models, including an evaluation of a zero-shot methodology, a fine-tuned model, and an assessment of a methodology that uses an InstructGPT-like model as a fallback when bespoke responses that are significantly similar to the current query (as determined by query classification) are not available in the knowledge base.

Over the past few months, large language models (LLMs) such as ChatGPT (Ouyang et al., 2022), have been garnering attention due to their impressive ability to understand instructions and generate human-like responses. The InstructGPT-like models are trained on massive amounts of natural language data in auto-regressive fashion and then fine-tuned to follow large-scale human instructions (Wang et al., 2022). They exhibit robust performance across a wide range of natural language processing tasks and can generalize to unseen tasks, making them promising unified solutions for text generation and conversational AI.

We hope to leverage the strength of open-source LLMs to generate answers by understanding assessor questions and responding with human-like reasoning about functioning. However, given that publicly available models are generally pre-trained on data outside of the ADL domains, it is necessary to create a dataset explicitly for our task. By further fine-tuning an InstructGPT on our ADL specific dataset, we can benefit from the model's conversation capability while also adapting to the style of an assessment interview. Researchers recently found that achieving the best performance with a fixed computer budget does not solely depend on model size. In some cases, smaller models that have been pre-trained with a greater amount of data can outperform larger models (Hoffmann et al., 2022). This is important to the deployment of applications like dialogue systems in the real world as they need to interact with users with very low latency. This requires models to have high computation efficiency at inference time. LLaMA (Touvron et al., 2023) is a set of fundamental instruct-based language models, varying in size from 7 billion to 65 billion parameters. The models were trained on a mixture data source consists of roughly 1.4 trillion unique tokens. It has been reported LLaMA 7B models demonstrated competitive performances against GPT-3 on multiple tasks such as Common-Sense Reasoning and Closed-book Question Answering. (Touvron et al., 2023). Considering the computational burden, we decided to investigate the 7B LLaMA model and experiment under several settings to evaluate its factual consistency with the grounded documents.

As described earlier in Section 3.1.4, the historical assessments were transformed into numbers of synthetic profiles with certain age, gender and various levels of daily living functioning in different domains. We rely on these synthetic profiles to establish the knowledge base, which currently contains 10 sampled profiles.

When InstructGPT models are used in the dialogue system, it is essential to feed the model with a well-designed prompt which embeds factual context and also provides a clear description of the task. We first translated numerical ratings of functioning for each assessment into plain English, then inserted that information into tailored prompt templates. We designed one template for typical interrogative sentences and another for follow up questions.

1. General: Write your next response in the following conversation about `{domain}` as if you `{plain English functioning}` and you are `{age}` `{gender}`.

2. Follow-up: Provide more details to this statement about `{domain}` as if you `{plain English functioning}` and you are `{age}` `{gender}`.

The fine-tuning data was derived from both the human written synthetic dialogues from survey data and annotated historical assessments introduced above. The instruction-following fine-tuning data format contains 3 fields: context, input, and output. The context field is filled with one of the prompts above, while the input and output fields are filled with one question answer pair. To accommodate multi-turn conversation from the source data, we concatenated all previous turns with a newline separator "`\n`" to account for dialogue history. The resultant dataset has 6,123 question/answer pairs and examples of short conversations. The dataset covers diverse profiles and questions from all the

ADL domains of interest. While fine-tuning the whole 7B models is prohibitively costly, there exist a family of methods called Parameter Efficient Fine-Tuning methods(PEFT) that only train a tiny number of parameters, but which result in comparable performance to whole-model fine-tuning (Mangrulkar et al., 2022). Low-Rank Adaptation(LoRA) (Hu et al., 2021) is the one of those methods we selected for our task. The idea behind LoRA is to fix the pre-trained model weights and add trainable rank decomposition matrices to every layer of the transformer architecture. In order to train the LoRA adapter with conversational capabilities for activities of daily living context, we apply the strategy demonstrated in Figure 3. We first trained a LoRA adapter using the public Stanford Alpaca dataset (Taori et al., 2023) to take advantage of the 52K instruction-following dataset, and then merged the LoRA weights back into LLaMA to create a single base model. We then trained another LoRA adapter with our ADL conversation specific instruction-following dataset described above. This training strategy is similar to the one employed in ChatDoctor (Li et al., 2023), but at this time we have only investigated the LoRA training approach, while Chatdoctor did a concurrent investigation of fine-tuning the whole model with the Stanford Alpaca dataset. All of our locally trained models were quantized using 8-bit precision to allow for fine-tuning on a single GPU.

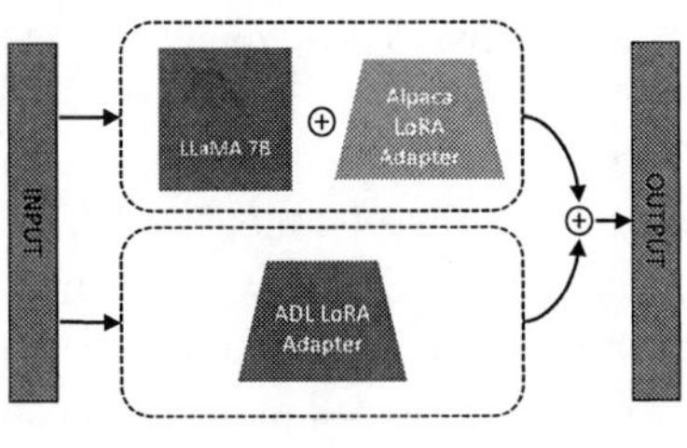

Figure 3: Diagram of LoRA training

3.3 Evaluation Methods

3.3.1 Query Classification

In order to generate sensible responses from our knowledge base of pre-prepared facts, the domain of a given query needed to be classified so that the system could accurately identify candidate responses. We assessed domain classification performance, across 4 different metrics, including weighted F_1, micro F_1 and macro F_1 for multi-classification task. The accuracy measures how the model performs regardless of the domain differences and the other 3 aggregated f-measures implies the performance when imbalance exists across domains.

3.3.2 Response Generation

In dialogue system research, evaluating the quality of the conversation automatically is still an open problem (Deriu et al., 2020). There have been efforts to develop reference-free metrics for evaluating factual consistency in knowledge grounded dialogue systems (Honovich et al., 2021) based on automatic question generation paired with a question answering model. However, given the style of the knowledge base in our system and various possible definitions of factuality, we only pursued human ratings at this time to evaluate the quality of conversations. We evaluated text excerpts through the notion of sensibleness and specificity, and provided a separate evaluation of factual consistency. Sensibleness and specificity average (SSA) is a metric to capture human likeness of generated responses (Adiwardana et al., 2020). Sensibleness measures whether the generated response is coherent and makes sense given the context while specificity measures whether the generated response seems uniquely suited to the questions that are asked, rather than just sensible in general. We generated a short conversation snippet using each NLG method with a fixed set of questions in an effort to keep the style of conversation consistent across methods. Two domains for which we had the most data (bathing, dressing) were selected and we created 5 questions for each. The 5 questions comprise 1 general question, 1 follow up question and 3 questions for detailed aspects. Next we randomly selected one profile and filled those questions into the prompt by design. Besides our fine-tuned LLaMA model, we also tested a 13B Vicuna model (Chiang et al., 2023) with a zero-shot configuration. In total, three models (Fine-tuned 7B LLaMA only, Fine-tuned 7B LLaMA + knowledge base, 13B Vicuna demo[3]) were accessed to generate conversations. When combining the fine-tuned LLaMA model with grounded knowledge, we used a heuristic rule to determine whether to utilize knowledge directly from the knowledge base, or to generate a response using the LLM. Mathematically, the heuristic can

[3] `https://chat.lmsys.org`

Experiments	Accuracy	F1-weighted	F1-micro	F1-macro
LR + Original	$0.703_{(0.702-0.704)}$	$0.708_{(0.707-0.709)}$	$0.703_{(0.702-0.704)}$	$0.606_{(0.604-0.608)}$
LR + Augmented	$0.696_{(0.694-0.705)}$	$0.702_{(0.700-0.711)}$	$0.696_{(0.694-0.705)}$	$0.615_{(0.613-0.623)}$
BERT$_{base}$ + Original	$0.747_{(0.729-0.760)}$	$0.744_{(0.727-0.756)}$	$0.747_{(0.729-0.760)}$	$0.649_{(0.635-0.670)}$
BERT$_{base}$ + Augmented	$0.726_{(0.720-0.733)}$	$0.729_{(0.723-0.738)}$	$0.726_{(0.720-0.733)}$	$0.639_{(0.630-0.651)}$
RoBERTa$_{base}$ + Original	$0.759_{(0.745-0.767)}$	$0.757_{(0.740-0.766)}$	$0.759_{(0.745-0.767)}$	$0.667_{(0.629-0.698)}$
RoBERTa$_{base}$ + Augmented	$0.727_{(0.720-0.732)}$	$0.731_{(0.725-0.737)}$	$0.727_{(0.720-0.732)}$	$0.641_{(0.633-0.648)}$
DeBERTa$_{v3}$ + Original	$\mathbf{0.762}_{(0.752-0.782)}$	$\mathbf{0.759}_{(0.746-0.781)}$	$\mathbf{0.762}_{(0.752-0.782)}$	$\mathbf{0.683}_{(0.652-0.708)}$
DeBERTa$_{v3}$ + Augmented	$0.732_{(0.728-0.738)}$	$0.736_{(0.732-0.741)}$	$0.732_{(0.728-0.738)}$	$0.646_{(0.643-0.651)}$

Table 1: Experimental results of testing classification models. The best performer for each metric is marked in bold.

be expressed as:

$$R = \begin{cases} \arg\max_{c \in \mathcal{C}} \sigma(q, c) & \text{if } \max_{c \in \mathcal{C}} \sigma(q, c) \geq \lambda \\ r_l & \text{otherwise} \end{cases}$$

Where σ is any similarity measurement(e.g. Bertscore), λ is an arbitrary cutoff and $\mathcal{C}$ is the collection of all candidates from the knowledge base. q denotes the incoming query and r_l denotes the response generated from LLM. A note about generation: in most cases, the fine-tuned LLaMA model tended to generate complete conversations rather than single responses, which could be due to the fact that the Alpaca fine-tuning data does not represent an obvious conversational form. To mitigate this, we manually selected the first sentence from the entire output as the response to the question. After assembling these excerpts we asked 6 colleagues who have limited background of this project to score sensibleness and specificity for each conversation on a scale of 1-6 and had them pick their favorite conversations based both on realistic quality and personal preference. The evaluation form is also publicly available. This resulted in 12 total SSA ratings of each method (2 conversation snippets per method, 6 raters) and 6 opinions on total quality and reality. For our factual consistency evaluation, two co-authors conversed freely with the chatbot systems for a fixed number of dialogue turns. This provided a chat history in which the dialogue systems would be free to "hallucinate" factual content about the synthetic profile, or forget about details that were already present in the conversation several turns ago. This method was selected for conversation generation in order to assure that the human turns were natural—allowing for things like specific follow-up questions, requests for further information, attempts to repair disfluent conversation turns, and other intricacies of human conversation. The co-authors then counted the number of contradictions that the conversations made against the knowledge base and also counted the number of factual self-contradictions in the dialogue history. This combination of two sorts of human-rated metrics (sensibility & specificity, and external grounding & internal consistency) formed our baseline for evaluating a systems ability to respond fluently and factually to an assessor's queries.

4 Results

4.1 Query Classification

The experimental results for 4 different metrics are reported in Table 1. We show the range of each metric instead of standard deviation as the numbers are too small compared to the mean value. The results indicate that the transformer family outperforms the simple logistic regression model with bag of word features. DeBERTa$_{v3}$, the largest transformer model among the candidates, achieves the best performance for all 4 metrics. When comparing model training results between the training with an augmented corpus and training with the original corpus, we observe that all the models consistently perform better with the original corpus. This finding can indicate that larger quantities of data does not necessarily bring advantages to learning classification rules and we suspect the paraphrasing potentially introduces noise that lowers the quality of the training corpus. Comparisons across the 4 metrics suggests there is an imbalance in performance across the domains. Higher weighted F_1 score and micro F_1 score than macro F_1 score implies the model performs poorly on domains with less available data. Such performance imbalances can also arise when domains share a high degree of overlap in their conceptual definition (such as categories like *light housekeeping* and *heavy house-*

Model	Sensibleness	Specificity	Realness	Favorite	¬ Knowledge	¬ History
Fine-tuned LLaMA 7B	3.67	3.92	1	1	4	1
Zero shot Vicuna 13B	4.50	5.00	0	1	5	2
Fine-tuned LLaMA 7B + Knowledge base	4.92	4.33	5	4	1	0

Table 2: Human Evaluation Results. The numbers in the *Sensibleness* and *Specificity* columns represent the average rating across evaluators. Numbers in the remaining columns are simple counts. "¬" indicates a contradiction against an existing knowledge source.

keeping), or when there are differences in the size or variability of the available data. If interested, a per-domain breakdown of F_1 score can be found in Figure 4 (appendix).

4.2 Response Generation

Human functioning is not easily reduceable to an array of numbers, so grounding the knowledge in a way that respects the "functional levels" of the ADL, but also embeds knowledge of specific human details that differ from person to person is a challenge. In our evaluation of response generation using InstructGPT-like models, the knowledge-grounding process that we employed had a modest impact on system's ability to speak fluently and to speak into topics in which we did not have our own training data, such as regular open-domain conversation and non-functioning related conversation topics about home life. In the authors' opinion the open-domain response generation of raw LLMs provided a more pleasurable chat experience across a long conversation (something that our numeric evaluation across five and ten turn excerpts could not capture), but the tradeoff for factual and internal consistency provides value in the application of these technologies for the simulation of a factually grounded profile. The results in Table 2 indicate that despite the immense power of LLMs, facts stored as natural language snippets in a database may be used to improve factual and internal consistency, and this does not come at a penalty to a simulation's sensibleness, specificity, or realistic behavior in all cases. It is also interesting to note that when evaluating our LLM generated responses, we experimented with different hyperparameters and found that though the models provided different occasionally during this exploration, the knowledge conveyed from each run was consistent. For example, it was unlikely in our experience that a change to the decoding hyperparameters would cause the LLM to generate "I have no problem bathing on my own," when under another hyperparameter configuration it had responded "I need a lot of help with bathing."

5 Conclusions and Limitations

In this paper, we present a comprehensive framework for measuring the quality of a dialogue system dedicated to activities of daily living assessments. We have created a new high-quality dataset of human-written questions and answers with corresponding profile information. We are currently working on expanding the dataset by adding more profiles and removing any factual inconsistencies resulting from human error. Although more complex models showed better query classification performances, we need to consider the trade-offs between model size and generation time in the deployment environment to ensure a smooth user experience. We also identify areas where LLM performance can be augmented by a knowledge base filled with human written natural language facts, and that this augmentation need not come at a penalty to sensibleness, specificity, or the realistic quality of conversation. General conclusions based on our initial work here may not be possible given the limited number of evaluators and small amount of evaluated dialogues, and this is a major limitation of our contribution. Future work is needed to develop a more robust and replicatable evaluation framework, especially to perform evaluations of long and complex conversations like the type that assessors perform in the field. Such an evaluation will need to include larger numbers of human raters to improve the statistical power of the surveys. Recent automatic evaluations may also help improve development efforts, as a sufficiently powerful LLM such as GPT-4 may be able to monitor the chatbot for regressions in its ability to speak fluently, sensibly or specifically. This assessment, known informally as the "Vicuna Assessment"(Chiang et al., 2023), cannot give an evaluation of the chatbot's fit-for-purpose, but could be used to compare short conversations from several versions of the same chatbot. This could free up more human resources to evaluate the knowledge-groundedness and fit-for-purpose of future versions. In addition, given more computing budget and more time to engineer prompts, larger language models beyond LLaMA 7B could be further studied or fine-tuned while experimenting with fine-tuning datasets and process. There are also many thresholds and parameters that could be further tested in the development of the knowledge-grounding system, wherein similarity measures inform the system's decision to answer using a generative model versus responding with language directly from the knowledge base.

6 Acknowledgements

Work on this paper was supported by funding from the Minnesota Department of Human Services. We would like to thank the people at DSD and MNIT for help with project specifications, gathering of historical data, and expert guidance on domain-specific aspects of the project. We would also like to thank Pamela Miller, Sidney Kiltie, and Elise Moore for help with transforming certified assessor notes to natural language format and Julia Garbuz for helping to develop and conduct the surveys of DHS assessors.

References

Daniel Adiwardana, Minh-Thang Luong, David R. So, Jamie Hall, Noah Fiedel, Romal Thoppilan, Zi Yang, Apoorv Kulshreshtha, Gaurav Nemade, Yifeng Lu, and Quoc V. Le. 2020. Towards a human-like open-domain chatbot.

Oshin Agarwal, Heming Ge, Siamak Shakeri, and Rami Al-Rfou. 2021. Knowledge graph based synthetic corpus generation for knowledge-enhanced language model pre-training. In *Proceedings of the 2021 Conference of the North American Chapter of the Association for Computational Linguistics: Human Language Technologies*, pages 3554–3565, Online. Association for Computational Linguistics.

Wei-Lin Chiang, Zhuohan Li, Zi Lin, Ying Sheng, Zhanghao Wu, Hao Zhang, Lianmin Zheng, Siyuan Zhuang, Yonghao Zhuang, Joseph E. Gonzalez, Ion Stoica, and Eric P. Xing. 2023. Vicuna: An open-source chatbot impressing gpt-4 with 90%* chatgpt quality.

Alexis Conneau, Kartikay Khandelwal, Naman Goyal, Vishrav Chaudhary, Guillaume Wenzek, Francisco Guzmán, Edouard Grave, Myle Ott, Luke Zettlemoyer, and Veselin Stoyanov. 2019. Unsupervised cross-lingual representation learning at scale. *CoRR*, abs/1911.02116.

Jan Deriu, Alvaro Rodrigo, Arantxa Otegi, Guillermo Echegoyen, Sophie Rosset, Eneko Agirre, and Mark Cieliebak. 2020. Survey on evaluation methods for dialogue systems. *Artificial Intelligence Review*, 54(1):755–810.

Jacob Devlin, Ming-Wei Chang, Kenton Lee, and Kristina Toutanova. 2018. BERT: pre-training of deep bidirectional transformers for language understanding. *CoRR*, abs/1810.04805.

Emily Dinan, Stephen Roller, Kurt Shuster, Angela Fan, Mary Williamson Auli, and Jason Weston. 2019. Wizard of wikipedia: Knowledge-powered conversational agents. In *International Conference on Learning Representations*.

Narjes Dziri, Erfan Kamalloo, Simon Milton, Osmar R. Zaïane, Mengzhou Yu, Emanuele Ponti, and Siva Reddy. 2022. Faithdial: A faithful benchmark for information-seeking dialogue. *Transactions of the Association for Computational Linguistics*, 10:1473–1490.

Precious F Edemekong, Dana L Bomgaars, Shaji Sukumaran, and Christopher Schoo. 2023. *Activities of Daily Living*. StatPearls Publishing. PMID: 29261878.

Ahmed Fadhil. 2018. Beyond patient monitoring: Conversational agents role in telemedicine and healthcare support for home-living elderly individuals. *arXiv preprint arXiv:1803.06000*.

Raymond Finzel, Aditya Gaydhani, Sheena Dufresne, Maria Gini, and Serguei Pakhomov. 2021. Conversational agent for daily living assessment coaching demo. In *Proceedings of the 16th Conference of the European Chapter of the Association for Computational Linguistics: System Demonstrations*, pages 321–328, Online. Association for Computational Linguistics.

Aditya Gaydhani, Raymond Finzel, Sheena R Dufresne, Maria Gini, and Serguei Pakhomov. 2020. Conversational agent for daily living assessment coaching. *CEUR Workshop Proceedings*, 2760:8–13.

Pengcheng He, Xiaodong Liu, Jianfeng Gao, and Weizhu Chen. 2021. Deberta: Decoding-enhanced bert with disentangled attention. In *International Conference on Learning Representations*.

Jordan Hoffmann, Sebastian Borgeaud, Arthur Mensch, Elena Buchatskaya, Trevor Cai, Eliza Rutherford, Diego de Las Casas, Lisa Anne Hendricks, Johannes Welbl, Aidan Clark, Tom Hennigan, Eric Noland, Katie Millican, George van den Driessche, Bogdan Damoc, Aurelia Guy, Simon Osindero, Karen Simonyan, Erich Elsen, Jack W. Rae, Oriol Vinyals, and Laurent Sifre. 2022. Training compute-optimal large language models. *arXiv preprint arXiv:2202.09743*.

Or Honovich, Roee Aharoni, Jonathan Herzig, Hagai Taitelbaum, Doron Kukliansy, Vered Cohen, Thomas Scialom, Idan Szpektor, Avinatan Hassidim, and

Yossi Matias. 2022. TRUE: Re-evaluating factual consistency evaluation. In *Proceedings of the Second DialDoc Workshop on Document-grounded Dialogue and Conversational Question Answering*, pages 161–175, Dublin, Ireland. Association for Computational Linguistics.

Or Honovich, Leshem Choshen, Roee Aharoni, Ella Neeman, Idan Szpektor, and Omri Abend. 2021. q^2: Evaluating factual consistency in knowledge-grounded dialogues via question generation and question answering. In *Proceedings of the 2021 Conference on Empirical Methods in Natural Language Processing*, pages 7856–7870, Online and Punta Cana, Dominican Republic. Association for Computational Linguistics.

Edward J. Hu, Yelong Shen, Phillip Wallis, Zeyuan Allen-Zhu, Yuanzhi Li, Shean Wang, Lu Wang, and Weizhu Chen. 2021. Lora: Low-rank adaptation of large language models.

Evan Jaffe, Michael White, William Schuler, Eric Fosler-Lussier, Alex Rosenfeld, and Douglas Danforth. 2015. Interpreting questions with a log-linear ranking model in a virtual patient dialogue system. In *Proceedings of the Tenth Workshop on Innovative Use of NLP for Building Educational Applications*, pages 86–96, Denver, Colorado. Association for Computational Linguistics.

Rik Koncel-Kedziorski, Dhanush Bekal, Yi Luan, Mirella Lapata, and Hannaneh Hajishirzi. 2019. Text Generation from Knowledge Graphs with Graph Transformers. In *Proceedings of the 2019 Conference of the North American Chapter of the Association for Computational Linguistics: Human Language Technologies, Volume 1 (Long and Short Papers)*, pages 2284–2293, Minneapolis, Minnesota. Association for Computational Linguistics.

Fréjus A. A. Laleye, Gaël de Chalendar, Antonia Blanié, Antoine Brouquet, and Dan Behnamou. 2020. A French medical conversations corpus annotated for a virtual patient dialogue system. In *Proceedings of the Twelfth Language Resources and Evaluation Conference*, pages 574–580, Marseille, France. European Language Resources Association.

Liliana Laranjo, Adam G Dunn, Huong Ly Tong, Ahmet Baki Kocaballi, Jessica Chen, Rabia Bashir, Didi Surian, Blanca Gallego, Farah Magrabi, Annie Y S Lau, and Enrico Coiera. 2018. Conversational agents in healthcare: a systematic review. *Journal of the American Medical Informatics Association*, 25(9):1248–1258.

Yunxiang Li, Zihan Li, Kai Zhang, Ruilong Dan, and You Zhang. 2023. Chatdoctor: A medical chat model fine-tuned on llama model using medical domain knowledge.

Ye Liu, Yao Wan, Lifang He, Hao Peng, and Philip S. Yu. 2021. Kg-bart: Knowledge graph-augmented bart for generative commonsense reasoning.

Leonardo Campillos Llanos, Dhouha Bouamor, Éric Bilinski, Anne-Laure Ligozat, Pierre Zweigenbaum, and Sophie Rosset. 2015. Description of the patient-genesys dialogue system. In *Proceedings of the 16th Annual Meeting of the Special Interest Group on Discourse and Dialogue*, pages 438–440, Prague, Czech Republic. Association for Computational Linguistics.

Michael Lucke. 2023. Using text-based representations of knowledge graphs to improve the consistency of generated text. Retrieved from the University of Minnesota Digital Conservancy, `https://hdl.handle.net/11299/253403`.

Sourab Mangrulkar, Sylvain Gugger, Lysandre Debut, Younes Belkada, and Sayak Paul. 2022. Peft: State-of-the-art parameter-efficient fine-tuning methods. `https://github.com/huggingface/peft`.

Feng Nan, Cicero Nogueira dos Santos, Henghui Zhu, Patrick Ng, Kathleen McKeown, Ramesh Nallapati, Dejiao Zhang, Zhiguo Wang, Andrew O. Arnold, and Bing Xiang. 2021. Improving factual consistency of abstractive summarization via question answering. In *Proceedings of the 59th Annual Meeting of the Association for Computational Linguistics and the 11th International Joint Conference on Natural Language Processing (Volume 1: Long Papers)*, pages 6881–6894, Online. Association for Computational Linguistics.

Sergei Nirenburg, Stephen Beale, Marjorie McShane, Bruce Jarrell, and George Fantry. 2008. Language understanding in maryland virtual patient. In *Coling 2008: Proceedings of the workshop on Speech Processing for Safety Critical Translation and Pervasive Applications*, pages 36–39, Manchester, UK. Coling 2008 Organizing Committee.

Long Ouyang, Jeff Wu, Xu Jiang, Diogo Almeida, Carroll L. Wainwright, Pamela Mishkin, Chong Zhang, Sandhini Agarwal, Katarina Slama, Alex Ray, John Schulman, Jacob Hilton, Fraser Kelton, Luke Miller, Maddie Simens, Amanda Askell, Peter Welinder, Paul Christiano, Jan Leike, and Ryan Lowe. 2022. Training language models to follow instructions with human feedback.

Fabio Petroni, Tim Rocktäschel, Sebastian Riedel, Patrick Lewis, Anton Bakhtin, Yuxiang Wu, and Alexander Miller. 2019. Language models as knowledge bases? In *Proceedings of the 2019 Conference on Empirical Methods in Natural Language Processing and the 9th International Joint Conference on Natural Language Processing (EMNLP-IJCNLP)*, pages 2463–2473, Hong Kong, China. Association for Computational Linguistics.

Hannah Rashkin, Vitaly Nikolaev, Matthew Lamm, Lora Aroyo, Michael Collins, Dipanjan Das, Slav Petrov, Gaurav Singh Tomar, Iulia Turc, and David Reitter. 2022. Measuring attribution in natural language generation models.

Victor Sanh, Lysandre Debut, Julien Chaumond, and Thomas Wolf. 2019. Distilbert, a distilled version of BERT: smaller, faster, cheaper and lighter. *CoRR*, abs/1910.01108.

Alex Sciuto, Arnita Saini, Jodi Forlizzi, and Jason Hong. 2018. Hey alexa, what's up?: A mixed-methods studies of in-home conversational agent usage. In *Proceedings of the 2018 Designing Interactive Systems Conference*, pages 857–868.

Derek Tam, Anisha Mascarenhas, Shiyue Zhang, Sarah Kwan, Mohit Bansal, and Colin Raffel. 2022. Evaluating the factual consistency of large language models through summarization.

Rohan Taori, Ishaan Gulrajani, Tianyi Zhang, Yann Dubois, Xuechen Li, Carlos Guestrin, Percy Liang, and Tatsunori B. Hashimoto. 2023. Stanford alpaca: An instruction-following llama model. `https://github.com/tatsu-lab/stanford_alpaca`.

Hugo Touvron, Thibaut Lavril, Gautier Izacard, Xavier Martinet, Marie-Anne Lachaux, Timothée Lacroix, Baptiste Rozière, Naman Goyal, Eric Hambro, Faisal Azhar, Aurelien Rodriguez, Armand Joulin, Edouard Grave, and Guillaume Lample. 2023. Llama: Open and efficient foundation language models.

Chenguang Wang, Xiao Liu, and Dawn Song. 2020. Language models are open knowledge graphs.

Yizhong Wang, Yeganeh Kordi, Swaroop Mishra, Alisa Liu, Noah A. Smith, Daniel Khashabi, and Hannaneh Hajishirzi. 2022. Self-instruct: Aligning language model with self generated instructions.

Jingqing Zhang, Yao Zhao, Mohammad Saleh, and Peter J. Liu. 2019. Pegasus: Pre-training with extracted gap-sentences for abstractive summarization.

A Domains of Interest

1. dressing 2. grooming 3. bathing 4. toileting 5. incontinence accident management 6. housekeeping light 7. housekeeping heavy 8. laundry 9. finance 10. food consumption 11. meal preparation 12. meal planing 13. mobility 14. transfer 15. mode of transfer 16. positioning 17. mode of positioning 18. fine motor skills

B Example Labeled Survey Form

Domain	Grooming
Ability	Physical Assistance
Age	65-84
Gender	Female
Assessor-1	"Can you tell me about how you take care of your grooming needs?" *intent - generic*
Participant-1	"I have a hard time"
Assessor-2	"Can you brush your hair?"*intent - challenges*
Participant-2	"No, I can't reach my hair to get it brushed in the back."
Assessor-3	"Who helps you to brush your hair?"*intent - helper*
Participant-2	"My daughter helps me to brush my hair."

Table 3: Sample dialogue from the survey.

C Profile Information

ID	Age	Gender	Avg rating	#utterances
3b1	27	Female	3.67	252
3b108	64	Male	3.00	259
3b77	71	Female	3.50	196
3b84	84	Male	2.78	148
3b86	52	Male	3.78	206
4d18	86	Female	3.94	233
4d23	60	Male	4.11	114
4d26	96	Female	3.89	81
4d29	42	Female	1.83	50
4d4	63	Female	3.27	213

Table 4: Synthetic profile summary

D Evaluation Questions

D.1 Test questions

Bathing

1. Tell me about how bathing goes for you.
2. Can you elaborate more on that?
3. Can you get in and out of the shower easily?
4. Do you need any help with drying off?
5. Can you wash your back okay?

Dressing

1. Tell me about how you get dressed in the morning.
2. Is there anything else I should know about that?
3. What about buttons and zippers specifically? Do you struggle at all with them?
4. Can you manage your shoes on your own?
5. Do you prefer any particular type of clothing?

D.2 Example of long casual talks for factuality evaluation

Bathing assessment

[Assessor]: Tell me about how bathing goes for you?

[Chatbot]: I have to get my wife or a caregiver to help me bathe. I can't do it myself.

[Assessor]: What sort of help does your wife give you?

[Chatbot]: She helps me undress, wash, dry off, dress, and put on my clothes. She also helps me shave.

[Assessor]: What parts of washing do you struggle with?

[Chatbot]: I can't reach my back.

[Assessor]: But you can manage to turn on the water yourself?

[Chatbot]: Yes, but I can't reach the soap.

[Assessor]: Have you thought about getting a caddy or something to bring the soap closer to you?

[Chatbot]: No, I haven't.

[Assessor]: Okay. Good to know. Is it easy to dry off after you shower?

[Chatbot]: It is hard to dry off because I am not able to stand up by myself.

[Assessor]: How long does it take you to shower and how often do you get to do it?

[Chatbot]: I don't like to take too much time in the shower because I get cold easily. It takes me about 15 minutes to shower.

[Assessor]: How frequently are you able to shower?

[Chatbot]: I am able to shower every other day.

[Assessor]: Do you prefer when your caregiver helps? Or your wife?

[Chatbot]: My wife helps me.

[Assessor]: Do you have any grab bars or anti-slip mats or other things that help you stay steady in the shower?

[Chatbot]: I have a bench in the shower.

E Domain F1 score

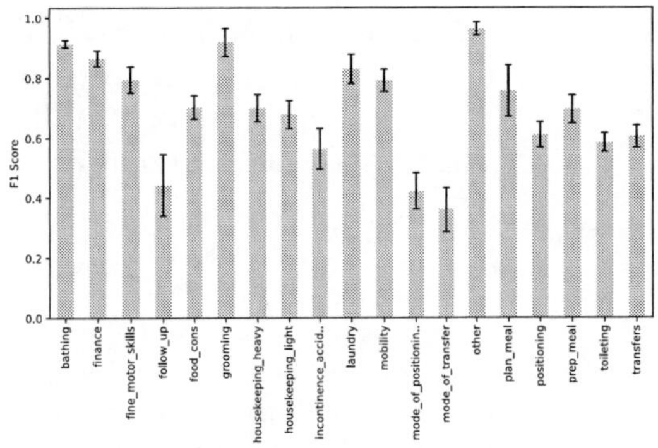

Figure 4: F1 score for each domain, aggregated across experiments. (Dressing domain is not included because we didn't derive the test data. And the results for bathing domain is from augmented set only as the original set does not have test data either.)

C-PMI: Conditional Pointwise Mutual Information for Turn-level Dialogue Evaluation

Liliang Ren*, **Mankeerat Sidhu***, **Qi Zeng**, **Revanth Gangi Reddy**, **Heng Ji**, **ChengXiang Zhai**
University of Illinois Urbana-Champaign
{liliang3, mssidhu2, qizeng2, revanth3, hengji, czhai}@illinois.edu

Abstract

Existing reference-free turn-level evaluation metrics for chatbots inadequately capture the interaction between the user and the system. Consequently, they often correlate poorly with human evaluations. To address this issue, we propose a novel model-agnostic approach that leverages Conditional Pointwise Mutual Information (C-PMI) to measure the turn-level interaction between the system and the user based on a given evaluation dimension. Experimental results on the widely used FED dialogue evaluation dataset demonstrate that our approach significantly improves the correlation with human judgment compared with existing evaluation systems. By replacing the negative log-likelihood-based scorer with our proposed C-PMI scorer, we achieve a relative 60.5% higher Spearman correlation on average for the FED evaluation metric. Our code is publicly available at https://github.com/renll/C-PMI.

1 Introduction

Evaluating dialogues is a multi-faceted task that demands consideration of diverse dimensions, which distinguishes it from the evaluation of task-oriented dialogue systems. Traditional n-gram-based evaluation metrics, such as ROUGE (Lin, 2004) and BLEU (Papineni et al., 2002), demonstrate weak correlation with human-annotated judgments due to the broad spectrum of potential responses in dialogues. As a result, researchers often resort to human evaluations to ascertain the quality and effectiveness of their generated system responses, especially for knowledge-guided dialog systems (Li et al., 2022; Fung et al., 2023; Lai et al., 2023).

Substantial research has been conducted on automatic evaluation metrics for dialogue (Yeh et al., 2021). These metrics can be classified into reference-based and reference-free categories. Reference-based metrics, which depend on comparing the system response to a human-written reference response, are generally inadequate for dialogue evaluation due to the inherent one-to-many nature of dialogues. The reference-free metric instead uses a computational model to generate a score for the system response with a given context.

Early models predominantly focus on a limited set of general features of dialogue generation quality, such as context coherency and fluency. Subsequent evaluation metrics investigated additional dimensions, such as USL-H (Phy et al., 2020), which combines relevance evaluation with fact-to-response selection. Holistic-eval (Pang et al., 2020) assesses content coherence, language fluency, self-consistency, and semantic appropriateness. D-Score (Zhang et al., 2021b) and Predictive Engage (Ghazarian et al., 2020) introduce response diversity and engagement scores. The recent FED (Mehri and Eskenazi, 2020a) metric encompasses 18 turn-level and dialogue-level metrics, including interestingness, likeability, and response flexibility. However, all of these methods do not model the interaction between the turn-level response and the dialogue history and regard them as an integrated context for score calculation.

In this paper, we focus on directly modeling user-system interactions through the lens of Mutual Information (Shannon, 1948; Ghassami and Kiyavash, 2017) and propose a novel scorer based on Conditional Pointwise Mutual Information (C-PMI), which effectively captures the turn-level interactions between the system and user with respect to a given hypothesis. We demonstrate that our approach results in a reference-free, training-free, automatic turn-level dialogue evaluation that significantly outperforms state-of-the-art methods with a comparable number of model parameters. Our contributions in this work are three-fold:

- A novel dialogue evaluation metric based on Conditional Pointwise Mutual Information (C-PMI) that effectively captures turn-level in-

*Equal contribution.

Proceedings of the Third DialDoc Workshop on Document-grounded Dialogue and Conversational Question Answering, pages 80–85
July 13, 2023

teractions between the system and user with respect to a given hypothesis.

- An unreferenced, training-free, automatic turn-level dialogue evaluation that significantly outperforms state-of-the-art methods with a comparable number of model parameters.
- A model-agnostic approach that can be served as a generalized alternative to the Negative Log-Likelihood (NLL) based evaluation metrics when interactions between previous turns need to be considered.

2 Related Work

Developing automatic evaluation metrics for dialog is challenging for several reasons: 1) Dialogues often have a one-to-many nature, rendering word-overlap metrics ineffective. To address this issue, metrics should be designed to be reference-free. 2) Given the limitless nature of conversation topics in open-domain dialogues, the dialogue evaluation metrics are expected to understand the semantic meaning of both the dialogue context and the generated responses. This necessitates a metric that can leverage pre-trained large language models and self-supervised training objectives. 3) Training dialogue evaluation metrics solely on labeled data can significantly restrict the metric's range, risking over-fitting to the training data in terms of conversation topics and response generation models. As such, recent metrics have started to incorporate self-supervised training objectives designed to capture various aspects of a dialogue, such as relevance, fluency, and interestingness among others.

Given the aforementioned challenges, large language models have become an integral part of dialogue evaluation. DialogRPT (Gao et al., 2020) employs an extended GPT-2 model trained on 147 million conversation-like interactions from Reddit. USR (Mehri and Eskenazi, 2020b) is an unsupervised, reference-free tool that takes advantage of the RoBERTa (Liu et al., 2019) model. USR employs a dialogue retrieval metric for assessing dialogue, where the metric is trained to differentiate between a ground truth response and a randomly sampled response. The FED metric (Mehri and Eskenazi, 2020a) utilizes DialoGPT (Zhang et al., 2020) due to its capacity for capturing knowledge, specifically within the context of conversations. It ignores the interaction between the user and the system and consider the dialogue history and the system response as an integral context, while our method explicitly captures such interaction through conditional mutual information.

3 Background

FED (Mehri and Eskenazi, 2020a) measures eighteen fine-grained qualities of dialogue without requiring comparison to a reference response or training data with ground-truth human ratings. The method leverages DialoGPT and uses the follow-up hypotheses as a means of evaluation, based on the assumption that the language model has learned to accurately measure the likelihood of the input sequence. Given a dialog context c, a system response r, and a scorer $\mathcal{L}$ that computes the average Negative Log-Likelihood (NLL) of a sequence with a language model θ, the predicted score for a pair of positive and negative hypotheses (p_i, n_i) is calculated as,

$$\sum_{i=1}^{|n|} \mathcal{L}\left(\{c, r, n_i\}, \theta\right) - \sum_{i=1}^{|p|} \mathcal{L}\left(\{c, r, p_i\}, \theta\right),$$

where $\{a, b\}$ means text b is appended to text a,and for each of the evaluation dimensions, $|p|$ and $|n|$ number of positive and negative hypothetical sentences are respectively pre-defined and used for reducing evaluation variance. For example, given a combined history $\{c, r\}$, the response is regarded as more interesting if the probability of DialoGPT generating a positive hypothesis (e.g., "That's really interesting!") is greater than the probability of it generating a negative one (e.g., "That's really boring.").

4 Conditional Pointwise Mutual Information based Turn-level Metric

For each of the dialogue turn t, our Pointwise Mutual Information (PMI) based metric is considering the dependencies between the following three random variables: the full dialogue history $\mathbf{r}_t = \{u_0, x_0, u_1, x_1, ..., u_t\} \sim R$ (where u_t is the user utterance), the system response $x_t \sim X$ and a hypothesis $h \sim H$. Ideally, we want to know how much correlation between the dialogue history and the system response causes the hypothesis to be a plausible entailment of the combined history, $\{\mathbf{r}_t, x_t\}$. We measure such correlation by calculating the Conditional Mutual Information (CMI) between the response and the history with a given hypothesis, *i.e.*,

$$I(R, X|H) = \mathbb{E}_{R,X,H}[\log \frac{p(\mathbf{r}_t, x_t|h)}{p(\mathbf{r}_t|h)p(x_t|h)}] = \mathbb{E}_{R,X,H}[\log \frac{p(\mathbf{r}_t, x_t, h)p(h)}{p(\mathbf{r}_t, h)p(x_t, h)}].$$

Intuitively, if $I(R, X|H)$ is large, the hypothesis is less likely to be caused by the interaction (*i.e.*, the shared information) between R and X.

Since sampling the history on a turn-by-turn basis needs exponentially increasing computation, an accurate estimation of the CMI between these random variables is intractable. Therefore, we propose to measure the CMI by calculating the point-wise mutual information contained between the observed dialogue history and the system response when the hypothesis is appended to the combined history. Formally, we define our Conditional PMI (C-PMI) score between the observed dialogue history, the system response, and the hypothesis as follows,

$$\text{C-PMI}(\mathbf{r}_t, x_t|h) = \log \frac{p(\mathbf{r}_t, x_t, h)p(h)}{p(\mathbf{r}_t, h)p(x_t, h)}.$$

In practice, we estimate the probability of each sequence using the averaged Log-Likelihood (LL) obtained from a language model P_θ, *i.e.*,

$$\text{LL}(\mathbf{s}) = \frac{1}{n}\sum_{i=1}^{n} \log P_\theta(s_i|\mathbf{s}_{<i}),$$

and our score is then computed as,

$$\text{C-PMI}(\mathbf{r}_t, x_t|h) = \text{LL}(\mathbf{r}_t, x_t, h) + \text{LL}(h) - \text{LL}(\mathbf{r}_t, h) - \text{LL}(x_t, h),$$

which can be efficiently implemented using the modern deep learning framework. To retain the symmetric property of the mutual information, we also define a symmetric version of our score, C-PMI-SYM, by interchanging the response and the dialogue history, *i.e.*,

$$\text{C-PMI-SYM}(\mathbf{r}_t, x_t|h) = \frac{1}{2}(\text{C-PMI}(\mathbf{r}_t, x_t|h) + \text{C-PMI}(x_t, \mathbf{r}_t|h)).$$

For integrating our scorer with the existing evaluation system such as FED, we simply replace its NLL scoring function with our C-PMI scorer, and follow the original pipeline to get the final score for each of the data samples.

5 Experiments

5.1 Dataset

We evaluate our model on the turn-level annotated subset of the FED (Mehri and Eskenazi, 2020a) dataset. This subset consists of 455 data samples, each of which includes a dialog context, a system response, and eight human-annotated turn-level labels: Interesting, Fluent, Engaging, Specific, Relevant, Correct, Appropriate, and Understandable. The annotations are obtained through a survey with the options of No, Somewhat, Yes, or N/A. An additional overall impression label is measured using a five-point Likert Scale. The FED dataset is proposed to evaluate metrics as it is annotated with human quality judgments with conversations from Meena and Mitsuku bots (Adiwardana et al., 2020).

5.2 Baseline Metrics

We primarily compare our proposed reference-free and unsupervised metric with FED, but other baselines are also included as follows.

BARTScore (Yuan et al., 2021) is a text-scoring model based on BART (Lewis et al., 2020) and does not requiring any fine-tuning. BARTScore calculates the weighted log probability of text $\mathbf{y}$ given text $\mathbf{x}$:

$$\text{BARTSCORE} = \sum_{t=1}^{m} \omega_t \log P_\theta(\mathbf{y}_t \mid \mathbf{y}_{<t}, \mathbf{x}),$$

where the weighted sum of the log probability of one text $\mathbf{y}$ given the other text $\mathbf{x}$ is used for scoring.

DynaEval (Zhang et al., 2021a) is an automatic evaluation framework for dialogue response generation tasks, designed to evaluate both turn-level and dialogue-level. The framework utilizes structured graph representations of dialogues and is trained on datasets that contain ground-truth human ratings.

5.3 Implementation Details

We follow the data pre-processing procedure as used by Yeh et al. (2021) for the FED dataset , and modify the scorer function as in the original FED repository. Following Yeh et al. (2021), we use a special "<|endoftext|>" token to connect each turn of the system responses and the user utterances for constructing a full sequence. The sequence is then fed into the *DialoGPT-large* language model to obtain the log-likelihood for calculating both the FED score and our C-PMI score.

Metrics	Interesting	Fluent	Engaging	Specific	Relevant	Correct	Appro.	Und.	Avg.
Supervised with Human Evaluations									
DynaEval	32.7	17.1	30.0	34.6	26.3	24.2	20.2	20.0	25.6
Unsupervised									
BARTSCORE	15.9	14.0	22.6	8.3	11.9	7.6	10.0	**12.0**	12.8
FED	32.4	-13.4	24.0	14.1	**19.9**	**26.2**	-9.4	1.3	11.9
FED*	32.5	*1.5*	17.6	23.0	13.4	15.9	*7.7*	*6.0*	14.7
FED + C-PMI-SYM	**48.2**	16.0	36.3	27.9	11.4	15.4	**17.8**	*9.8*	22.8
FED + C-PMI	**48.2**	**16.4**	**36.4**	**28.8**	13.5	17.4	**17.8**	*10.0*	**23.6**

Table 1: The Spearman correlations with human judgment on the FED Turn-level dataset. Italicized values indicate that they are not statistically significant (p > 0.05). We include the results from the supervised metric to showcase the power of our method. For the unsupervised metrics, the highest correlation is shown in bold and the second highest is underlined. * indicates our reimplementation. The results for DynaEval, BARTSCORE, and FED are from Fu et al. (2023). Appro. and Und. are respectively the abbreviations of the evaluation dimensions: Semantically Appropriate and Understandable.

6 Results & Analysis

Table 1 shows that our proposed metrics, FED+C-PMI-SYM and FED+C-PMI, outperform other methods in most of the evaluation dimensions, and is comparable to DynaEval which requires training on the evaluation dataset. Both FED+C-PMI-SYM and FED+C-PMI show substantial improvements in Interesting, Engaging, Specific, Semantically Appropriate and the Understable dimensions compared to our re-implemented FED metric. Notably, our metric even substantially outperforms DynaEval on the Interesting and the Engaging dimensions which conceptually needs an accurate measure of the interaction between the user and the system. This demonstrates the effectiveness of our approach in capturing turn-level interactions.

The performance of FED+C-PMI-SYM and FED+C-PMI is quite similar across most dimensions. However, FED+C-PMI shows slightly better performance in the Relevant, Correct, and Understandable dimensions, suggesting that the asymmetrical variant of the C-PMI calculation might provide more accurate evaluation scores in certain cases. We suspect that this is because interchanging the positions of the response and the dialogue history results in unnatural dialogue, which leads to worse probability estimation from the language models.

The results indicate that the proposed C-PMI-based turn-level metrics are capable of providing a more accurate evaluation of dialogue system responses compared to existing state-of-the-art methods. Moreover, our metric is unreferenced and training-free, which makes it particularly suitable for practical applications, such as responses selection and re-ranking.

7 Conclusion

In this paper, we introduce a novel dialogue evaluation metric based on Conditional Pointwise Mutual Information (C-PMI) that captures turn-level interactions between the system and user across various evaluation dimensions. The proposed metric is reference-free and training-free, outperforming state-of-the-art methods with a comparable number of model parameters. For turn-level dialogue evaluations, our experimental results demonstrate that this metric can serve as a generalized alternative to the Negative Log-Likelihood scorer for multi-dimensional evaluation metrics. We plan to extend our approach to other dialogue evaluation methods and explore its applicability to general text generation problems. We are also interested to see if our measure can improve the factual consistency evaluation for document-grounded dialogue or conversational question answering. Additionally, we will investigate incorporating our C-PMI-based metric into the fine-tuning process of LLMs.

Limitations

While our proposed method demonstrates promising results and outperforms several state-of-the-art techniques, it is important to acknowledge certain limitations.

- **Dependence on pre-trained LLMs:** Our method relies heavily on the pre-trained LLM's quality and the knowledge it has captured. As a result, any biases, inaccuracies, or limitations present in the LLM may directly impact the performance of our evaluation metric.

- **Lack of diversity in the dataset:** The FED dataset, which we use for evaluation, is primarily derived from conversations with the Meena and Mitsuku chatbots. Consequently, it is possible that our evaluation might not have better correlation with human ratings for other dialogue systems or more diverse conversational contexts.
- **Adaptability to new evaluation dimensions:** Our method currently focuses on eight turn-level metrics. Extending the method to incorporate additional or novel evaluation dimensions might require further investigation and calibration.
- **Computational cost:** The current implementation of our approach is around twice as slow as the baseline NLL-based method due to multiple times of the inferences of the language model. The efficiency of the implementation can be improved in the future by re-using the log-likelihood of the dialogue history.
- **Subjectivity in human judgments:** Our evaluation metric's correlation with human judgments serves as a key performance indicator. However, human judgments are inherently subjective, which could lead to inconsistencies or discrepancies in the evaluation results.

Despite these limitations, our proposed method presents a significant step forward in dialogue evaluation, offering a model-agnostic, unreferenced, and training-free approach that captures the human and the system interaction. Future work could address these limitations and explore additional dimensions of evaluation, further refining the method and its applicability across a broader range of dialogue systems and text evaluation systems.

Ethics Statement

In this study, we recognize the importance of ethical considerations in natural language processing and dialogue systems research. Acknowledging the potential biases in pre-trained LLMs and human judgments, we advocate for future research to investigate and mitigate these biases in evaluation metrics. We strive for fairness and inclusivity by designing our method to be generalizable and adaptable to various settings. As researchers, we are committed to responsible AI development and contribute to the ongoing discourse on evaluating dialogue systems, enabling the creation of more effective and ethical AI-powered conversational agents. We encourage the research community to continue discussing ethical considerations and promoting transparency in the field.

Acknowledgements

We would like to acknowledge support from the Amazon Alexa Prize as part of SocialBot Grand Challenge 5.

References

Daniel Adiwardana, Minh-Thang Luong, David R. So, Jamie Hall, Noah Fiedel, Romal Thoppilan, Zi Yang, Apoorv Kulshreshtha, Gaurav Nemade, Yifeng Lu, and Quoc V. Le. 2020. Towards a human-like open-domain chatbot. *CoRR*, abs/2001.09977.

Jinlan Fu, See-Kiong Ng, Zhengbao Jiang, and Pengfei Liu. 2023. Gptscore: Evaluate as you desire. *arXiv preprint arXiv:2302.04166*.

Yi Fung, Han Wang, Tong Wang, Ali Kebarighotbi, Prem Natarajan, Mohit Bansal, and Heng Ji. 2023. Deepmaven: Deep question answering on long-distance movie/tv show videos with multimedia knowledge extraction and synthesis. In *Proc. The 17th Conference of the European Chapter of the Association for Computational Linguistics (EACL2023)*.

Xiang Gao, Yizhe Zhang, Michel Galley, Chris Brockett, and Bill Dolan. 2020. Dialogue response ranking-training with large-scale human feedback data. In *EMNLP*.

AmirEmad Ghassami and Negar Kiyavash. 2017. Interaction information for causal inference: The case of directed triangle. In *2017 IEEE International Symposium on Information Theory (ISIT)*, pages 1326–1330. IEEE.

Sarik Ghazarian, Ralph Weischedel, Aram Galstyan, and Nanyun Peng. 2020. Predictive engagement: An efficient metric for automatic evaluation of open-domain dialogue systems. In *Proceedings of the AAAI Conference on Artificial Intelligence*, volume 34, pages 7789–7796.

Tuan M. Lai, Giuseppe Castellucci, Saar Kuzi, Heng Ji, and Oleg Rokhlenko. 2023. External knowledge acquisition for end-to-end document-oriented dialog systems. In *Proc. The 17th Conference of the European Chapter of the Association for Computational Linguistics (EACL2023)*.

Mike Lewis, Yinhan Liu, Naman Goyal, Marjan Ghazvininejad, Abdelrahman Mohamed, Omer Levy,

Veselin Stoyanov, and Luke Zettlemoyer. 2020. BART: Denoising sequence-to-sequence pre-training for natural language generation, translation, and comprehension. In *Proceedings of the 58th Annual Meeting of the Association for Computational Linguistics*, pages 7871–7880, Online. Association for Computational Linguistics.

Sha Li, Mahdi Namazifar, Di Jin, Mohit Bansal, Heng Ji, Yang Liu, and Dilek Hakkani-Tur. 2022. Enhancing knowledge selection for grounded dialogues via document semantic graphs. In *Proc. The 2022 Conference of the North American Chapter of the Association for Computational Linguistics - Human Language Technologies (NAACL-HLT2022)*.

Chin-Yew Lin. 2004. ROUGE: A package for automatic evaluation of summaries. In *Text Summarization Branches Out*, pages 74–81, Barcelona, Spain. Association for Computational Linguistics.

Yinhan Liu, Myle Ott, Naman Goyal, Jingfei Du, Mandar Joshi, Danqi Chen, Omer Levy, Mike Lewis, Luke Zettlemoyer, and Veselin Stoyanov. 2019. Roberta: A robustly optimized BERT pretraining approach. *CoRR*, abs/1907.11692.

Shikib Mehri and Maxine Eskenazi. 2020a. Unsupervised evaluation of interactive dialog with DialoGPT. In *Proceedings of the 21th Annual Meeting of the Special Interest Group on Discourse and Dialogue*, pages 225–235, 1st virtual meeting. Association for Computational Linguistics.

Shikib Mehri and Maxine Eskenazi. 2020b. USR: An unsupervised and reference free evaluation metric for dialog generation. In *Proceedings of the 58th Annual Meeting of the Association for Computational Linguistics*, pages 681–707, Online. Association for Computational Linguistics.

Bo Pang, Erik Nijkamp, Wenjuan Han, Linqi Zhou, Yixian Liu, and Kewei Tu. 2020. Towards holistic and automatic evaluation of open-domain dialogue generation. In *Proceedings of the 58th Annual Meeting of the Association for Computational Linguistics*, pages 3619–3629, Online. Association for Computational Linguistics.

Kishore Papineni, Salim Roukos, Todd Ward, and Wei-Jing Zhu. 2002. Bleu: a method for automatic evaluation of machine translation. In *Proceedings of the 40th Annual Meeting of the Association for Computational Linguistics*, pages 311–318, Philadelphia, Pennsylvania, USA. Association for Computational Linguistics.

Vitou Phy, Yang Zhao, and Akiko Aizawa. 2020. Deconstruct to reconstruct a configurable evaluation metric for open-domain dialogue systems. In *Proceedings of the 28th International Conference on Computational Linguistics*, pages 4164–4178, Barcelona, Spain (Online). International Committee on Computational Linguistics.

Claude Elwood Shannon. 1948. A mathematical theory of communication. *The Bell System Technical Journal*, 27:379–423.

Yi-Ting Yeh, Maxine Eskenazi, and Shikib Mehri. 2021. A comprehensive assessment of dialog evaluation metrics. In *The First Workshop on Evaluations and Assessments of Neural Conversation Systems*, pages 15–33, Online. Association for Computational Linguistics.

Weizhe Yuan, Graham Neubig, and Pengfei Liu. 2021. Bartscore: Evaluating generated text as text generation. In *Advances in Neural Information Processing Systems*, volume 34, pages 27263–27277. Curran Associates, Inc.

Chen Zhang, Yiming Chen, Luis Fernando D'Haro, Yan Zhang, Thomas Friedrichs, Grandee Lee, and Haizhou Li. 2021a. Dynaeval: Unifying turn and dialogue level evaluation. In *The Joint Conference of the 59th Annual Meeting of the Association for Computational Linguistics and the 11th International Joint Conference on Natural Language Processing (ACL-IJCNLP 2021)*, Online.

Chen Zhang, Grandee Lee, Luis Fernando D'Haro, and Haizhou Li. 2021b. D-score: Holistic dialogue evaluation without reference. *IEEE ACM Trans. Audio Speech Lang. Process.*, 29:2502–2516.

Yizhe Zhang, Siqi Sun, Michel Galley, Yen-Chun Chen, Chris Brockett, Xiang Gao, Jianfeng Gao, Jingjing Liu, and Bill Dolan. 2020. Dialogpt: Large-scale generative pre-training for conversational response generation. In *ACL, system demonstration*.

ConvRGX: Recognition, Generation, and Extraction for Self-trained Conversational Question Answering

Tianhua Zhang[†1,2], Liping Tang[†*1], Wei Fang[3], Hongyin Luo[3],
Xixin Wu[1,2], Helen Meng[1,2], and James Glass[3]

[1]Centre for Perceptual and Interactive Intelligence, Hong Kong SAR, China
[2]The Chinese University of Hong Kong, Hong Kong SAR, China
[3]Massachusetts Institute of Technology, Cambridge MA, USA
[1]{thzhang, lptang}@cpii.hk

Abstract

Collecting and constructing human-annotated corpora for training conversational question-answering (CQA) models has recently been shown to be inefficient and costly. To solve this problem, previous works have proposed training QA models with automatically generated QA data. In this work, we extend earlier studies on QA synthesis, and propose an efficient QA data generation algorithm under conversational settings. Our model recognizes potential dialogue topics, generates corresponding questions, and extracts answers from grounding passages. To improve the quality of generated QAs and downstream self-training of CQA models, we propose dropout and agreement-based QA selection methods. We conduct experiments on both data augmentation and domain adaptation settings. Experiments on the QuAC and Doc2Dial tasks show that the proposed method can significantly improve the quality of generated QA data, and also improves the accuracy of self-trained CQA models based on the constructed training corpora.

1 Introduction

Recent progress on pre-trained language models (Devlin et al., 2019; Clark et al., 2020; Liu et al., 2019; He et al., 2020) has significantly improved the performance of different natural language understanding tasks, including question answering (QA). However, task-specific fine-tuning of pre-trained models still requires human-annotated training corpora, especially for QA. For example, training a QA model on the Wikipedia domain needs a training set of over 80,000 human-annotated question-answer pairs (Rajpurkar et al., 2016). Annotating such a training corpus is too costly to be generalized for other domains and QA tasks. Moreover, many real-life agents answer questions in a conversational style. However, collecting data for training conversational question-answering (CQA) models is much more challenging. Recent studies have collected such corpora, but with human annotations on less than 1,000 documents (Choi et al., 2018; Feng et al., 2020).

Due to the limited amount of labeled training data and questions for conversational QA tasks being more complicated, there is a significant performance gap between single-turn and conversational QA models. As a coarse reference rather than a direct comparison, single-turn QA models achieve over 90% exact match score on SQuAD (Rajpurkar et al., 2016), and the accuracy of most CQA models is below 70% on the Doc2dial benchmark (Feng et al., 2020).

To address this problem of insufficient conversational QA for training, we propose an automatic conversational question-answering data annotation method. Inspired by the recognition-generation-extraction (RGX) pipeline (Luo et al., 2022), we design a conversation generation algorithm (named ConvRGX), which generates dialogues based on grounding documents. To generate a question and the corresponding answer in a conversation, the model first recognizes a possible dialogue topic from the grounding document, which provides information about the answer. Given the topic, a number of questions are generated. We then use a pre-trained question-answering model to verify the generated questions by comparing the selected dialogue topic and the answer extracted by the QA model given the generated questions, or the agreement between CQA models with different dropout. Among all generated QA pairs, we filter out low-quality data, samples high-quality QA pairs as the current dialogue turn, and continue to generate the next question. Compared to the baseline RGX model, we improve the answer recognition module and apply a dropout-based data selection strategy to improve the model under conversational settings.

[†]These authors contributed equally to this work and share first authorship.

[*]Now affiliated with Mohamed bin Zayed University of Artificial Intelligence. Email: liping.tang@mbzuai.ac.ae

Proceedings of the Third DialDoc Workshop on Document-grounded Dialogue and Conversational Question Answering, pages 86–100
July 13, 2023

To prove the effectiveness of ConvRGX, we evaluate the generated QA data along different dimensions. We first evaluate the question quality using Bleu (Papineni et al., 2002), RougeL (Lin, 2004), and Q-metric (Nema and Khapra, 2018). Experiments show that ConvRGX generates high-quality questions. We also conduct self-training for the CQA models with the generated QA data. Experiments show that the data generation and selection framework can constantly improve the data synthesis quality and QA self-training performance.

2 Related Work

Conversational Question Answering Recently, CQA has garnered a lot of interest, in which a QA agent answers questions from users given a piece of text as the context in a multi-turn conversation. Numerous benchmark datasets have been proposed to support investigations into different challenging facts of the CQA problem, introducing increasingly challenging aspects such as unanswerability (Reddy et al., 2019), dialogue acts (Choi et al., 2018), interpreting rules (Saeidi et al., 2018), dialogue flows (Feng et al., 2020), multiple grounding documents (Feng et al., 2021), etc. Conventional sequence models that apply various mechanisms such as attention (Choi et al., 2018) and flow (Huang et al., 2019) were explored to tackle CQA challenges. With the emergence of pre-trained language models, traditional sequence models were replaced and methods were devised to adapt these large LMs for conversations (Ohsugi et al., 2019; Qu et al., 2019). Still, challenges such as long conversational history and the lack of large training corpora exist, with various works attempting to tackle these problems (Zhao et al., 2021; Kim et al., 2021). More recently, CQA challenges have been extended with open domain retrieval (ORCQA) (Qu et al., 2020), wherein ground truth contexts are not available, which presents the need to retrive information from other sources, such as Wikipedia.

Self-trained Question Answering Recent work have studied the potential for improving QA models with question generation. A question generator benefits mutual information-based QA (Tang et al., 2017; Duan et al., 2017), in-domain data augmentation (Sachan and Xing, 2018; Puri et al., 2020; Liu et al., 2020; Klein and Nabi, 2019), and out-of-domain adaptation of QA models. Lewis et al. (2019) and Lee et al. (2020) introduced QA generation frameworks for self-trained question answering. Shakeri et al. (2020) proposed an end-to-end QA generation model, and Bartolo et al. (2021) showed that the quality and diversity of generated QA can be improved by difficult QA cases. Luo et al. (2022) proposed a cooperative self-training strategy that benefits both question generation and answering. Lewis et al. (2021); Jia et al. (2022) presented additional applications for QA generation systems.

Document-Grounded Conversation Generation In view of the prohibitive cost of manually constructing datasets, automatic conversation generation has attracted increasing research interest. One line of research (Gao et al., 2019; Gu et al., 2021) focuses on conversational question generation to produce follow-up questions based on the current dialogue context. Gao et al. (2019) generates questions with specific coreference alignment and conversation flow modeling modules, simply assuming the required answer for question generation is already predefined as input. A few efforts (Wu et al., 2022; Kim et al., 2022) attend to generate question-answering style conversations from scratch, the framework of which typically involve three components: a rationale extractor to detect the most possible text span from the grounding documents for subsequent question generation, a question generator to produce a natural question asking for information from the selected span, and an answer generator to produce answers for the questions.

3 Method

For automatically generating conversational QA data on unlabeled grounding documents, we propose a 3-step pipeline named ConvRGX. In order to generate a dialogue turn, we first recognize the upcoming possible topic from the grounding document and then generate a number of candidate questions. The generated questions are then filtered, and a pre-trained CQA model is applied to predict refined answers for the generated questions. The pipeline is illustrated in Figure 1. In this section, we introduce the details of each step of ConvRGX.

3.1 Dialogue Topic Recognition

High-quality document discourse structure are leveraged for informing dialogue flow as we synthesize question-answering conversations rather than a separate hard-to-train rationale extractor. Inspired by the findings in Gao et al. (2019) that as

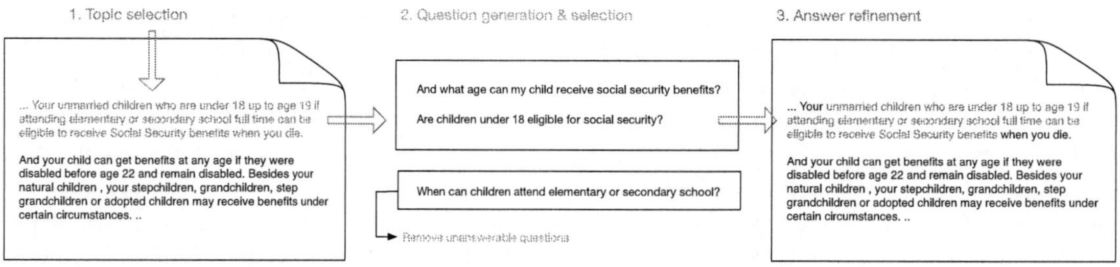

Figure 1: The 3-step pipeline of the ConvRGX model, including dialogue topic selection, question generation & filtering, and answer refinement.

conversations progress, the focus of most questions transit from the beginning of the grounding document to the end, we design the conversation flow by heuristically following the topic flow along the document. For each document $d = \{s_1, s_2, ..., s_N\}$, we sample K instances with T ordered sentences, i.e., $I_k = \{s_{o1}, s_{o2}, ..., s_{oT}\}$, where $\{o_j\}_{j=1}^{T}$ is an increasing sequence. Inspired by Dai et al. (2022), a dialogue template $C_k = \{(\triangle, s_{o1}), (\triangle, s_{o2}), ..., (\triangle, s_{oT})\}$ is constructed for each instance, where $\triangle$ indicates the conversational question to be generated grounded on sentence s_{o_j} and s_{o_j} will be replaced with a refined answer a_j.

A complete conversation is generated following the determined dialogue flow in an auto-regressive manner: in the first turn, the question generator described in Section 3.2 takes as input $(\{d'\}\texttt{</s>}\{s_{o1}\})$ with empty history $h = \varnothing$ and generates multiple diversified questions $q_1 = \{q_1^1, q_1^2, ...\}$ with text dropout at different positions. The refinement and selection module in Section 3.3 replaces s_{o1} with a polished answer span a_1 and determines whether (q_1^i, a_1) is an answerable QA pair worth keeping. It can remove low-quality QA pairs (e.g., unanswerable QA pair) to avoid misleading the models to be trained on. The input to the question generator in the next turn is $(\{(q_1^i, a_1)\}\{d'\}\texttt{</s>}\{s_{o2}\})$ or $(\{d'\}\texttt{</s>}\{s_{o2}\})$, depending on whether (q_1^i, a_1) is retained or not in the previous step. The process will continue until the dialogue is complete.

To verify the effectiveness of dialogue topic flow, we also experiment with a *random* version, where the grounding passage structure is not maintained in the dialog, by shuffling the *sequential* I_k.

3.2 Conversational Question Generation

In this work, we propose a question-generation method for conversational QA. Given a document d, the related dialogue history h, and the selected dialogue topic, which is a sentence s in d, we apply an end-to-end language model to generate a question: $q = BART(\{h\}\{d'\}\ \texttt{</s>}\ \{s\})$, where d' stands for a masked document that removes s from d. In practice, we train BART models (Lewis et al., 2020) for the question generation task with human-annotated CQA data and generate questions using the trained model with top-k sampling.

To improve the diversity in the generated questions, we propose a text dropout strategy. We randomly replace up to $len(grounding\, sentence)/10$ tokens for each selected grounding sentence with `<mask>`. This method is applied in the training stage of the question generator, while no text dropout is applied in the evaluation stage to maintain as much information as possible for question synthesis.

3.3 Data Selection and Answer Refinement

To ensure the quality of generated questions, we train a CQA model on human-annotated data and then utilize it to perform data selection. Specifically, given the generated question q_i^j and the dialogue history h, the pre-trained CQA model is used to extract answers from the grounding passage P. Based on the extracted answers, we propose the following two data selection strategies[1]:

Overlap-based Data Selection was previously used by Wu et al. (2022) and Kim et al. (2022). Under this strategy, we keep all questions that produce answers that overlap with QG-grounding sentences.

Dropout-based Data Selection is inspired by test-time dropout (Kamath et al., 2020), which ensembles the prediction across multiple dropout masks to deal with out-of-domain data. During the inference stage, we enable the standard dropout

[1]CQA extracted answers instead of the QG-selected sentences are kept in the generated data.

(Srivastava et al., 2014) in Transformers (Vaswani et al., 2017). We use the pre-trained CQA model to extract M answers from M different dropout masks given the same input and keep the generated question if there are at least C consistent answers among the M extracted answers.[2]

Answer Refinement After selecting high-quality questions, we propose to refine the answer using the aforementioned pre-trained conversational QA model. Specifically, after obtaining a consistent answer from the dropout-based data selection step or an answer overlapping with the QG-grounding sentence, we extend the answer to compact sentences and add one sentence before and one sentence after the answer sentences given the entire passage. The motivation is that it may be easier for the conversational QA model to predict a more accurate answer from a shorter span than from a long passage.

3.4 QA Self-training

After selecting high-quality QA data, we construct synthetic training corpora for fine-tuning the pre-trained QA models. In this work, we train extractive question-answering models with the RoBERTa (Liu et al., 2019) backbone. A linear model is stacked on the pre-trained RoBERTa model to predict the starting and ending positions of the answers as standard extractive QA baselines.

4 Experimental Setup

4.1 Datasets

Doc2Dial (Feng et al., 2020) contains goal-oriented dialogues that are grounded in documents. It consists of two subtasks: 1) grounding span identification based on dialogue context; and 2) agent response generation based on extracted spans. In this paper, we focus on the first subtask and evaluate the performance of ConvRGX under the machine reading comprehension setting. During training and auto-regressive dialogue generation, we replace the agent response in dialogue history by its *oracle* and *identified* grounding spans respectively since no agent response generation module is involved in ConvRGX.

Question Answering in Context (QuAC) (Choi et al., 2018) is a standard CQA benchmark that contains questions that are complex, highly context-dependent and sometimes unanswerable. Dialogue answers in this dataset, if available, are spans within the given grounding context. We evaluate our approach with the standard split. Dataset statistics for the two experimental settings described in Section 4.3 are shown in Appendix A.

4.2 Question Generation Evaluation

We first evaluate the quality of questions generated by ConvRGX on the two CQA datasets. Since there has always been criticism for evaluating the performance of automatic generation by common n-gram-based similarity metrics only, Q-metric was proposed to measure the answerability of generated question-answer pairs. It scores the quality of a generated question by assigning different importance to four types of information: named entity, question type, relevant content and function words, which correlates better with human judgment. We refer interested readers to Nema and Khapra (2018) for more details. We report the question generation performance using 1) traditional automatic evaluation metrics: Bleu (Papineni et al., 2002) and RougeL (Lin, 2004); and 2) their corresponding Q-Metrics: Q-Bleu and Q-RougeL.

4.3 Question Answering Evaluation

To show the effectiveness of ConvRGX on addressing the data scarcity issue for conversational QA tasks, we evaluate ConvRGX on downstream CQA tasks under two settings: 1) extractive-based CQA, and 2) retrieval-based CQA.

Extractive-based CQA The extractive-based CQA follows the general evaluation step of QA systems. Specifically, we concatenate the conversational question, i.e., the concatenation of the entire dialogue history and the current question, with the grounding passage as input to a Roberta-large model. We then stack a linear model on the Roberta-large model to predict the starting and ending positions of the answers. Under this setting, we follow Feng et al. (2020) to evaluate ConvRGX with Exact match (EM) and F1 score for Doc2Dial. Following Choi et al. (2018), we report results with F1 score and human equivalence score (HEQ) for QuAC.

Retrieval-based CQA Besides the commonly used extractive-based CQA setting, we further consider the retrieval-based CQA tasks. Specifically, given a new conversational question, we search via BM25[3] (Robertson et al., 2009) from the database

[2]In our setting, M is set as 5 and C is set as 4.

[3]In our preliminary experiments, SimCSE (Gao et al., 2021) was also used for training the representations of con-

that consists of all conversational queries in the dataset (original training dataset or the dataset augmented by synthetic data). Then we treat the answer of the retrieved conversational query as the final answer. To be consistent with the EM and F1 values in extractive CQA, we measure the retrieval-based CQA with EM@k (EM@1, EM@5, EM@10) and F1@k (F1@1, F1@5, F1@10), i.e., the highest EM and F1 values among top k retrieved answers.

For both extractive and retrieval CQA, we perform experiments under the following two settings:

Data Augmentation Under this setting, we use the original dataset splits that are given and train on the training set. During evaluation, ConvRGX generates new QA pairs using documents from both the training and validation sets, which are then used to augment the original training set. The augmented dataset is finally used to train the QA model.

Unseen Documents We also evaluate our approach on a set of unseen documents to investigate the generalization performance. To prevent leakage, we remove the training dialogues that are based on documents in the validation set for Doc2Dial. For QuAC, the documents do not overlap between training and validation, so the original splits already correspond to this setting.

Implementation details for both QG and QA settings can be found in Appendix B.

4.4 Baselines

Since there is no prior performance benchmark that is readily available[4], we compare the proposed model against three baselines typically used for natural language data augmentation, as done by Wu et al. (2022).

Easy Data Augmentation (EDA) EDA is proposed by Wei and Zou (2019) to augment data through text editing operations. In particular, EDA consists of four simple operations: synonym replacement, random insertion, random swap, and random deletion.

Back-translation Back-translation augments natural language data by first translating the text into a second language and then back-translating them to the original language. Following BERT-QA (Chadha and Sood, 2019) and DG2 (Wu et al., 2022), we translate all user utterances to French and then translate them back to English.[5]

Paraphrase Paraphrasing rewrites text using different words or sentence structures. In particular, we use the BART-large model (Lewis et al., 2020) trained on the MRPC (Dolan and Brockett, 2005), QQP (Shankar et al., 2017) and PAWS (Zhang et al., 2019) datasets.[6]

5 Results

5.1 Question Generation Quality

We conduct intrinsic evaluation of question generation when text dropout is (*w/*) and is not (*w/o*) introduced during the training and validation process with Q-metric and n-gram-based metrics. As shown in Table 1(a), the text dropout strategy in question generator during training achieves significant performance improvement at all metrics when evaluated on the Doc2Dial validation set under both *w/* and *w/o* dropout settings. On QuAC in Table 1(b), text dropout training obtains performance comparable to the baseline when evaluated *w/o* dropout, and improves the performance when evaluated *w/* dropout. Training with explicit dropout introduces variations to the input and enhances the robustness of the question generator.

Comparing *w/* and *w/o* dropout during the validation process, text dropout on the validation input decreases the performance since keywords in the grounding span might be masked, resulting in information loss and failure to derive the ground-truth question. On the other hand, text dropout during auto-regressive dialogue generation can boost the downstream CQA performance. Specifically, by masking different input positions, questions focusing on different information will be generated, which enriches the diversity of synthesized dialogues. It reveals the discrepancy between the intrinsic question generator performance measurements and the actual need for high-quality and diverse conversations to increase CQA performance, showing the necessity of evaluating data quality by extrinsic downstream CQA performance. We report the corresponding results in Section 6.2.

versational queries, which gave us similar results but required more training time than BM25.

[4]The two works that we have found to be closest to our settings are Wu et al. (2022) and Kim et al. (2022). However, the codes of these two works are not publicly available.

[5]Translated via the Google Translate API.

[6]https://huggingface.co/eugenesiow/bart-paraphrase

Train	Val	Q-Bleu1	Q-Bleu2	Q-Bleu3	Q-Bleu4	Q-RougeL	Bleu1	Bleu2	Bleu3	Bleu4	RougeL
(a) Doc2Dial											
w/o	w/o	0.321	0.28	0.262	0.252	0.333	0.272	0.153	0.099	0.068	0.309
w/	w/o	**0.327**	**0.287**	**0.268**	**0.257**	**0.339**	**0.282**	**0.164**	**0.108**	**0.078**	**0.318**
w/o	w/	0.318	0.279	0.260	0.250	0.332	0.269	0.152	0.097	0.067	0.308
w/	w/	**0.323**	**0.283**	**0.265**	**0.254**	**0.336**	**0.279**	**0.162**	**0.106**	**0.076**	**0.316**
(b) QuAC											
w/o	w/o	0.332	0.296	**0.274**	**0.263**	0.341	0.288	**0.182**	**0.116**	**0.085**	0.315
w/	w/o	**0.333**	0.296	0.273	0.262	**0.342**	**0.289**	0.180	0.112	0.080	**0.316**
w/o	w/	0.325	0.289	0.267	0.257	0.335	0.279	0.174	0.109	0.079	0.306
w/	w/	**0.329**	**0.292**	**0.270**	**0.259**	**0.339**	**0.285**	**0.177**	**0.110**	**0.079**	**0.313**

Table 1: Question generator performance on the Doc2Dial and QuAC validation sets. *w/* and *w/o* indicate whether text dropout is introduced during training and validation process of the question generator.

Training Data		*Data Augmentation*				*Unseen Documents*			
Original	**Generated**	**best EM**	**cor F1**	**cor EM**	**best F1**	**best EM**	**cor F1**	**cor EM**	**best F1**
✓	✗	62.93	75.78	62.87	75.90	49.07	67.43	48.46	67.86
✓	EDA	64.07	75.35	63.29	75.88	50.07	67.70	49.66	68.16
✓	Back-translation	63.92	75.82	62.98	75.91	49.66	67.95	49.18	68.17
✓	Paraphrase	63.98	75.89	63.82	76.07	49.37	68.01	49.25	68.15
✓	ConvRGX	**64.62**	**77.05**	**64.39**	**77.31**	**50.91**	**69.26**	**50.80**	**69.34**
✗	ConvRGX	50.88	67.84	50.80	67.87	43.67	63.00	43.28	63.06

Table 2: Extractive-based question answering performance on the Doc2Dial validation set. We report the best EM together with the corresponding F1 scores and the best F1 together with the corresponding EM scores.

Training Data		*Unssen Documents*		
Original	**Generated**	**best F1**	**HEQ-Q**	**HEQ-D**
✓	✗	71.12	67.46	11.17
✓	EDA	70.46	66.88	10.80
✓	Back-translation	70.67	66.88	9.70
✓	Paraphrase	70.47	66.54	10.00
✓	ConvRGX	**71.64**	**68.37**	**12.70**
✗	ConvRGX	55.58	49.57	3.80

Table 3: Extractive-based question answering performance on the QuAC validation set.

5.2 Self-trained CQA Results

In this section, we validate the data generation quality of ConvRGX by training QA models on the generated data and compare the self-training performance. We assess the accuracy of extractive and retrieval-based QA models.

5.2.1 Extractive-based CQA

Doc2dial The experiments on the Doc2dial benchmark is shown in Table 2. We report the best EM together with the corresponding F1 scores and the best F1 together with the corresponding EM scores. We first show the in-domain self-training results, where ConvRGX generates synthetic data on seen documents. The experiment results show that most data augmentation models outperforms the model trained only with the human-generated training set, validating our hypothesis that augmenting the training corpus can benefit CQA models. On the other hand, ConvRGX outperforms all data augmentation models across different metrics. Among all baseline models, EDA achieves the best EM score but the corresponding F1 is worse than the unaugmented baseline. On the other hand, the paraphrase method achieves the best F1. We found that the F1 improvement of ConvRGX over paraphrasing is higher than the performance gap between paraphrasing and the base CQA model, indicating that the improvement of the ConvRGX model is more significant.

To test the generalization ability of this approach, we train the models on a subset of documents and generate data on unseen documents. The results shown in Table 2 indicate that the ConvRGX model achieves more improvement than the in-domain setting. This validates our hypothesis that CQA performance can benefit from the QA data synthesis approach on unlabeled documents.

QuAC We evaluate the model performance on the QuAC and present the experiment results in Table 3, where all test documents are unseen in the training process. The ConvRGX model still outperforms all baselines, but the improvement is not as high as the Doc2dial model, because the

Training Data		*Data Augmentation*						*Unseen Documents*					
Original	**Generated**	**EM@1**	**EM@5**	**EM@10**	**F1@1**	**F1@5**	**F1@10**	**EM@1**	**EM@5**	**EM@10**	**F1@1**	**F1@5**	**F1@10**
✓	✗	11.86	26.18	33.06	23.30	43.13	51.05	0.86	2.14	2.82	12.07	22.75	26.75
✓	EDA	11.66	22.08	28.73	23.06	38.15	46.12	0.81	1.74	2.42	11.95	20.27	24.27
✓	Back-translation	11.98	21.90	28.05	23.38	37.98	45.44	0.88	1.74	2.24	12.08	20.19	24.01
✓	Paraphrase	11.98	22.51	28.15	23.40	38.55	45.62	0.83	1.76	2.32	12.13	20.41	24.03
✓	ConvRGX	**13.17**	**30.72**	**39.35**	**26.22**	**48.02**	**56.85**	**6.34**	**12.71**	**17.15**	**20.59**	**34.43**	**40.92**

Table 4: Retrieval-based question answering performance on the Doc2Dial validation set.

number of annotated QuAC QA samples is much larger than Doc2dial, which reduces the potential of data augmentation. The result further validates our conclusion that the performance of CQA models is significantly affected by the data annotation effort.

5.2.2 Retrieval-based CQA

We report the retrieval-based CQA performance on Doc2Dial dataset in Table 4. ConvRGX outperforms all baselines across all evaluation metrics under both data augmentation and unseen documents settings for retrieval-based CQA tasks. Different from the results of extractive CQA setting, adding more data generated from the three baselines leads to a performance reduction on EM@k and F1@k (k=5,10) under the retrieval-based CQA setting. The reason is that the three data augmentation baselines cannot improve the answer text coverage of conversational questions in the dataset and can only generate semantically similar questions.

Under the unseen documents setting, the EM values of data augmentation baselines and the baseline of no data augmentation are almost zero. This is because the grounding documents in the testing dataset are invisible in the training dataset. Thus almost no conversational questions are grounded on the answer texts in the testing dataset.[7] After data augmentation via the three baselines, no new answer text is involved. On the contrary, ConvRGX obtains higher EM and F1 values because it can generate conversational questions on the documents of the testing dataset to cover more possible answer texts. More experimental results on QuAC are in Appendix D.

6 Analysis

In this section, we report results with extractive-based CQA models trained with only generated dialogues on the Doc2Dial dataset to further explore the contribution of different factors to the quality of synthesized conversations.

[7]The EM values are close to zero but not exactly zero because there are some sentences overlapping among the documents in the training dataset and testing dataset even under the unseen documents setting.

(a) No Data Selection				
Dial-Num	**Selection**	**Flow-Order**	**EM**	**F1**
single	-	random	**2.69**	**31.31**
		sequential	2.44	22.39

(b) Best Setting without Answer Refinement			
Setting	**Flow-Order**	**EM**	**F1**
Data Augmentation	random	50.71	66.70
	sequential	**51.49**	**66.81**
Unseen Documents	random	43.03	62.99
	sequential	**43.67**	**63.00**

Table 5: Ablation study of different topic recognition strategies (*random* versus *sequential*). Best setting without answer refinement refers to QG Dropout, *dropout* selection and *multi* Dial-Num.

6.1 Effect of Topic Recognition Strategies

Since the synthesized dialogue flows are constructed from high-quality documents, we analyze the effect of topic recognition from two aspects.

Document Sentence Sampling (*Dial-Num*) We examine the performance of using all sentences in a short truncated passage to derive a single dialogue template (*single*), i.e., $K = 1, T = N$ and sampling different sets of sentences to construct multiple dialogue templates from a enlarged passage (*multi*), i.e., $K > 1, T < N$. Intuitively, the *multi* setting considers different possible combinations of sentences and hence increases the information-coverage and diversity of subsequent dialogue generation. The EM and F1 scores are raised from 47.03 to 50.71 and 62.56 to 66.70 respectively when the setting is changed from *single* to *multi*, in line with our expectations. More implementation details are in Appendix C.

Document Sentence Order (*Flow-Order*) We further analyze how the sentence usage order affect the data quality. The *sequential* approach derives dialogue topic flow following the document discourse and aims to generate dialogues conversing each topic (possibly in depth) before shifting to another one. On the contrary, the *random* approach increases the variability to the possible dialogues

Selection	Dial-Num	QG Dropout	EM	F1
overlap	single	✗	35.96	54.44
		✓	**41.99**	**59.99**
overlap	multi	✗	41.21	60.00
		✓	**44.24**	**62.56**
dropout	single	✗	42.21	59.01
		✓	**47.03**	**62.56**
dropout	multi	✗	49.10	65.37
		✓	**50.71**	**66.70**

Table 6: Ablation study of QG Text Dropout (✗ versus ✓) and Data Selection strategies (*overlap* versus *dropout*). This table reports the best EM and corresponding F1 scores with *random* flow. (Remark: if *sequential* flow were used, similar results are observed.)

Flow-Order	Answer Refinement	EM	F1
random	✗	35.96	54.44
	✓	**40.05**	**58.07**
sequential	✗	36.71	54.15
	✓	**38.61**	**56.18**

Table 7: Ablation study of answer refinement (✗ versus ✓). We use *overlap* selection and *single* Dial-Num, *without* QG dropout.

and is closer to information-asymmetric situation, where no pre-knowledge of the document is given to questioners. We found that there is no single conclusion that one setting is superior to the other in all cases since the performance depends on the overall design. In particular, *sequential* relies heavily on the data selection strategy. Without turn-level filtering, the *single-sequential* strategy produces conversations strictly following the grounding document structure, which hurts the QA self-training since the QA model can simply predict next sentence in the document as the answer. Experimental results in Table 5(a) verifies this hypothesis. In our best setting for *Data Augmentation* and *Unseen Documents*, *sequential* results exceed *random* setting with well-designed selection strategy eliminating low-quality QA pairs and introducing variations to resolve the aforementioned limitation.

6.2 Effect of Text Dropout

Table 6 presents the extrinsic evaluation results of the synthesized conversations when text dropout is (✓) and is not (✗) introduced during the question generation process. We measure the quality of generated dialogues using the extractive-based QA performance. Introducing text dropout in question generation gave marked improvement under all four settings. In particular, 16.8% improvement is observed when QG text dropout is involved in the *overlap-selection* and *single-Dial-Num* settings. By masking different positions of the input grounding span, ConvRGX generates not only diverse questions of various forms with similar semantic meanings, but also information-seeking questions for different knowledge. An example is shown in Appendix E. The contrasting results to Section 5.1 imply that evaluating the generated question quality by intrinsic Q-metric is not sufficient.

6.3 Effect of Data Selection and Anwer Refinement

Table 6 also shows how the data selection in conversation generation contributes to the improvement of CQA performance. First, the QA model performs poorly on both EM and F1 when trained on generated conversations without data selection. Introducing data selection boosts the performance drastically, with the EM score increasing from 2.69 to 42.21 (35.96) and F1 score from 31.31 to 59.01 (54.44) if dropout(overlap)-based selection is involved. Although the question generator can produce diverse questions of fluency and coherence, the generated questions may not be answerable by the given grounding text s. We design selection strategies that replace the grounding span with a fine-grained answer a and filter out low-quality, especially unanswerable QA pairs. An example is shown in Appendix E. We also find that the dropout-based selection strategy outperforms the overlap-based strategy significantly in all settings listed in Table 6. It implies that the data selection strategies has a significant effect on the CQA generation quality.

Table 7 shows how answer refinement affects the performance of CQA. As shown in Table 7, adding answer refinement improve the performance of CQA, with the EM score increasing from 35.96 (36.71) to 40.05 (38.61) and F1 score from 54.44 (54.15) to 58.07 (56.18) with the *random* (*sequential*) flow-order, which implies the positive effect of answer refinement in improving generation quality.

7 Conclusion

We propose ConvRGX, an automatic CQA data annotation method extended from the recognition-generation-extraction (RGX) framework for conversational applications, which can generate high-quality CQA data that can be used for question generation and data augmentation. We demonstrate the effectiveness of ConvRGX on standard conversational benchmarks, which show improvements over current data generation and augmentation methods for both question quality and self-training performance. In summary, ConvRGX presents a scalable and effective way to approach CQA problems that have limited human annotation.

Acknowledgement

This research was supported by the Center for Perceptual and Interactive Intelligence (CPII) Ltd under the Innovation and Technology Commission's InnoHK Scheme.

Limitations

This paper proposes a conversational QA generation system and evaluates the generated QA quality on two publicly available benchmarks. Although the improved Q-metric indicates that the ConvRGX generates better QA data than previous methods, the QA generation pipeline can still generate noisy conversations and hence cannot be entirely trusted. On the other hand, if we force the model such that only QA pairs with high confidence are selected, the diversity of generated data would be limited. In the future, we will investigate the trafeoff between reliability and diversity in CQA generation tasks.

Ethics Statement

The CQA generation system proposed in this work can augment the performance of CQA models, but also introduce the following risks. Firstly, the questions are generated according to grounding documents. As a result, they might deliver social biases and misinformation contained in the documents. Secondly, the method increases the size of CQA corpora and the computational cost of model training. Lastly, since the system can automatically annotate unlabeled documents, it might reduce the number of jobs in manual data annotation.

References

Max Bartolo, Tristan Thrush, Robin Jia, Sebastian Riedel, Pontus Stenetorp, and Douwe Kiela. 2021. Improving question answering model robustness with synthetic adversarial data generation. In *Proceedings of the 2021 Conference on Empirical Methods in Natural Language Processing*, pages 8830–8848, Online and Punta Cana, Dominican Republic. Association for Computational Linguistics.

Ankit Chadha and Rewa Sood. 2019. BERTQA - attention on steroids. *CoRR*, abs/1912.10435.

Eunsol Choi, He He, Mohit Iyyer, Mark Yatskar, Wentau Yih, Yejin Choi, Percy Liang, and Luke Zettlemoyer. 2018. QuAC: Question answering in context. In *Proceedings of the 2018 Conference on Empirical Methods in Natural Language Processing*, pages 2174–2184, Brussels, Belgium. Association for Computational Linguistics.

Kevin Clark, Minh-Thang Luong, Quoc V. Le, and Christopher D. Manning. 2020. ELECTRA: pre-training text encoders as discriminators rather than generators. In *8th International Conference on Learning Representations, ICLR 2020, Addis Ababa, Ethiopia, April 26-30, 2020*. OpenReview.net.

Zhuyun Dai, Arun Tejasvi Chaganty, Vincent Zhao, Aida Amini, Qazi Mamunur Rashid, Mike Green, and Kelvin Guu. 2022. Dialog inpainting: Turning documents into dialogs.

Jacob Devlin, Ming-Wei Chang, Kenton Lee, and Kristina Toutanova. 2019. BERT: Pre-training of deep bidirectional transformers for language understanding. In *Proceedings of the 2019 Conference of the North American Chapter of the Association for Computational Linguistics: Human Language Technologies, Volume 1 (Long and Short Papers)*, pages 4171–4186, Minneapolis, Minnesota. Association for Computational Linguistics.

William B. Dolan and Chris Brockett. 2005. Automatically constructing a corpus of sentential paraphrases. In *Proceedings of the Third International Workshop on Paraphrasing (IWP2005)*.

Nan Duan, Duyu Tang, Peng Chen, and Ming Zhou. 2017. Question generation for question answering. In *Proceedings of the 2017 Conference on Empirical Methods in Natural Language Processing*, pages 866–874, Copenhagen, Denmark. Association for Computational Linguistics.

Song Feng, Siva Sankalp Patel, Hui Wan, and Sachindra Joshi. 2021. MultiDoc2Dial: Modeling dialogues grounded in multiple documents. In *Proceedings of the 2021 Conference on Empirical Methods in Natural Language Processing*, pages 6162–6176, Online and Punta Cana, Dominican Republic. Association for Computational Linguistics.

Song Feng, Hui Wan, Chulaka Gunasekara, Siva Patel, Sachindra Joshi, and Luis Lastras. 2020. doc2dial: A goal-oriented document-grounded dialogue dataset. In *Proceedings of the 2020 Conference on Empirical Methods in Natural Language Processing (EMNLP)*, pages 8118–8128, Online. Association for Computational Linguistics.

Tianyu Gao, Xingcheng Yao, and Danqi Chen. 2021. Simcse: Simple contrastive learning of sentence embeddings. In *Proceedings of the 2021 Conference on Empirical Methods in Natural Language Processing*,

EMNLP 2021, Virtual Event / Punta Cana, Dominican Republic, 7-11 November, 2021, pages 6894–6910. Association for Computational Linguistics.

Yifan Gao, Piji Li, Irwin King, and Michael R. Lyu. 2019. Interconnected question generation with coreference alignment and conversation flow modeling. In *Proceedings of the 57th Annual Meeting of the Association for Computational Linguistics*, pages 4853–4862, Florence, Italy. Association for Computational Linguistics.

Jing Gu, Mostafa Mirshekari, Zhou Yu, and Aaron Sisto. 2021. ChainCQG: Flow-aware conversational question generation. In *Proceedings of the 16th Conference of the European Chapter of the Association for Computational Linguistics: Main Volume*, pages 2061–2070, Online. Association for Computational Linguistics.

Pengcheng He, Xiaodong Liu, Jianfeng Gao, and Weizhu Chen. 2020. Deberta: Decoding-enhanced bert with disentangled attention. *arXiv preprint arXiv:2006.03654*.

Hsin-Yuan Huang, Eunsol Choi, and Wen-tau Yih. 2019. Flowqa: Grasping flow in history for conversational machine comprehension. In *7th International Conference on Learning Representations, ICLR 2019, New Orleans, LA, USA, May 6-9, 2019*. OpenReview.net.

Robin Jia, Mike Lewis, and Luke Zettlemoyer. 2022. Question answering infused pre-training of general-purpose contextualized representations. In *Findings of the Association for Computational Linguistics: ACL 2022*, pages 711–728, Dublin, Ireland. Association for Computational Linguistics.

Amita Kamath, Robin Jia, and Percy Liang. 2020. Selective question answering under domain shift. In *Proceedings of the 58th Annual Meeting of the Association for Computational Linguistics*, pages 5684–5696, Online. Association for Computational Linguistics.

Gangwoo Kim, Hyunjae Kim, Jungsoo Park, and Jaewoo Kang. 2021. Learn to resolve conversational dependency: A consistency training framework for conversational question answering. In *Proceedings of the 59th Annual Meeting of the Association for Computational Linguistics and the 11th International Joint Conference on Natural Language Processing (Volume 1: Long Papers)*, pages 6130–6141, Online. Association for Computational Linguistics.

Gangwoo Kim, Sungdong Kim, Kang Min Yoo, and Jaewoo Kang. 2022. Towards more realistic generation of information-seeking conversations. *CoRR*, abs/2205.12609.

Tassilo Klein and Moin Nabi. 2019. Learning to answer by learning to ask: Getting the best of gpt-2 and bert worlds. *arXiv preprint arXiv:1911.02365*.

Dong Bok Lee, Seanie Lee, Woo Tae Jeong, Donghwan Kim, and Sung Ju Hwang. 2020. Generating diverse and consistent QA pairs from contexts with information-maximizing hierarchical conditional VAEs. In *Proceedings of the 58th Annual Meeting of the Association for Computational Linguistics*, pages 208–224, Online. Association for Computational Linguistics.

Mike Lewis, Yinhan Liu, Naman Goyal, Marjan Ghazvininejad, Abdelrahman Mohamed, Omer Levy, Veselin Stoyanov, and Luke Zettlemoyer. 2020. BART: Denoising sequence-to-sequence pre-training for natural language generation, translation, and comprehension. In *Proceedings of the 58th Annual Meeting of the Association for Computational Linguistics*, pages 7871–7880, Online. Association for Computational Linguistics.

Patrick Lewis, Ludovic Denoyer, and Sebastian Riedel. 2019. Unsupervised question answering by cloze translation. In *Proceedings of the 57th Annual Meeting of the Association for Computational Linguistics*, pages 4896–4910, Florence, Italy. Association for Computational Linguistics.

Patrick Lewis, Yuxiang Wu, Linqing Liu, Pasquale Minervini, Heinrich Küttler, Aleksandra Piktus, Pontus Stenetorp, and Sebastian Riedel. 2021. PAQ: 65 million probably-asked questions and what you can do with them. *Transactions of the Association for Computational Linguistics*, 9:1098–1115.

Chin-Yew Lin. 2004. ROUGE: A package for automatic evaluation of summaries. In *Text Summarization Branches Out*, pages 74–81, Barcelona, Spain. Association for Computational Linguistics.

Dayiheng Liu, Yeyun Gong, Jie Fu, Yu Yan, Jiusheng Chen, Jiancheng Lv, Nan Duan, and Ming Zhou. 2020. Tell me how to ask again: Question data augmentation with controllable rewriting in continuous space. In *Proceedings of the 2020 Conference on Empirical Methods in Natural Language Processing (EMNLP)*, pages 5798–5810, Online. Association for Computational Linguistics.

Yinhan Liu, Myle Ott, Naman Goyal, Jingfei Du, Mandar Joshi, Danqi Chen, Omer Levy, Mike Lewis, Luke Zettlemoyer, and Veselin Stoyanov. 2019. Roberta: A robustly optimized bert pretraining approach. *arXiv preprint arXiv:1907.11692*.

Hongyin Luo, Shang-Wen Li, Mingye Gao, Seunghak Yu, and James Glass. 2022. Cooperative self-training of machine reading comprehension. In *Proceedings of the 2022 Conference of the North American Chapter of the Association for Computational Linguistics: Human Language Technologies*, pages 244–257, Seattle, United States. Association for Computational Linguistics.

Preksha Nema and Mitesh M. Khapra. 2018. Towards a better metric for evaluating question generation systems. In *Proceedings of the 2018 Conference on*

Empirical Methods in Natural Language Processing, pages 3950–3959, Brussels, Belgium. Association for Computational Linguistics.

Yasuhito Ohsugi, Itsumi Saito, Kyosuke Nishida, Hisako Asano, and Junji Tomita. 2019. A simple but effective method to incorporate multi-turn context with BERT for conversational machine comprehension. In *Proceedings of the First Workshop on NLP for Conversational AI*, pages 11–17, Florence, Italy. Association for Computational Linguistics.

Kishore Papineni, Salim Roukos, Todd Ward, and Wei-Jing Zhu. 2002. Bleu: a method for automatic evaluation of machine translation. In *Proceedings of the 40th Annual Meeting of the Association for Computational Linguistics*, pages 311–318, Philadelphia, Pennsylvania, USA. Association for Computational Linguistics.

Raul Puri, Ryan Spring, Mohammad Shoeybi, Mostofa Patwary, and Bryan Catanzaro. 2020. Training question answering models from synthetic data. In *Proceedings of the 2020 Conference on Empirical Methods in Natural Language Processing (EMNLP)*, pages 5811–5826, Online. Association for Computational Linguistics.

Chen Qu, Liu Yang, Cen Chen, Minghui Qiu, W Bruce Croft, and Mohit Iyyer. 2020. Open-retrieval conversational question answering. In *Proceedings of the 43rd International ACM SIGIR conference on research and development in Information Retrieval*, pages 539–548.

Chen Qu, Liu Yang, Minghui Qiu, Yongfeng Zhang, Cen Chen, W Bruce Croft, and Mohit Iyyer. 2019. Attentive history selection for conversational question answering. In *Proceedings of the 28th ACM International Conference on Information and Knowledge Management*, pages 1391–1400.

Pranav Rajpurkar, Jian Zhang, Konstantin Lopyrev, and Percy Liang. 2016. SQuAD: 100,000+ questions for machine comprehension of text. In *Proceedings of the 2016 Conference on Empirical Methods in Natural Language Processing*, pages 2383–2392, Austin, Texas. Association for Computational Linguistics.

Siva Reddy, Danqi Chen, and Christopher D. Manning. 2019. CoQA: A conversational question answering challenge. *Transactions of the Association for Computational Linguistics*, 7:249–266.

Stephen Robertson, Hugo Zaragoza, et al. 2009. The probabilistic relevance framework: Bm25 and beyond. *Foundations and Trends® in Information Retrieval*, 3(4):333–389.

Mrinmaya Sachan and Eric Xing. 2018. Self-training for jointly learning to ask and answer questions. In *Proceedings of the 2018 Conference of the North American Chapter of the Association for Computational Linguistics: Human Language Technologies, Volume 1 (Long Papers)*, pages 629–640, New Orleans, Louisiana. Association for Computational Linguistics.

Marzieh Saeidi, Max Bartolo, Patrick Lewis, Sameer Singh, Tim Rocktäschel, Mike Sheldon, Guillaume Bouchard, and Sebastian Riedel. 2018. Interpretation of natural language rules in conversational machine reading. In *Proceedings of the 2018 Conference on Empirical Methods in Natural Language Processing*, pages 2087–2097, Brussels, Belgium. Association for Computational Linguistics.

Siamak Shakeri, Cicero Nogueira dos Santos, Henghui Zhu, Patrick Ng, Feng Nan, Zhiguo Wang, Ramesh Nallapati, and Bing Xiang. 2020. End-to-end synthetic data generation for domain adaptation of question answering systems. In *Proceedings of the 2020 Conference on Empirical Methods in Natural Language Processing (EMNLP)*, pages 5445–5460, Online. Association for Computational Linguistics.

Iyer Shankar, Dandekar Nikhil, and Csernai Kornel. 2017. First quora dataset release: question pairs (2017). *URL https://www. quora. com/q/quoradata/First-Quora-Dataset-Release-Question-Pairs*.

Nitish Srivastava, Geoffrey E. Hinton, Alex Krizhevsky, Ilya Sutskever, and Ruslan Salakhutdinov. 2014. Dropout: a simple way to prevent neural networks from overfitting. *J. Mach. Learn. Res.*, 15(1):1929–1958.

Duyu Tang, Nan Duan, Tao Qin, Zhao Yan, and Ming Zhou. 2017. Question answering and question generation as dual tasks. *arXiv preprint arXiv:1706.02027*.

Ashish Vaswani, Noam Shazeer, Niki Parmar, Jakob Uszkoreit, Llion Jones, Aidan N. Gomez, Lukasz Kaiser, and Illia Polosukhin. 2017. Attention is all you need. In *Advances in Neural Information Processing Systems 30: Annual Conference on Neural Information Processing Systems 2017, December 4-9, 2017, Long Beach, CA, USA*, pages 5998–6008.

Jason W. Wei and Kai Zou. 2019. EDA: easy data augmentation techniques for boosting performance on text classification tasks. In *Proceedings of the 2019 Conference on Empirical Methods in Natural Language Processing and the 9th International Joint Conference on Natural Language Processing, EMNLP-IJCNLP 2019, Hong Kong, China, November 3-7, 2019*, pages 6381–6387. Association for Computational Linguistics.

Thomas Wolf, Lysandre Debut, Victor Sanh, Julien Chaumond, Clement Delangue, Anthony Moi, Pierric Cistac, Tim Rault, Rémi Louf, Morgan Funtowicz, and Jamie Brew. 2019. Huggingface's transformers: State-of-the-art natural language processing. *CoRR*, abs/1910.03771.

Qingyang Wu, Song Feng, Derek Chen, Sachindra Joshi, Luis A. Lastras, and Zhou Yu. 2022. DG2: data augmentation through document grounded dialogue generation. In *Proceedings of the 23rd Annual Meeting of the Special Interest Group on Discourse and Dialogue, SIGDIAL 2022, Edinburgh, UK, 07-09 September 2022*, pages 204–216. Association for Computational Linguistics.

Yuan Zhang, Jason Baldridge, and Luheng He. 2019. PAWS: Paraphrase adversaries from word scrambling. In *Proceedings of the 2019 Conference of the North American Chapter of the Association for Computational Linguistics: Human Language Technologies, Volume 1 (Long and Short Papers)*, pages 1298–1308, Minneapolis, Minnesota. Association for Computational Linguistics.

Jing Zhao, Junwei Bao, Yifan Wang, Yongwei Zhou, Youzheng Wu, Xiaodong He, and Bowen Zhou. 2021. RoR: Read-over-read for long document machine reading comprehension. In *Findings of the Association for Computational Linguistics: EMNLP 2021*, pages 1862–1872, Punta Cana, Dominican Republic. Association for Computational Linguistics.

A Dataset Statistics

Table 8 shows the statistics of the Doc2dial and QuAC benchmarks.

B Implementation Details

All model training and inference in this work are conducted on a single NVIDIA RTX A6000 (48G).

CQG We implement the question generator using Bart-large based on the Transformers library (Wolf et al., 2019). For QG text dropout, we randomly replace $max(1, len(grounding\ span)/10)$ tokens with `<mask>`. For Doc2Dial, the number of training epochs is set as 8 with a batch size of 4 and evaluation is conducted after each epoch. We use a learning rate of 3e-5 with a weight decay of 0.001. Maximum input sequence length is set as 1024 with dialogue history length no longer than 128 due to the long document. Maximum target length length is set as 128. During inference time, we initiate multi-generation. For each grounding sentence, we generate 5 questions. If text dropout is introduced during dialogue generation, we randomly mask the grounding sentence 5 times to introduce different variations to the input.

CQA Roberta-large based on the Transformers library (Wolf et al., 2019) is used as the model backbone of CQA tasks. The number of training epochs is set as 5 and the number of evaluation steps is set as 2000 with a batch size of 15. We use a learning rate of 3e-5 with a weight decay of 0.01. Maximal sequence length is set as 512 and maximal answer length is set as 50. The number of tokens for document stride is set as 128 and the number of warmup steps is set as 1000. The whole training process takes about 3.5 hours for Doc2Dial and 8 hours for QuAC without any synthetic data.

C Details of Document Sentence Sampling

Table 9 shows the data statistics of the passage truncation and dialogue template construction for Doc2Dial datasets reported in this paper.

Single Dial-Num We truncate each Doc2Dial document into passages with $N = 6$ sentences and obtain 6979 unique passages in total. Then following the ConvRGX generation pipeline, each document sentence is regarded as the grounding span to generate a QA turn in an auto-regressive manner. Hence, we produce a single dialogue template with 6 turns (i.e., QA pairs) per passage.

Multi Dial-Num We first enlarge each passage to $N = 12$ sentences to enable multi-template construction. For each truncated passage, we sample at most $K = 3$ sets of sentences, with $T = 8$ sentences for each set and let any two sets have 4 different sentences. Overall, we get 2794 truncated passages and 7162 dialogue templates. To verify the contribution of longer passage truncation and longer dialogue turn to the performance improvement of the extractive-based QA model, we also implement the setting of $K = 3$ and $T = 6$ as a comparison to the *single* setting. Experimental results indicate that both longer passage and longer dialogue turn can bring benefits to the quality of synthesized conversations since the *multi* setting is closer to the statistics of human annotated Doc2Dial dataset.

D Retrieval-based CQA Results on QuAC

Table 10 shows the retrieval-based CQA results on QuAC dataset.

E Qualitative Results

Table 11(a) shows an example where ConvRGX generates multiple information-seeking questions with different text dropout. Table 11(b) shows an example that our question generator produces a grammatically correct but unanswerable question by the passage with the text in italics as grounding span. Our data selection module succeeds in identifying and eliminating such kinds of instances.

Doc2Dial	Train				Val				# doc overlap
	# dial	**# doc**	**# tok/doc**	**# tok/usr**	**# dial**	**# doc**	**# tok/doc**	**# tok/usr**	
Data Augmentation	3474	402	833	10.2	661	272	821	10.0	237
Unseen Documents	1345	166	899	10.4					0

QuAC	Train				Val				# doc overlap
	# dial	**# doc**	**# tok/doc**	**# tok/usr**	**# dial**	**# doc**	**# tok/doc**	**# tok/usr**	
Unseen Documents	11567	6843	396.8	6.5	1000	1000	440	6.5	0

Table 8: Data statistics of Doc2Dial and QuAC datasets used in our experiments. The number of documents are obtained after document deduplication. Models are trained on the *Train* set and evaluated on the *Val* set.

	# s/psg	# turn	# dial/psg	# diff s	# psg	# template
single	6	6	1	/	6979	6979
multi	12	8	3	4	2794	7162

Table 9: Data statistics of passage truncation and dialogue template construction on Doc2Dial dataset.

Training Data		Unseen Documents		
Original	**Generated**	**F1@1**	**F1@5**	**F1@10**
✓	✗	2.98	8.13	10.39
✓	EDA	2.98	6.89	8.93
✓	Back-translation	2.89	7.06	9.14
✓	Paraphrase	3.04	7.09	9.15
✓	ConvRGX	**4.69**	**9.06**	**11.02**

Table 10: Retrieval-based question answering performance on the QuAC validation set.

Table 12 demonstrates a complete dialogue generated by ConvRGX grounded on the given passage in an auto-regressive manner.

(a) Diverse question generation example
[Passage]: ... *Your unmarried children who are under 18 up to age 19 if attending elementary or secondary school full time can be eligible to receive Social Security benefits when you die.* And your child can get benefits at any age if they were disabled before age 22 and remain disabled. Besides your natural children , your stepchildren, grandchildren, step grandchildren or adopted children may receive benefits under certain circumstances. ...
[Generated questions]: And what about my unmarried children, who are under 18 years old? And at what age can my child receive Social Security benefits? And what about my children who are not in school? Are children under 18 eligible for Social Security?
(b) Unswerable question filtering example
[Passage]: Your loan servicer can help you understand your options. You may be able to switch repayment plans to get a lower monthly payment , consider an income - driven repayment plan , change your payment due date , or get a deferment or forbearance. NEVER ignore delinquency or default notices from your loan servicer. Consider Simplifying Repayment with Consolidation You might wish to combine your multiple federal student loans into a single Direct Consolidation Loan to simplify repayment. *There may be tradeoffs, so understand the advantages and possible disadvantages of consolidation before you apply.*
[Generated question]: What are the advantages and disadvantages of consolidation?

Table 11: Examples of (a) diverse question generation and (b) unanswerable question filtering. The question generator of ConvRGX generates the questions taking the text in *italics* as grounding span.

ConvRGX Dialogue Generation
[Passage]: In addition to meeting our definition of disability , you must have worked long enough and recently enough under Social Security to qualify for disability benefits. Social Security work credits are based on your total yearly wages or self - employment income. You can earn up to four credits each year. The amount needed for a work credit changes from year to year. In 2019 , for example , you earn one credit for each $1,360 in wages or self - employment income. When you've earned $5,440 , you've earned your four credits for the year. The number of work credits you need to qualify for disability benefits depends on your age when you become disabled. Generally , you need 40 credits , 20 of which were earned in the last 10 years ending with the year you become disabled. However , younger workers may qualify with fewer credits. For more information on whether you qualify , read our publication ; How You Earn Credits. What We Mean By Disability The definition of disability under Social Security is different than other programs.
[Generated Dialogue]: q1 : What are Social Security work credits based on? a1 : Social Security work credits are based on your total yearly wages or self - employment income. You can earn up to four credits each year. q2 : How much do I need for a work credit? a2 : You can earn up to four credits each year. The amount needed for a work credit changes from year to year. In 2019 , for example , you earn one credit for each $1,360 in wages or self - employment income. q3 : What if I earn $5,440 for the year? a3 : you've earned your four credits for the year. q4 : Where can I find more information on whether I qualify? a4 : read our publication ; How You Earn Credits. q5 : Is disability the same as illness? a5 : The definition of disability under Social Security is different than other programs.

Table 12: Example of synthesized dialogue by ConvRGX on the grounding passage.

Language-Agnostic Transformers and Assessing ChatGPT-Based Query Rewriting for Multilingual Document-Grounded QA

Srinivas Gowriraj* , **Soham Dinesh Tiwari***, **Mitali Potnis***, **Srijan Bansal**, **Teruko Mitamura**, and **Eric Nyberg**
{sgowrira, sohamdit, mpotnis, srijanb, teruko, en09}@andrew.cmu.edu
Language Technologies Institute, Carnegie Mellon University

Abstract

The DialDoc 2023 shared task has expanded the document-grounded dialogue task to encompass multiple languages, despite having limited annotated data. This paper assesses the effectiveness of both language-agnostic and language-aware paradigms for multilingual pre-trained transformer models in a bi-encoder-based dense passage retriever (DPR), concluding that the language-agnostic approach is superior. Additionally, the study investigates the impact of query rewriting techniques using large language models, such as ChatGPT, on multilingual, document-grounded question-answering systems. The experiments conducted demonstrate that, for the examples examined, query rewriting does not enhance performance compared to the original queries. This failure is due to topic switching in final dialogue turns and irrelevant topics being considered for query rewriting.

1 Introduction

English dominates as the most widely used language on the internet, and for communicating with virtual assistants [1]. However, the prevalence of English-centric content creates a language barrier for non-English speakers who wish to access information and services online. To bridge this gap, there is a growing need for multilingual knowledge-grounded question-answering dialogue systems that can enable individuals to access the internet and utilize virtual assistants in their native language. While the development of English document-grounded dialogue systems (Feng et al., 2021) has been extensively explored, the exploration of other languages remains limited.

In response to this, DialDoc 2023 shared task extends the task of document-grounded dialogue to include multiple languages with limited annotated data, such as Vietnamese and French. The development of multilingual dialogue systems poses two significant challenges: (i) understanding queries in any language and retrieving relevant passages from a collection of documents in multiple languages (ii) generating appropriate responses in the same language. Prior works (Clark et al., 2020; Asai et al., 2021a) in open-domain multilingual question-answering models have addressed these challenges using a retriever-reader approach. Specifically, the multilingual DPR (mDPR) model, an extension of DPR (Karpukhin et al., 2020), is used to retrieve documents from a corpus. A multilingual reader based on multilingual T5 (Xue et al., 2021a), generates suitable responses in the target language based on the retrieved multilingual passages. In contrast to conventional retrieval tasks, passage retrieval in conversational question answering (QA) presents new challenges as each question must be interpreted within the context of the ongoing dialogue. Previous studies (Wu et al., 2022) have shown that rewriting the question using the dialogue context into a standalone question can enhance the retrieval process, surpassing the performance of current state-of-the-art retrievers.

The mDPR model employs a bi-encoder architecture, utilizing a pre-trained multilingual model to encode the questions and passages independently. The encoded representations are then compared using a maximum inner product search to identify relevant passages for a given question. In this study, we evaluate two paradigms for multilingual pre-trained transformer models as mDPR bi-encoders, namely, a language-agnostic paradigm and a language-aware paradigm. Specifically, we consider two models for multilingual sentence embedding: Language-Agnostic BERT Sentence Embedding (LaBSE) (Feng et al., 2022) and XLM-RoBERTa (XLM-R) (Conneau et al., 2020). LaBSE combines masked language modeling with translation language modeling to produce language-

[1]Usage Statistics and Market Share of Content Languages for Websites, February 2023 — w3techs.com.

*These authors contributed equally to this work.

Proceedings of the Third DialDoc Workshop on Document-grounded Dialogue and Conversational Question Answering, pages 101–108
July 13, 2023 ©2023 Association for Computational Linguistics

agnostic sentence embeddings, while XLM-R is a cross-lingual version of RoBERTa (Liu et al., 2019) pre-trained on a large corpus of text in over 100 languages using a self-supervised approach. Although both models are beneficial for multilingual sentence embeddings, based on our experiments, it has been observed that LaBSE outperforms XLM-R. Additionally, we examine the impact of query rewriting techniques using large language models (LLMs) such as ChatGPT to summarize the conversational history more concisely and use transfer learning to generalize to French and Vietnamese rewritten queries.

Therefore, in this study, we investigate the performance difference between the language-aware and language-agnostic paradigms, where we found that the language-agnostic LaBSE retriever outperforms the language-aware XLM-R retriever. Additionally, we explore the impact of query rewriting on the performance of such systems. While query rewriting has been proposed as a potential solution for improving performance, our results indicate that rewriting queries did not significantly improve performance for the considered sub-samples. Our code is available on GitHub [2].

2 Related Work

2.1 Language-agnostic Multilingual Model

Language-agnostic BERT Sentence Embedding (LaBSE) model is essentially the BERT (Devlin et al., 2019) model trained with a cross-lingual training technique to create language agnostic sentence embeddings for many languages. By training on parallel data consisting of pairs of sentences expressing the same meaning in different languages, LaBSE is able to learn how to map sentences from different languages onto a shared high-dimensional space, where similar sentences are located close to each other and dissimilar ones are far apart. LaBSE outperforms previous state-of-the-art models in a range of cross-lingual and multilingual natural language processing tasks, including cross-lingual sentence retrieval, cross-lingual document classification, and multilingual question answering, owing to its cross-lingual training approach. Language agnosticism enables LaBSE to transfer knowledge across different languages and generate superior-quality sentence embeddings for texts in numerous languages, thereby making it a valuable instrument for researchers and practitioners dealing with multilingual text data. We have employed LaBSE in our work due to its shared embedding space and its ability to capture contextual information across multiple languages enabling strong cross-lingual performance and knowledge transfer across multiple languages.

2.2 Multilingual Query Rewriting

GPT models, including ChatGPT, possess a remarkable capability for comprehending and interpreting natural language (Haleem et al., 2023; Walid, 2023). ChatGPT has proven to be highly capable of high-quality responses to natural language queries. Additionally, it is also effective at rewriting long contextual information into compact queries (Wang et al., 2023). Prompting methods (White et al., 2023; Zuccon and Koopman, 2023) are used to steer the LLM's behaviour for desired outcomes without updating model weights. In this academic paper, we have used ChatGPT for the purpose of query rewriting. Query rewriting by prompting ChatGPT has potential to improve the effectiveness of conversational question-answering systems and aiding the retrieval of information from extensive text collections.

3 Dataset

DialDoc 2023 shared task dataset consists of 797 Vietnamese dialogues with an average turn count of 4 and 816 French dialogues with an average of 5 turns. These dialogues are grounded in multiple documents from nine different domains, namely Technology, Health, Health Care Services, Veterans Affairs, Insurance, Public Services, Social Security, Department of Motor Vehicles, and Student Financial Aid in the USA. Each dialogue turn in the dataset contains role annotations for the conversation between a human and a conversational agent, with the turns in reverse chronological order, the latest turn first in dialogue history. The retrieval dataset includes query, dialogue data, positive passages, and negative passages. Positive passages contain the answer to the given query and are within the document, while negative passages are closely related to the document but they do not contain the answer to the query in focus.

4 Methodology and Experiments

The prevailing paradigm for document-grounded question-answering models involves a retriever-

[2] https://github.com/srinivas-gowriraj/Multilingual_QA/

Model	Pretrained	Finetuned	Evaluated	R@1	R@5	R@10	R@20
LaBSE	zh + en	fr + vi	fr + vi	**0.65**	**0.82**	**0.86**	**0.90**
LaBSE	zh + en	fr + vi	fr	0.57	0.76	0.82	0.87
LaBSE	zh + en	fr + vi	vi	0.75	0.89	0.92	0.95
XLMR	zh + en	fr + vi	fr + vi	0.55	0.75	0.80	0.84
XLMR	zh + en	fr + vi	fr	0.45	0.67	0.72	0.78
XLMR	zh + en	fr + vi	vi	0.65	0.83	0.87	0.90

Table 1: Performance comparison of language-agnostic versus language-aware multilingual dense passage retrieval approaches pre trained on Chinese (zh) + English (en) and fine-tuned on French (fr) + Vietnamese (vi).

reader approach that comprises of a document retrieval module, a reranker module, and an answer generation module. However, in this study, our main focus has been on the multilingual retriever component, while fixing XLM-R as reranker. However, we did experiment with the Fusion-in-Decoder (FiD) approach (Raffel et al., 2020) to modify the mT5 model previously being used as the answer generator (Xue et al., 2021b).

4.1 Retrieval: Language Agnostic vs Language-aware

In this paper, we employ the multilingual dense passage retriever (mDPR) (Asai et al., 2021b) to retrieve passages from multilingual document collections. However, the bi-encoders used in mDPR consist of two different models: LaBSE, which is designed for the language-agnostic paradigm, and XLM-R, which is suitable for the language-aware setting. To prepare the models, we first pre-train them using the English and Chinese portions of a document-grounded dataset. We then fine-tune the models on three different combinations of target datasets, namely French and Vietnamese, French only, and Vietnamese only. Finally, we evaluate the performance of the models on the corresponding validation sets of each dataset combination.

The mDPR models are trained using the English and Chinese splits, employing gold passages along with 10 hard negatives mined through BM25. [3]. The dataset is divided into an 80-20 train-test split using a consistent seed. The training process for all configurations persists for 50 epochs.

4.2 Zero-Shot Multilingual Query Re-writing

To improve the efficiency of the retriever module, we postulated that converting the query and dialogue context history into more concise and informative questions would be advantageous. Drawing inspiration from the accomplishments of large language models, we utilized ChatGPT for query rewriting. A specific prompt structure was employed for the ChatGPT model, where the question was rewritten using the last turn in the query, and the context encompassed all preceding turns concatenated in reverse order. The template of the prompt that we employed is provided below:

Rewrite the question into an informative query explicitly mentioning relevant details from the provided context. Context : {dialogue history} Question : {last-turn} Re-written Question :

Our study's outcomes, which compared language-agnostic and multilingual paradigms, demonstrated that LaBSE-based retrievers outperformed other methods for multilingual retrieval tasks. As a result, we opted to utilize the LaBSE-based mDPR retriever module for all subsequent experiments. We also evaluated the impact of utilizing forward-order context, but the results indicated that it accentuated irrelevant information.

5 Results and Discussion

Language agnostic retrievers outperform language-aware retrievers. In Table 1, we present the results of our experiments, where we first pre-trained the retriever models LaBSE and XLM-R on Chinese (zh) + English (en) data, and then fine-tuned them on various combinations of French (fr) and Vietnamese (vi) document grounded datasets, as described in Section 4.1. The findings demonstrate that the LaBSE-based mDPR retriever model outperformed the XLM-R-based mDPR retriever model, in all metrics and training dataset combinations. Although XLM-R, which is based on RoBERTa (a more advanced version of BERT) and has 125M model parameters, was trained on unsupervised cross-lingual data, LaBSE still outperformed it. The BERT-based architecture has 110M trainable parameters.

[3]https://www.analyticsvidhya.com/blog/2021/05/build-your-own-nlp-based-search-engine-using-bm25.

Multilingual Query Rewriting does not lead to better performance. The results presented in Table 2 provide evidence that the incorporation of multilingual query rewriting does not lead to enhanced performance for the tested examples. More precisely, the LaBSE model, which was trained on unmodified subsets of English (en) data, demonstrated superior knowledge transfer abilities compared to models trained on queries that were rewritten by ChatGPT. Thus, further research is necessary to elucidate the reasons for this suboptimal performance.

Trained on	Eval On	R@1	R@5	R@10	R@20
en (Raw)	fr (Raw)	0.45	0.70	0.77	0.84
en (Raw)	vi (Raw)	0.51	0.78	0.84	0.89
en (ChatGPT)	fr (ChatGPT)	0.16	0.33	0.38	0.46
en (ChatGPT)	vi (ChatGPT)	0.26	0.49	0.58	0.65

Table 2: Comparison of transfer learning approaches using different query-rewriting approaches. **Raw** refers to the original dialogue query i.e. current turn + History while **ChatGPT** refers to the query re-written by ChatGPT using current turn and dialogue history. We use LaBSE-based mDPR for all the above settings.

5.1 Error Analysis of Rewritten Queries

This study focuses on the evaluation of the performance of rewritten queries generated by ChatGPT in comparison to the original queries consisting of a question and context. Moreover, a comprehensive error analysis is conducted to identify the gaps in the rewritten queries. Figure 1 presents notable observations. The findings reveal that the quality of the rewritten queries generated by ChatGPT is inferior to that of the original queries. Further investigation shows that topic switching often occurs in the last turn of the conversation, resulting in rewritten queries that incorporate non-relevant context. This phenomenon is illustrated in Figure 1. The switching of topics adversely affects the relevance and accuracy of the rewritten queries. Additionally, the rewriting process tends to summarize both relevant and non-relevant topics from the conversation, and hallucinate information, as shown in Figure 2. This approach lacks specificity and clarity in the rewritten queries, further impeding their quality and effectiveness. Furthermore, the prompts are created manually by visually inspecting the generated outputs. While this method allows for quality control of the prompts, it is inherently subjective and vulnerable to human biases. Thus, it is essential to explore advanced prompting methods to enhance the overall quality of the rewritten queries, as suggested in (Liu et al., 2023).

6 Conclusion

This paper investigates the effectiveness of language-agnostic and language-aware paradigms for multilingual pre-trained transformer models in a bi-encoder-based dense retriever. The paper also evaluates the impact of query rewriting on task performance. Our findings indicate that the language-agnostic approach outperforms the language-aware approach. However, for the considered subsamples, query rewriting did not improve the performance over the original queries. Furthermore, the observed topic switching in the conversations' last turns, and ChatGPT's tendency to summarize non-relevant topics and hallucination lead to less accurate rewritten queries compared to the original queries.

7 Limitations, Potential Risks, and Future Work

The limitations of this study are primarily due to budget and credit constraints. Consequently, our query rewriting observations are based on a sample size of 2000, leading to limited generalizability of findings. Another limitation of the limited resources was the limited context size of ChatGPT and the relatively long nature of the questions in our dataset. Hence, we could not test prompting ChatGPT with in-context examples for better query rewriting performance. Hence one potential future work is testing the performance of query rewriting using in-context examples. Finally, ChatGPT architecture is not open source, preventing us from testing advanced prompting methods. Hence another future work would be to test query rewriting using open source models and with advanced fine-tuning methods like Prefix Tuning (Li and Liang, 2021) and Prompt Tuning (Lester et al., 2021).

The study is also subject to the risk of "hallucinations" in ChatGPT's responses, which may lead to imprecision in query rewriting. The study suggests further investigation into these issues to improve the accuracy and reliability of the results. We recommend further investigation into these limitations and any potential societal biases present in our dataset to enhance the reliability and performance of query rewriting.

Original vietnamese query	Translated english query
Dialogue History: **user:** thiết bị tiêu dùng khác để làm gì? **agent:** để khuyến khích lối sống lành mạnh, chẳng hạn như, quy mô kết nối hoặc máy theo dõi tim mạch, cũng là một khả năng của IoT. **user**: Thiết bị IoT cũng có thể làm gì? **agent**: có thể được sử dụng để kiểm soát cơ sở hạ tầng quan trọng như cầu để cung cấp truy cập vào tàu. **user**: các ứng dụng của IoT có giới hạn trong các lĩnh vực này không? **agent**: các ứng dụng của IoT không chỉ giới hạn trong các lĩnh vực này. **Original Query:** ARM đã "nhanh chân" trong việc nhận ra rằng, ổ đĩa có xu hướng sử dụng các bộ vi điều khiển 32-bit là giải pháp cho những người như thế nào? **Rewritten Query:** Trong lĩnh vực IoT, các ứng dụng có giới hạn trong những lĩnh vực nào và thiết bị IoT có thể được sử dụng để làm gì, bao gồm cả việc khuyến khích lối sống lành mạnh và thiết bị tiêu dùng khác?	**Dialogue History** **user**: other consumer devices for what? **agent**: to promote healthy lifestyles, for example, connected scales or heart monitors, is also an IoT possibility. **user**: What can IoT devices do too? **agent**: can be used to control critical infrastructure such as bridges to provide access to ships. **user**: are IoT applications limited to these areas? **agent**: applications of IoT are not limited to these areas. **Original Query (translated):** ARM was "quick feet" in realizing that the drive tends to use 32-bit microcontrollers is the solution for those? **Rewritten Query (translated):** In the field of IoT, what areas are the applications limited to and what can IoT devices be used for, including promoting healthy lifestyles and other consumer devices?

Figure 1: An erroneous rewritten query (ChatGPT) occurred wherein the subject matter abruptly changed during the final exchange of dialogue, as highlighted in yellow.

Original french query	Translated english query
Dialogue History **user**: Qu'est-ce qui est fait avec une partie de l'énergie? **agent**: La climatisation, le chauffage, l'éclairage et autres. **user**: Quels facteurs limitent l'efficacité des trains à sustentation magnétique classiques? **agent**: La traînée aérodynamique. **agent**: Se déplacer linéairement le long de la voie. **user:** Qu'est-ce que le sujet peut faire le long de la voie? **Original Query:** Comment peut-on entraîner un train sans disposer d'une plaque de réaction séparée ? **Rewritten Query:** Quels facteurs limitent l'efficacité des trains à sustentation magnétique classiques, tels que la climatisation, le chauffage, l'éclairage et autres, et que fait-on avec une partie de l'énergie, sachant que l'agent se déplace linéairement le long de la voie et que la traînée aérodynamique est utilisée pour l'entraînement du train sans disposer d'une plaque de réaction séparée ?	**Dialog History:** **user**: What is done with part of the energy? **agent**: Air conditioning, heating, lighting and others. **user**: What factors limit the efficiency of conventional magnetic levitation trains? **agent**: Aerodynamic drag. **agent**: Move linearly along the lane. **user:** What can the subject do along the way? **Original Query:** How can you drive a train without having a separate reaction plate? **Rewritten Query:** What factors limit the efficiency of conventional magnetic levitation trains, such as air conditioning, heating, lighting and others, and what do we do with some of the energy, knowing that the agent moves linearly along of the track and that the aerodynamic drag is used for driving the train without having a separate reaction plate?

Figure 2: Erroneous rewritten query (ChatGPT) which considered non-relevant topics and hallucinated information

References

Sumit Agarwal, Suraj Tripathi, Teruko Mitamura, and Carolyn Penstein Rose. 2022. Zero-shot cross-lingual open domain question answering. In *Proceedings of the Workshop on Multilingual Information Access (MIA)*, pages 91–99, Seattle, USA. Association for Computational Linguistics.

Akari Asai, Jungo Kasai, Jonathan Clark, Kenton Lee, Eunsol Choi, and Hannaneh Hajishirzi. 2021a. XOR QA: Cross-lingual open-retrieval question answering. In *Proceedings of the 2021 Conference of the North American Chapter of the Association for Computational Linguistics: Human Language Technologies*, pages 547–564, Online. Association for Computational Linguistics.

Akari Asai, Xinyan Yu, Jungo Kasai, and Hannaneh Hajishirzi. 2021b. One question answering model for many languages with cross-lingual dense passage retrieval.

Jonathan H. Clark, Eunsol Choi, Michael Collins, Dan Garrette, Tom Kwiatkowski, Vitaly Nikolaev, and Jennimaria Palomaki. 2020. TyDi QA: A benchmark for information-seeking question answering in typologically diverse languages. *Transactions of the Association for Computational Linguistics*, 8:454–470.

Alexis Conneau, Kartikay Khandelwal, Naman Goyal, Vishrav Chaudhary, Guillaume Wenzek, Francisco Guzmán, Edouard Grave, Myle Ott, Luke Zettlemoyer, and Veselin Stoyanov. 2020. Unsupervised cross-lingual representation learning at scale.

Jacob Devlin, Ming-Wei Chang, Kenton Lee, and Kristina Toutanova. 2019. Bert: Pre-training of deep bidirectional transformers for language understanding.

Fangxiaoyu Feng, Yinfei Yang, Daniel Cer, Naveen Arivazhagan, and Wei Wang. 2022. Language-agnostic BERT sentence embedding. In *Proceedings of the 60th Annual Meeting of the Association for Computational Linguistics (Volume 1: Long Papers)*, pages 878–891, Dublin, Ireland. Association for Computational Linguistics.

Song Feng, Siva Sankalp Patel, Hui Wan, and Sachindra Joshi. 2021. MultiDoc2Dial: Modeling dialogues grounded in multiple documents. In *Proceedings of the 2021 Conference on Empirical Methods in Natural Language Processing*, pages 6162–6176, Online and Punta Cana, Dominican Republic. Association for Computational Linguistics.

Abid Haleem, Mohd Javaid, and Ravi Singh. 2023. An era of chatgpt as a significant futuristic support tool: A study on features, abilities, and challenges. *BenchCouncil Transactions on Benchmarks, Standards and Evaluations*, 2:100089.

Gautier Izacard and Edouard Grave. 2021a. Leveraging passage retrieval with generative models for open domain question answering.

Gautier Izacard and Edouard Grave. 2021b. Leveraging passage retrieval with generative models for open domain question answering. In *Proceedings of the 16th Conference of the European Chapter of the Association for Computational Linguistics: Main Volume*, pages 874–880, Online. Association for Computational Linguistics.

Vladimir Karpukhin, Barlas Oguz, Sewon Min, Patrick Lewis, Ledell Wu, Sergey Edunov, Danqi Chen, and Wen-tau Yih. 2020. Dense passage retrieval for open-domain question answering. In *Proceedings of the 2020 Conference on Empirical Methods in Natural Language Processing (EMNLP)*, pages 6769–6781, Online. Association for Computational Linguistics.

Brian Lester, Rami Al-Rfou, and Noah Constant. 2021. The power of scale for parameter-efficient prompt tuning. In *Proceedings of the 2021 Conference on Empirical Methods in Natural Language Processing*, pages 3045–3059, Online and Punta Cana, Dominican Republic. Association for Computational Linguistics.

Xiang Lisa Li and Percy Liang. 2021. Prefix-tuning: Optimizing continuous prompts for generation. In *Proceedings of the 59th Annual Meeting of the Association for Computational Linguistics and the 11th International Joint Conference on Natural Language Processing (Volume 1: Long Papers)*, pages 4582–4597, Online. Association for Computational Linguistics.

Pengfei Liu, Weizhe Yuan, Jinlan Fu, Zhengbao Jiang, Hiroaki Hayashi, and Graham Neubig. 2023. Pre-train, prompt, and predict: A systematic survey of prompting methods in natural language processing. 55(9).

Yinhan Liu, Myle Ott, Naman Goyal, Jingfei Du, Mandar Joshi, Danqi Chen, Omer Levy, Mike Lewis, Luke Zettlemoyer, and Veselin Stoyanov. 2019. Roberta: A robustly optimized BERT pretraining approach. *CoRR*, abs/1907.11692.

Colin Raffel, Noam Shazeer, Adam Roberts, Katherine Lee, Sharan Narang, Michael Matena, Yanqi Zhou, Wei Li, and Peter J. Liu. 2020. Exploring the limits of transfer learning with a unified text-to-text transformer. *Journal of Machine Learning Research*, 21(140):1–67.

Siamak Shakeri, Noah Constant, Mihir Sanjay Kale, and Linting Xue. 2021. Towards zero-shot multilingual synthetic question and answer generation for cross-lingual reading comprehension.

Hariri Walid. 2023. Unlocking the potential of chatgpt: A comprehensive exploration of its applications, advantages, limitations, and future directions in natural language processing.

Shuai Wang, Harrisen Scells, Bevan Koopman, and Guido Zuccon. 2023. Can chatgpt write a good boolean query for systematic review literature search?

Jules White, Quchen Fu, Sam Hays, Michael Sandborn, Carlos Olea, Henry Gilbert, Ashraf Elnashar, Jesse Spencer-Smith, and Douglas C. Schmidt. 2023. A prompt pattern catalog to enhance prompt engineering with chatgpt.

Zeqiu Wu, Yi Luan, Hannah Rashkin, David Reitter, Hannaneh Hajishirzi, Mari Ostendorf, and Gaurav Singh Tomar. 2022. CONQRR: Conversational query rewriting for retrieval with reinforcement learning. In *Proceedings of the 2022 Conference on Empirical Methods in Natural Language Processing*, pages 10000–10014, Abu Dhabi, United Arab Emirates. Association for Computational Linguistics.

Linting Xue, Noah Constant, Adam Roberts, Mihir Kale, Rami Al-Rfou, Aditya Siddhant, Aditya Barua, and Colin Raffel. 2021a. mT5: A massively multilingual pre-trained text-to-text transformer. In *Proceedings of the 2021 Conference of the North American Chapter of the Association for Computational Linguistics: Human Language Technologies*, pages 483–498, Online. Association for Computational Linguistics.

Linting Xue, Noah Constant, Adam Roberts, Mihir Kale, Rami Al-Rfou, Aditya Siddhant, Aditya Barua, and Colin Raffel. 2021b. mt5: A massively multilingual pre-trained text-to-text transformer.

Guido Zuccon and Bevan Koopman. 2023. Dr chatgpt, tell me what i want to hear: How prompt knowledge impacts health answer correctness.

A Appendix

A.1 Reader: mT5 and Fusion-in-Decoder

In recent years, the use of the multilingual Text-to-Text Transfer Transformer (mT5) (Xue et al., 2021b), a multilingual variant of Text-to-Text Transfer Transformer (T5) (Raffel et al., 2020) has gained popularity in multilingual question answering tasks (Shakeri et al., 2021). mT5 has the ability to learn the representations of text that capture the nuances of language across different languages and contexts, allowing it to excel in multilingual settings. To leverage this growing popularity of the mT5 generative reader model, our work involves employing a Fusion-in-Decoder (FiD) (Izacard and Grave, 2021a) as a reader in combination with mT5. FiD in combination with mT5 has been proven to boost the performance of answer extraction as compared to using mT5 alone (Agarwal et al., 2022) by encoding the reranked passages individually one-by-one and concatenating them together while passing them for the decoder stage.

We conducted further analysis on the impact of our language-agnostic multilingual retriever selection by employing a two-step process. Firstly, we retrieved relevant passages using the chosen retriever, and subsequently, we utilized the mT5 reader to generate responses based on these retrieved passages. Two different versions of the reader were employed: the vanilla mT5 and the mT5 with Fusion-in-Decoder (FiD) (Izacard and Grave, 2021b). The vanilla mT5 reader takes the query concatenated with the retrieved passages as its input. On the other hand, the FiD-mT5 reader independently encodes each retrieved passage along with the query. The encoded representations are then concatenated and passed to the decoder. As a result, the evidence fusion takes place solely within the decoder. To assess the quality of the generated responses, we employed BLEU, Rouge-L, and F1 metric scores.

We further evaluate the impact of our choice of language-agnostic multilingual retriever by passing retrieved passages to mT5 reader to generate response. We used two different readers which are mT5 (vanilla) and mT5 with Fusion-in-Decoder (FiD) (Izacard and Grave, 2021b). Vanilla mT5 takes query concatentate with retrieved passages as input while FiD-mT5 encodes each retrieved passage along with query independently which is then concatenated and passed to the decoder. The model thus performs evidence fusion in the decoder only. We evaluate the generated response using BLEU, Rouge-L, and F1 metric scores.

Model	Pre-trained	Evaluated	F1	BLEU	ROUGE-L
mT5	fr + vi	fr + vi	62.43	40.87	62.96
mT5 + FiD	fr + vi	fr + vi	64.83	42.22	64.73
mT5	fr	fr	59.89	39.42	58.55
mT5 + FiD	fr	fr	56.76	41.47	60.00
mT5	vi	vi	65.34	45.93	63.03
mT5 + FiD	vi	vi	68.22	45.72	65.61

Table 3: Reader performance comparison of vanilla mT5 versus mT5 in combination with FiD

Fusion-in-Decoder (FiD) improves the overall reader performance. As illustrated in Table 3 we observed an improvement of approximately 4.2%, 3.51%, and 2.80% in F1, BLEU, and Rouge-L scores, respectively when we include Fusion-in-Decoder along with mT5 in the case of both Vietnamese (vi) and French (fr) languages thus proving that Fusion-in-Decoder does indeed help in bolstering our Reader performance.

Follow the Knowledge: Structural Biases and Artefacts in Knowledge Grounded Dialog Datasets

Ehsan Lotfi, Maxime De Bruyn, Jeska Buhmann, Walter Daelemans
CLiPS Research Center
University of Antwerp, Belgium
firstname.lastname@uantwerpen.be

Abstract

Crowd-sourcing has been one of the primary ways to curate conversational data, specially for certain scenarios like grounding in knowledge. In this setting, using online platforms like AMT, non-expert participants are hired to converse with each other, following instructions which try to guide the outcome towards the desired format. The resulting data then is used for different parts of dialog modelling like knowledge selection and response selection/generation.

In this work, we take a closer look into two of the most popular knowledge grounded dialog (KGD) datasets. Investigating potential biases and artefacts in knowledge selection labels, we observe that in many cases the 'knowledge selection flow' simply follows the order of presented knowledge pieces. In Wizard of Wikipedia (the most popular KGD dataset) we use simple content-agnostic models based on this bias to get significant knowledge selection performance. In Topical-Chat we see a similar correlation between the knowledge selection sequence and the order of entities and their segments, as provided to crowd-source workers. We believe that the observed results, question the significance and origin of the presumed dialog-level attributes like 'knowledge flow' in these crowd-sourced datasets.

1 Introduction

Since the introduction of data hungry methods into dialog modeling, sizeable datasets have become an essential asset for researchers of the field. While generic conversational data can be harvested in large quantities from already existing resources like movie subtitles (Lison and Tiedemann, 2016) or website forums (Lowe et al., 2015), more specific datasets usually need to be curated under supervision. Knowledge grounded dialog is one of the fields that has remarkably benefited from crowd-sourced datasets like Wizard of Wikipedia or WoW (Dinan et al., 2018), Holl-E (Moghe et al., 2018) and Topical-Chat (Gopalakrishnan et al., 2019), which offer grounded utterances generated by non-expert annotators or Turkers. During the curation, participants are commonly asked to first choose a knowledge piece (or no knowledge) from a provided pool and then use the selected piece to ground their next utterance on.

Method	w/o response	w/ response
Random	2.7	2.7
GRU	20.0	66.0
Transformer	22.5	70.4
BERT	23.4	78.2
Human	17.1	83.7

Table 1: The prior-posterior gap in knowledge selection for the WoW seen-test dataset (from Kim et al. (2020)). Columns show the performance (accuracy) without and with access to the grounded response.

One common attribute in these datasets is the sizeable difference between the knowledge selection performance with and without access to the uttered response. The phenomenon –referred to as the prior-posterior gap– is demonstrated in Table 1 (from Kim et al. (2020)) for the WoW dataset. Looking for ways to improve the prior performance, studies have tried to design methods to capture higher-order patterns beyond the limiting (and seemingly insufficient) turn-level scope. A natural candidate for this, is modeling the 'knowledge flow'; i.e. how the history of knowledge selection affects the next selection.

In this work we investigate the potential spurious origins of 'knowledge flow' in crowd-sourced KGD datasets. Focusing on the most popular resources in the field, i.e. WoW, we show that competitive results can be obtained in the knowledge selection task, using very simple structural heuristics. We also show that these rudimentary patterns are not an isolated case and can be found in other knowledge grounded dialog datasets like Topical-

Proceedings of the Third DialDoc Workshop on Document-grounded Dialogue and Conversational Question Answering, pages 109–121
July 13, 2023 ©2023 Association for Computational Linguistics

Dataset	dialogs	utterances	Kn access	Kn gold label	Kn pool	citations
Wizard of Wikipedia	22,311	201,999	A	sentence	dynamic, multi-topic	620
CMU_DoG	4,112	130,000	S/A	-	static, single-topic	170
Holl-E	9,071	90,810	S	sentence	static, single-topic	131
Topical-Chat	9,058	198,306	S/A	section	static, multi-topic	219

Table 2: Four most popular (English) datasets for knowledge grounded conversation (Kn:knowledge, S:symmetric, A:asymmetric). Citations are from Google scholar as of April 2023.

Chat, which –in our opinion– connects knowledge selection patterns to dataset curation choices and design.

While dataset artifacts and their relation to the curation process have been widely studied in NLU tasks and especially NLI (Nangia et al., 2021; Gururangan et al., 2018), it is an under-studied topic in dialog modeling. We hope our work draws attention to the issue and contributes to having better dialog datasets, which we believe is necessary for properly modeling higher-order dialog attributes.

2 Knowledge Grounded Conversation

2.1 Problem Formulation

In general, the question of knowledge grounded dialog (KGD) modelling is defined over dialog and knowledge datasets $\mathcal{D}_d = \{(C_i, r_i)\}_{i=1}^{N}$ and $\mathcal{D}_k = \{(k_j)\}_{j=1}^{M}$ where $\forall i \in \{1, ..., N\}$, C_i and r_i represent context and response for a specific dialog turn, and $\forall j \in \{1, ..., M\}$, k_j is a knowledge piece (e.g. a sentence or paragraph). In most recent datasets, $\mathcal{D}_d$ and $\mathcal{D}_k$ are provided as parallel, which allows for a simpler formalization over $\mathcal{D} = \{(C_i, K_i, r_i)\}_{i=1}^{N}$, where K_i (or knowledge pool) is a subset of $\mathcal{D}_k$, and often includes one or more 'gold truth' (K_i^G), i.e. the knowledge piece(s) picked by the annotator during data curation.

The problem of knowledge selection (KS) in this context means designing a model f_{ks} to identify the relevant knowledge piece(s) in K_i: $f_{ks}(K_i) = K_i^G$. Ideally f_{ks} provides a ranking over K_i which can be used to retrieve top-k results for response generation.

2.2 Popular Datasets

The problem of modeling open-domain knowledge grounded conversation attracted increasing attention since the introduction and release of large scale crowd-sourced knowledge grounded dialog datasets with parallel dialog and knowledge corpora. Table 2 shows selected details of the four most popular KGD datasets: **Wizard of Wikipedia** (Dinan et al., 2018) includes conversations between a wizard (with access to knowledge) and an apprentice (no knowledge access) grounded on Wikipedia articles. **CMU_DoG** (Zhou et al., 2018) and **Holl-E** (Moghe et al., 2018) contain dialogs about movies grounded on Wikipedia information plus descriptions for 3 key scenes (CMU_DoG) or a selection of movie's plot, reviews, comments and facts (Holl-E). Finally **Topical-Chat** (Gopalakrishnan et al., 2019) includes conversations on various 'entities' and grounded in a combination of Wikipedia article, fun facts and news articles, in both symmetric and asymmetric knowledge access scenarios.

Among these, WoW is by far The most cited dataset in the field which can be attributed to qualities like proper size, gold knowledge labels and multi-topic knowledge pool. It is also the only dataset with dynamic pool, meaning that the knowledge choices are updated at each turn. Topical-Chat is another popular resource which creates distinction with pre-defined scenarios for knowledge access between collocutors. However it only provides section-level (and not sentence-level) labels for knowledge selection, which makes it less convenient for supervised knowledge selection modeling.

2.3 Knowledge Selection Methods

The popular approach of breaking the KGD problem into the knowledge selection (KS) and response generation (RG) tasks, became mainstream with WoW. Along with the dataset, the release paper (Dinan et al., 2018) also proposed a baseline model (Transformer MemNet) which addressed KGD in these two steps, acquiring 22.5% and 12.2% accuracy for knowledge selection on the seen and unseen test sets accordingly[1].

One of the first approaches to improve on this,

[1] In the seen set -unlike the unseen- dialog 'topics' are shared with the training set.

Model	Method	Seen	Unseen
Random	-	2.7	2.3
Baseline (Dinan et al., 2018)	memory network	22.5	12.2
PostKS (Lian et al., 2019)	posterior signal	22.5	15.8
SKT(BERT) (Kim et al., 2020)	sequential latent kn selection	26.8	18.3
DiffKS(BERT) (Zheng et al., 2020)	difference aware	25.6	20.1
DukeNet (Meng et al., 2020)	kn tracking & shifting	26.4	19.6
SKT+ (Chen et al., 2020)	SKT + posterior signal + distillation	27.7	19.4
MIKe (Meng et al., 2021)	initiative aware	28.4	21.5
SKT-KG (Zhan et al., 2021b)	kn transition with CRF	26	-
KMine* (Lotfi et al., 2021)	posterior signal via generation	27.9	27.0
CoLV (Zhan et al., 2021a)	collaborative latent spaces	30.1	18.9
DIALKI (Wu et al., 2021)	dial-doc contextualization	32.9	35.5
DSG (Li et al., 2022)	document semantic graph	29.4	30.8
TAKE (Yang et al., 2022)	modeling topic shift	28.8	25.8
RoBERTa-base	sequence classification (dialog+kn)	28.6	26.6

Table 3: Knowledge selection performance (accuracy) on the WoW seen and unseen test sets for various models. Numbers are for the highest performing variance (when multiples were present). All models except for Baseline and PostKS benefit from pretrained transformers. $*$: KMine is unsupervised (no gold knowledge labels).

was addressing and exploiting the prior-posterior gap, which uses the posterior knowledge distribution to provide additional learning signals for the KS module, usually via a KL-divergence loss (Lian et al., 2019; Chen et al., 2020; Zhan et al., 2021a; Lotfi et al., 2021).

But probably the most popular approach is trying to address the problem on the dialog level (rather than turn level), and model higher-order 'flows' or sequential patterns that could guide the knowledge selection process. Li et al. (2019) used an incremental transformer to incorporate the knowledge selection history. Jiang et al. (2020) enhanced the posterior signal by modeling the 'topic drift'. Kim et al. (2020) introduced sequential latent knowledge selection to incorporate the selection history. Zheng et al. (2020) took a more specific approach by providing a positive bias for new or different knowledge choices. Meng et al. (2020) explicitly modeled 'knowledge tracking' and 'knowledge shifting' during a conversation while Meng et al. (2021) tried to incorporate speakers' initiative. Zhan et al. (2021b) used conditional random fields to model knowledge transition and Wu et al. (2021) leveraged the document structure to provide dialog-contextualized passage encodings while adding an auxiliary loss to capture the history of dialog-document connections. Li et al. (2022) used document semantic graphs to guide the knowledge selection, and Yang et al. (2022) proposed a topic-shift aware knowledge selector.

More recently models like RAG (Lewis et al., 2020) and FID (Kim et al., 2020) improved the question answering performance by shifting the final knowledge selection to the decoding process. Extending this to dialog (which was implemented differently by Lin et al. (2020)), studies have incorporated the fine-grained decoding-stage selection for better knowledge grounding (Shuster et al., 2021) or combined it with the posterior signal (Paranjape et al., 2021).

Table 3 summarizes a selection of these approaches, which mostly try to incorporate dynamic knowledge patterns by modeling attributes like topic shift, knowledge transition, knowledge tracking/shifting, knowledge difference etc.

3 Knowledge Selection Biases and Artefacts

Our main objective in this work is to explore the structural biases and artefacts in the knowledge selection labels of popular KGD datasets. For this, we use different methods depending on the way knowledge pools are constructed and presented to crowd-source workers, but in both cases, we essentially investigate the same hypothesis:

> *Crowd-source workers often base their knowledge selection on the structure and order of the knowledge pool, as presented to them.*

In other words, when selecting the knowledge piece for the next utterance, they tend to just follow the knowledge document and pick the 'next' item, instead of coming up with a more sophisticated 'flow'. In the following sections, we explore this hypothesis separately for Wizard of Wikipedia and Topical-Chat.

3.1 Wizard of Wikipedia (WoW)

As mentioned before, in WoW, dialogs happen between a 'wizard' and 'apprentice', with the former having access to unstructured knowledge. For each dialog either the wizard or apprentice is picked to choose the topic and speak first (the other player receives the topic information). The conversation begins and at each turn the wizard (system) can select from a knowledge pool which has been curated from a collection of Wikipedia articles via basic retrieval methods. Then the (potentially) selected knowledge piece is used by the wizard to generate the next utterance (system response). Out of 83247 wizard turns in the training set, 77523 (93%) are 'knowledge-grounded'; i.e. turns where the annotator has chosen a knowledge piece to ground their next utterance on.

Figure 1 shows how the knowledge pool is created for the wizard: At each turn, the last two utterances are used as queries by a TF-IDF retrieval module to get 14 (7 for each) relevant articles from a Wikipedia collection (title + first paragraphs). The dialog-topic article (title + first 10 sentences) is added to this set to create the final pool, which on average contains 63 knowledge *sentences* from up to 15 *passages* or articles[2]. Figure 5 (Appendix A) shows how this pool is presented to annotators.

To investigate our hypothesis, we consider 3 heuristic content-agnostic models for knowledge selection:

- **Topic-First (T0)**: Picks the first sentence of the dialog-topic article in all turns.
- **Topic-Next (T+)**: Starts from the dialog-topic article's first sentence, but proceeds to the next sentence at each successive turn.
- **Last-Next (L+)**: Picks the next sentence in the (gold) passage that was selected in the previous turn[3].

[2]Since each passage corresponds to an article with a unique topic, passage, article and topic can be used interchangeably in the WoW context.

[3]If not available, the model returns the next (unused) sentence in the dialog-topic article (e.g. in the first turn, the dialog-topic article's first sentence will be selected.)

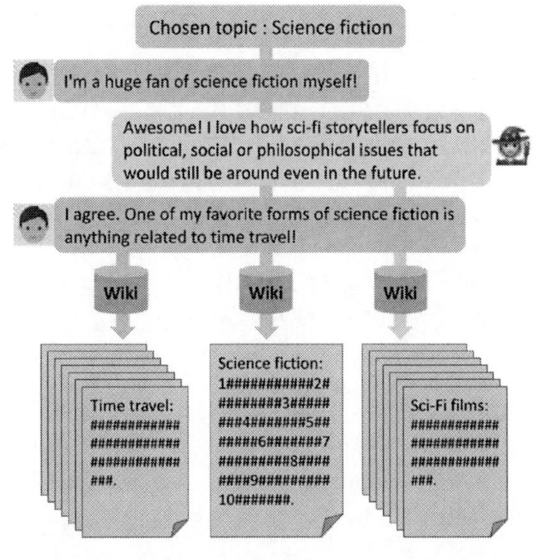

Figure 1: Curating the knowledge pool for wizard (right) in WoW dataset. At each turn a Wikipedia article collection is consulted using the last two utterances as queries, and the first paragraph of the 7 most relevant articles for each query plus the article for the dialog's chosen topic (first 10 sentences) are returned to create the knowledge pool to be used for the next wizard turn.

T0 is a static ('flow-less') model. T+ precisely and strictly follows the topic-article's narrative for dialog grounding, and L+ exploits the knowledge selection history for the next move.

Table 4 shows the performance of these 3 models in selecting the gold passage and sentence from the knowledge pool. T0 does not score very high but it offers a strong baseline for knowledge selection in WoW. In particular the T0 performance on the unseen test set already beats a handful of the models in Table 3 including the original baseline (18.9 vs. 12.2). Adding the basic 'flow' (T+) significantly improves the KS performance (an additional ~6% accuracy), and following the L+ selection policy adds another 5% boost to accuracy, making the content-agnostic L+ model highly competitive among the KS models. These performances show a strong bias towards picking the dialog-topic article among the passages, as well as picking the 'next' sentence within the current passage.

3.2 Topical-Chat

Unlike WoW, in Topical-Chat (Gopalakrishnan et al., 2019) the partners do not have explicitly defined roles. Instead, the authors leveraged infor-

Model	Train				Test-seen				Test-unseen			
	Pssg. Acc.		Sent. Acc.		Pssg. Acc.		Sent. Acc.		Pssg. Acc.		Sent. Acc.	
	all	kng	all	kng	all	kng	all	kng	all	kng	all	kng
T0	67.4	72.4	18.3	19.7	67.9	72.4	18.1	19.3	70.9	75.2	18.9	20.1
T+	67.4	72.4	23.3	25.0	67.9	72.4	24.0	25.6	70.9	75.2	24.6	26.2
L+	68.5	73.5	27.9	29.9	68.9	73.5	28.3	30.1	72.3	76.8	30.2	32.1

Table 4: Knowledge selection accuracy for the heuristic content-agnostic models T0, T+ and L+ on WoW subsets. 'kng' refers to the knowledge-grounded subset. Underlined values can be compared with Table 3.

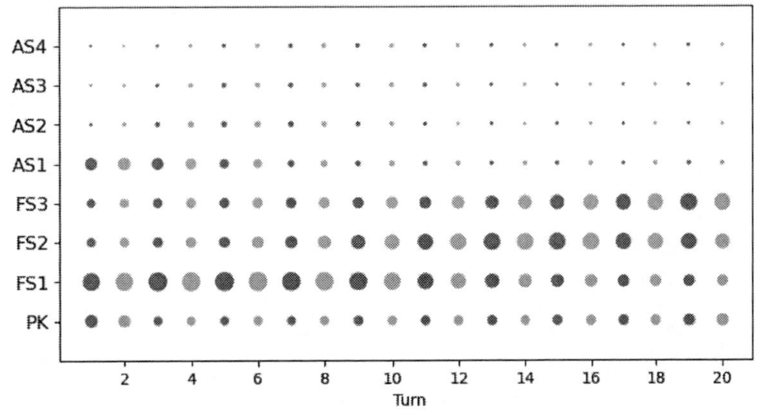

Figure 2: Grounding density for different knowledge sections at each turn in TopicalChat train set. Colors represent speakers. (PK: Personal Knowledge; FS: Factual Section; AS: Article Section.)

mation asymmetry to implicitly cause both partners to serve dual roles of a teacher and a participant which more accurately reflects real-world conversations.

For each dialog, 3 entities (from a pool of 300) were picked, plus their Wikipedia lead section, 8-10 fun facts, and a news article referencing all 3. These resources then were divided or modified according to one of 4 configurations (Figure 6 in Appendix B) to provide 2 identical (conf. A and B) or different (conf. C and D) knowledge pools. Finally Mechanical Turk workers were partnered up and assigned to these reading sets, and asked to chat about them for at least 20 turns. To present the reading set, information about an entity E (i.e. Wikipedia sections and fun facts) were displayed as a group titled Factual Section (FS), and the news article about the entities was chunked into 4 similar-sized sections (AS1-4). Turkers were asked to specify the knowledge source (FS1-3, AS1-4 and/or Personal Knowledge (PK)) used to generate their message at each turn. Selecting Personal Knowledge as the source means that the utterance is not grounded in external knowledge.

Figure 2 shows how the grounding evolves as conversations proceed in TopicalChat. Knowledge sections are arranged along the Y-axis, and point sizes represent normalized (per turn) frequency, or density. We can see that:

1. Grounding is mainly done on Factual Sections (FS), rather than Article Sections (AS).

2. The first part of the Article (AS1) is used significantly more than the rest for grounding, mainly in the beginning of the conversation[4].

3. As the conversation proceeds, the grounding density peak moves from FS1 to FS2 and FS3.

4. Personal Knowledge has a higher density in the beginning and ending turns which agrees with greeting patterns.

In other words, the 'average' TopicalChat conversation is likely to follow the PK-AS1-FS1-FS2-FS3-PK pattern for grounding. Since the numbering of entities and corresponding Factual Sections (i.e. FS1-3) in each conversation is independent

[4]This usually corresponds to opening utterances like *Do you know/Have you heard about X?*

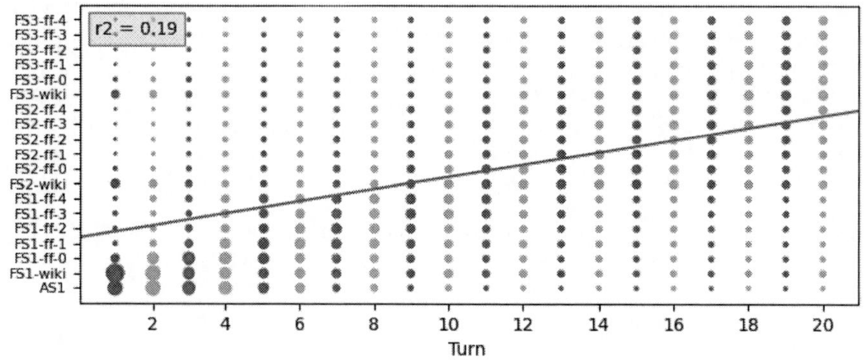

Figure 3: Fine-grained grounding density for different knowledge sections at each turn in TopicalChat train set. Colors indicate speakers.

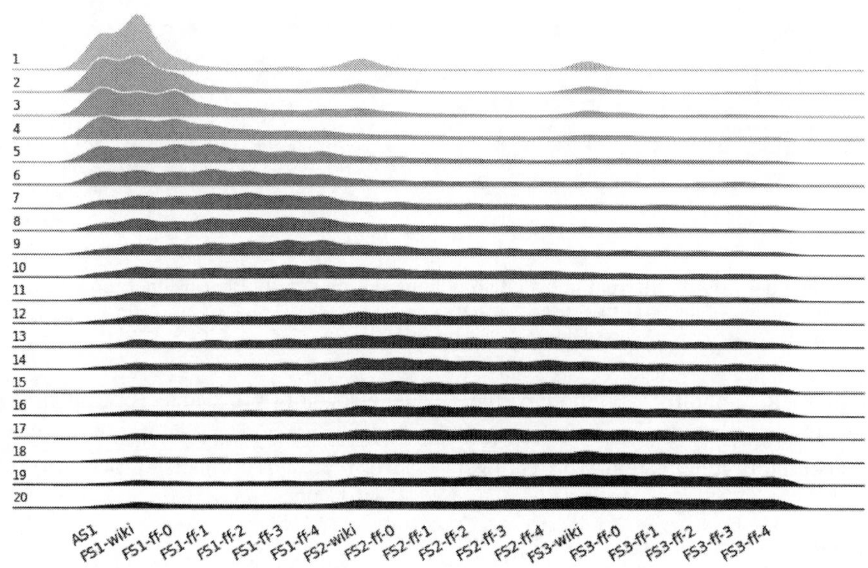

Figure 4: Grounding distribution over different knowledge parts (x-axis) for different turns (y-axis) in TopicalChat train set.

of the Article content[5], the observed pattern suggests that the grounding order is biased towards a pre-determined arbitrary parameter.

To have a more fine-grained view of this pattern, we exploit the response-knowledge overlap and employ a pre-trained sentence embedding model to estimate the gold knowledge sentence within the gold section (details in Appendix B). We then use these labels to expand each FS section into FS-wiki (the Wikipedia part) and FS-ff-{0-4} (the 5 fun facts). Figure 3 shows the resulting chart (limited to AS1, FS1, FS2 and FS3 sections), which demonstrates the same overall tendency of grounding on later sentences/sections as the conversation proceeds. The straight line is the linear regression fit (assuming sections' order as their value; i.e. 1, 2, ..., 19) with the slope and $r2$ value of 0.41 and 0.19 respectively (The slope of the diagonal line is 0.95).

The proceeding pattern is better illustrated in Ridgeline plots. For this, we switch the axes and invert the Y-axis direction so that the conversation starts at the top of the Y-axis. The result (Figure 4) displays a dispersing distribution with a clear tendency to 'move' forward; i.e. towards later sentences/sections. As Figure 7 (Appendix B) shows, this is shared in different knowledge configurations (i.e. A, B, C, D in Figure 6) with slight fluctuations.

[5]As opposed to –for example– numbered by importance or coverage order in the supporting Article.

3.3 WoW: A Markov View

As the final experiment, we revisit WoW dataset with a more complicated knowledge selection strategy. Inspired by the noticeable performance of content-agnostic models, we now consider a Markov model for KS with two stochastic parameters; Passage (P), and Line (L), with the following domains:

$$\begin{aligned} P &\in \{\texttt{None, DTopic, Other}\} \\ L &\in \{\texttt{None, Next, Other}\} \end{aligned} \tag{1}$$

P can be None (no grounding), DTopic (grounding on the dialog-topic passage) or Other (grounding on any other passage). Similarly, L can be None (no grounding), Next (picking the next sentence in the selected passage)[6], or Other (picking any other sentence. These choices follow the observed biases towards picking the dialog-topic article among the passages, and the 'next' sentence within the current passage, as discussed in 3.1.

Using this model, we can calculate initial state and transition probabilities from the WoW training set. Table 5 shows $P0$ and $L0$ probabilities for the initial state (S0); i.e first turn. 0/0 and 0/1 refer to the first turns in which wizard (0/0) or apprentice (0/1) start the conversation. As one can see, there is a strong bias towards picking the dialog-topic passage (DTopic) which is expected, especially for 0/0 where DTopic is the only grounding choice. More interesting is the tendency to start from the first sentence, especially when DTopic is chosen as passage (random probability: ~0.1).

P0	Turn = 0	0/0	0/1
None	0.048	0.061	0.034
DTopic	0.909	0.939	0.880
Other	0.043	0.0	0.085

L0	Turn = 0	0/0	0/1
Next (= first)	0.647	0.712	0.584
Other	0.353	0.288	0.416

Table 5: Initial state (S0) probabilities for the Passage (P) and Line (L) variables in WoW (here Next is equivalent to picking the first line in the passage).

Table 6 shows the transition probabilities for Passage (P) and Line (L) between successive states

P	None	DTopic	Other
None	0.208	0.415	0.377
DTopic	0.055	0.754	0.191
Other	0.102	0.192	0.704

L	Next	Other
	0.348	0.652

Table 6: Transition probabilities for the Passage (P) and Line (L) variables with full grounding memory.

(full grounding memory), which demonstrates a strong tendency to 'stay' in DTopic (~0.75) and an overall preference for picking the Next sentence ((random probability: ~0.19).

Equation 1 along with the $P0$, $L0$, P and L values provides a fine-grained content-agnostic distribution (CAG) over the knowledge choices at each turn, which can be used in combination with any content-aware (CAW) KS model. Here we examine three ways to do so (all CAW models are based on RoBERTa-base):

- **Ensemble**: We simply use the CAG predictions in a mean-value ensemble.
- **TokenCues**: Instead of directly incorporating the CAG values, we provide corresponding bias cues as special tokens in the input sequences. In particular we add <topic>, <next> and <prev_next> to respectively mark the topic-article sentences, the successive sentence in each passage (w.r.t the last visited one in that passage) and the sentence after the one selected in the previous turn.
- **Both**: We use the token-cues model in combination with CAG in a mean-value ensemble.

Model	S	U
Baseline	28.6	26.6
Ensemble (CAG + Baseline)	31.9	33.8
TokenCues	32.8	33.8
Ensemble (CAG + TokenCues)	32.9	34.6

Table 7: Knowledge selection accuracy on WoW test subsets (S: seen, U:unseen) for various incorporations of the content-agnostic knowledge.

Table 7 shows the KS performance of these variations compared with the conventional sequence classification approach (Baseline). As one can see,

[6]Here Next is meant with respect to the grounding history; i.e. picking up from the last time the passage was visited. In the case of no grounding memory (first-order Markov), L starts from 0 every time the grounding topic changes.

incorporating the content-agnostic knowledge (directly or indirectly), results in a significant performance improvement. Moreover it seems that the transformer model is capable of learning the KS biases once proper cues are provided in the training data: the TokenCues model matches the Baseline Ensemble while gaining only marginal improvement from the explicit CAG values.

4 Discussion and Conclusion

In this work we investigated the potential knowledge selection biases and artefacts in two popular KGD datasets. Our central governing hypothesis was that crowd-source workers tend to simply follow the structure and order of knowledge pieces, as presented to them. For the WoW dataset, we showed that using this hypothesis, content-agnostic models can achieve noticeable knowledge selection performance, and combined with simple sequence classification training are able to compete with sophisticated solutions. For Topical-Chat we observed a noisy alignment between the KS sequence and the order of entities and their segments, as provided to crowd-sources.

Although following the existing order of knowledge pieces is not strange or unexpected (at least within one document), we believe that the way knowledge options are curated and presented to crowd-source workers can be an exacerbating factor. All 4 datasets provide a large number of retrieved knowledge pieces at each turn (usually more than 60) which is statistically beneficial to the dataset, but it could also encourage an 'easy solution' regime in which annotators opt for the safe and convenient choice of following the already existing structure of knowledge articles, instead of trying to create and maintain a novel 'flow'. In its extreme case, this leads to conversations similar to reciting an article line by line[7].

In terms of dialog modeling, these results can suggest that the origin and significance of higher-order attributes in the dataset can be questioned. In particular, the concept of 'flow' as governing the dialog-level pattern of knowledge selection seems to be rooted substantially in the structure of knowledge documents. This does not rule out the existence or learnability of genuine patterns/flows, but the very low human performance for this task (~17%; Table 1) imposes a serious higher-bound on its discerning power; i.e. in most cases, there seems to be not enough semantic cues in the conversational history to uniquely and clearly bound it to a single knowledge piece.

Although the ultimate goal in KGD modeling is generating proper responses (and not mastering the knowledge selection part), but in order to model higher-order and dialog-level conversational phenomena, we probably need better datasets. One important factor in producing such resources is considering the process from annotators' point of view, and how design choices (e.g. annotation interface and instructions, size of knowledge pool, etc.) can persuade them towards or away from 'easy solution' regimes which are prone to artifacts. Another approach is providing explicit 'scenarios' for the way dialogs are supposed to unfold. This is how DuConv (Wu et al., 2019) and NaturalConv (Wang et al., 2021) datasets (both Chinese) have been curated, but whether this mitigates the problem or introduces new artifacts should be studied.

5 Limitations

The main limitation of our work is its focus on English datasets. While this was due to their popularity and extensive usage (and our limited language skills), it overlooks datasets like DuConv (Wu et al., 2019) and NaturalConv (Wang et al., 2021) (both Chinese) which employ more explicit annotation instructions regarding dialog 'path' and topic transitions. Studying the way these restrictions affect conversational attributes, is necessary for a more comprehensive understanding of the problem.

Another limitation is the lack of an empirical investigation on how/if these artefacts and biases affect the final objective of KGD modeling, i.e. response generation. This of course is not easy in the absence of a less biased dataset, but synthetic datasets –which have become much better in quality and flexibility thanks to large language models– can probably provide reliable estimations, which we plan to explore in future studies.

Acknowledgements

This research received funding from the Flemish Government under the "Onderzoeksprogramma Artificiële Intelligentie (AI) Vlaanderen" programme.

[7]There are also case-specific factors. for example in WoW the utterance-based knowledge pieces are subject to change at each turn, and therefore there is no guarantee that the passage used for grounding in the current turn will be present in the provided pool for the next turn. This makes grounding on the dialog-topic article a safe choice, since it is always in the pool.

References

Xiuyi Chen, Fandong Meng, Peng Li, Feilong Chen, Shuang Xu, Bo Xu, and Jie Zhou. 2020. Bridging the gap between prior and posterior knowledge selection for knowledge-grounded dialogue generation. In *Proceedings of the 2020 Conference on Empirical Methods in Natural Language Processing (EMNLP)*, pages 3426–3437, Online. Association for Computational Linguistics.

Emily Dinan, Stephen Roller, Kurt Shuster, Angela Fan, Michael Auli, and Jason Weston. 2018. Wizard of wikipedia: Knowledge-powered conversational agents. *CoRR*, abs/1811.01241.

Karthik Gopalakrishnan, Behnam Hedayatnia, Qinlang Chen, Anna Gottardi, Sanjeev Kwatra, Anu Venkatesh, Raefer Gabriel, and Dilek Hakkani-Tür. 2019. Topical-Chat: Towards Knowledge-Grounded Open-Domain Conversations. In *Proc. Interspeech 2019*, pages 1891–1895.

Suchin Gururangan, Swabha Swayamdipta, Omer Levy, Roy Schwartz, Samuel Bowman, and Noah A. Smith. 2018. Annotation artifacts in natural language inference data. In *Proceedings of the 2018 Conference of the North American Chapter of the Association for Computational Linguistics: Human Language Technologies, Volume 2 (Short Papers)*, pages 107–112, New Orleans, Louisiana. Association for Computational Linguistics.

Bin Jiang, Jingxu Yang, Chao Yang, Wanyue Zhou, Liang Pang, and Xiaokang Zhou. 2020. Knowledge augmented dialogue generation with divergent facts selection. *Knowledge-Based Systems*, 210:106479.

Byeongchang Kim, Jaewoo Ahn, and Gunhee Kim. 2020. Sequential latent knowledge selection for knowledge-grounded dialogue.

Patrick Lewis, Ethan Perez, Aleksandra Piktus, Fabio Petroni, Vladimir Karpukhin, Naman Goyal, Heinrich Küttler, Mike Lewis, Wen-tau Yih, Tim Rocktäschel, Sebastian Riedel, and Douwe Kiela. 2020. Retrieval-augmented generation for knowledge-intensive nlp tasks. In *Proceedings of the 34th International Conference on Neural Information Processing Systems*, NIPS'20, Red Hook, NY, USA. Curran Associates Inc.

Sha Li, Mahdi Namazifar, Di Jin, Mohit Bansal, Heng Ji, Yang Liu, and Dilek Hakkani-Tur. 2022. Enhancing knowledge selection for grounded dialogues via document semantic graphs. In *Proceedings of the 2022 Conference of the North American Chapter of the Association for Computational Linguistics: Human Language Technologies*, pages 2810–2823, Seattle, United States. Association for Computational Linguistics.

Zekang Li, Cheng Niu, Fandong Meng, Yang Feng, Qian Li, and Jie Zhou. 2019. Incremental transformer with deliberation decoder for document grounded conversations. In *Proceedings of the 57th Annual Meeting of the Association for Computational Linguistics*, pages 12–21, Florence, Italy. Association for Computational Linguistics.

Rongzhong Lian, Min Xie, Fan Wang, Jinhua Peng, and Hua Wu. 2019. Learning to select knowledge for response generation in dialog systems. In *Proceedings of the Twenty-Eighth International Joint Conference on Artificial Intelligence, IJCAI-19*, pages 5081–5087. International Joint Conferences on Artificial Intelligence Organization.

Xiexiong Lin, Weiyu Jian, Jianshan He, Taifeng Wang, and Wei Chu. 2020. Generating informative conversational response using recurrent knowledge-interaction and knowledge-copy. In *Proceedings of the 58th Annual Meeting of the Association for Computational Linguistics*, pages 41–52, Online. Association for Computational Linguistics.

Pierre Lison and Jörg Tiedemann. 2016. OpenSubtitles2016: Extracting large parallel corpora from movie and TV subtitles. In *Proceedings of the Tenth International Conference on Language Resources and Evaluation (LREC'16)*, pages 923–929, Portorož, Slovenia. European Language Resources Association (ELRA).

Ehsan Lotfi, Maxime De Bruyn, Jeska Buhmann, and Walter Daelemans. 2021. Teach me what to say and I will learn what to pick: Unsupervised knowledge selection through response generation with pretrained generative models. In *Proceedings of the 3rd Workshop on Natural Language Processing for Conversational AI*, pages 254–262, Online. Association for Computational Linguistics.

Ryan Lowe, Nissan Pow, Iulian Serban, and Joelle Pineau. 2015. The Ubuntu dialogue corpus: A large dataset for research in unstructured multi-turn dialogue systems. In *Proceedings of the 16th Annual Meeting of the Special Interest Group on Discourse and Dialogue*, pages 285–294, Prague, Czech Republic. Association for Computational Linguistics.

Chuan Meng, Pengjie Ren, Zhumin Chen, Zhaochun Ren, Tengxiao Xi, and Maarten de Rijke. 2021. Initiative-aware self-supervised learning for knowledge-grounded conversations. In *Proceedings of the 44th International ACM SIGIR Conference on Research and Development in Information Retrieval*, SIGIR '21, page 522–532, New York, NY, USA. Association for Computing Machinery.

Chuan Meng, Pengjie Ren, Zhumin Chen, Weiwei Sun, Zhaochun Ren, Zhaopeng Tu, and Maarten de Rijke. 2020. Dukenet: A dual knowledge interaction network for knowledge-grounded conversation. In *Proceedings of the 43rd International ACM SIGIR Conference on Research and Development in Information Retrieval*, SIGIR '20, page 1151–1160, New York, NY, USA. Association for Computing Machinery.

Nikita Moghe, Siddhartha Arora, Suman Banerjee, and Mitesh M. Khapra. 2018. Towards exploiting background knowledge for building conversation systems. In *Proceedings of the 2018 Conference on Empirical Methods in Natural Language Processing*, pages 2322–2332, Brussels, Belgium. Association for Computational Linguistics.

Nikita Nangia, Saku Sugawara, Harsh Trivedi, Alex Warstadt, Clara Vania, and Samuel R. Bowman. 2021. What ingredients make for an effective crowdsourcing protocol for difficult NLU data collection tasks? In *Proceedings of the 59th Annual Meeting of the Association for Computational Linguistics and the 11th International Joint Conference on Natural Language Processing (Volume 1: Long Papers)*, pages 1221–1235, Online. Association for Computational Linguistics.

Ashwin Paranjape, Omar Khattab, Christopher Potts, Matei Zaharia, and Christopher D. Manning. 2021. Hindsight: Posterior-guided training of retrievers for improved open-ended generation.

Nils Reimers and Iryna Gurevych. 2019. Sentence-bert: Sentence embeddings using siamese bert-networks. In *Proceedings of the 2019 Conference on Empirical Methods in Natural Language Processing*. Association for Computational Linguistics.

Kurt Shuster, Spencer Poff, Moya Chen, Douwe Kiela, and Jason Weston. 2021. Retrieval augmentation reduces hallucination in conversation. In *Findings of the Association for Computational Linguistics: EMNLP 2021*, pages 3784–3803, Punta Cana, Dominican Republic. Association for Computational Linguistics.

Xiaoyang Wang, Chen Li, Jianqiao Zhao, and Dong Yu. 2021. Naturalconv: A chinese dialogue dataset towards multi-turn topic-driven conversation. In *AAAI Conference on Artificial Intelligence*.

Wenquan Wu, Zhen Guo, Xiangyang Zhou, Hua Wu, Xiyuan Zhang, Rongzhong Lian, and Haifeng Wang. 2019. Proactive human-machine conversation with explicit conversation goal. In *Proceedings of the 57th Annual Meeting of the Association for Computational Linguistics*, pages 3794–3804, Florence, Italy. Association for Computational Linguistics.

Zeqiu Wu, Bo-Ru Lu, Hannaneh Hajishirzi, and Mari Ostendorf. 2021. DIALKI: Knowledge identification in conversational systems through dialogue-document contextualization. In *Proceedings of the 2021 Conference on Empirical Methods in Natural Language Processing*, pages 1852–1863, Online and Punta Cana, Dominican Republic. Association for Computational Linguistics.

Chenxu Yang, Zheng Lin, Jiangnan Li, Fandong Meng, Weiping Wang, Lanrui Wang, and Jie Zhou. 2022. TAKE: Topic-shift aware knowledge sElection for dialogue generation. In *Proceedings of the 29th International Conference on Computational Linguistics*, pages 253–265, Gyeongju, Republic of Korea. International Committee on Computational Linguistics.

Haolan Zhan, Lei Shen, Hongshen Chen, and Hainan Zhang. 2021a. CoLV: A collaborative latent variable model for knowledge-grounded dialogue generation. In *Proceedings of the 2021 Conference on Empirical Methods in Natural Language Processing*, pages 2250–2261, Online and Punta Cana, Dominican Republic. Association for Computational Linguistics.

Haolan Zhan, Hainan Zhang, Hongshen Chen, Zhuoye Ding, Yongjun Bao, and Yanyan Lan. 2021b. Augmenting knowledge-grounded conversations with sequential knowledge transition. In *Proceedings of the 2021 Conference of the North American Chapter of the Association for Computational Linguistics: Human Language Technologies*, pages 5621–5630, Online. Association for Computational Linguistics.

Chujie Zheng, Yunbo Cao, Daxin Jiang, and Minlie Huang. 2020. Difference-aware knowledge selection for knowledge-grounded conversation generation. In *Findings of the Association for Computational Linguistics: EMNLP 2020*, pages 115–125, Online. Association for Computational Linguistics.

Kangyan Zhou, Shrimai Prabhumoye, and Alan W Black. 2018. A dataset for document grounded conversations. In *Proceedings of the 2018 Conference on Empirical Methods in Natural Language Processing*, pages 708–713, Brussels, Belgium. Association for Computational Linguistics.

A Appendix: WoW Interface

Figure 5 shows the annotation interface used in curating Wizard of Wikipedia.

B Appendix: Topical-Chat

Considering the absence of sentence-level gold labels in Topical-Chat, we exploit the response-knowledge overlap and employ a pre-trained sentence embedding model to estimate the gold knowledge sentence within the gold section. More specifically, we use the `all-mpnet-base-v2` model from the 'sentence-transformers' library (Reimers and Gurevych, 2019) which shows the highest performance on benchmarks, and pick the sentence which has the highest cosine similarity with the response. Manually checking the performance on a small subset (500 grounded samples) shows an error rate of 18% (accuracy =~82%) of which 10% is due to incorrect gold section labels. Enforcing an acceptance similarity threshold of 0.2, filters out 13% of samples including 88% of errors, which improves the accuracy to 93%. We apply this setting to the train set[8], and –to keep conversations in reasonable lengths (and therefore less likely to be damaged by the filtering)–, we remove dialogs with less than 80% of accepted utterances. This, results in a more reliable subset of 7922 (out of 8,628) conversations, with 150564 utterances.

[8]We consider the first 20 utterances in each dialog, which is the minimum required length during crowd-sourcing.

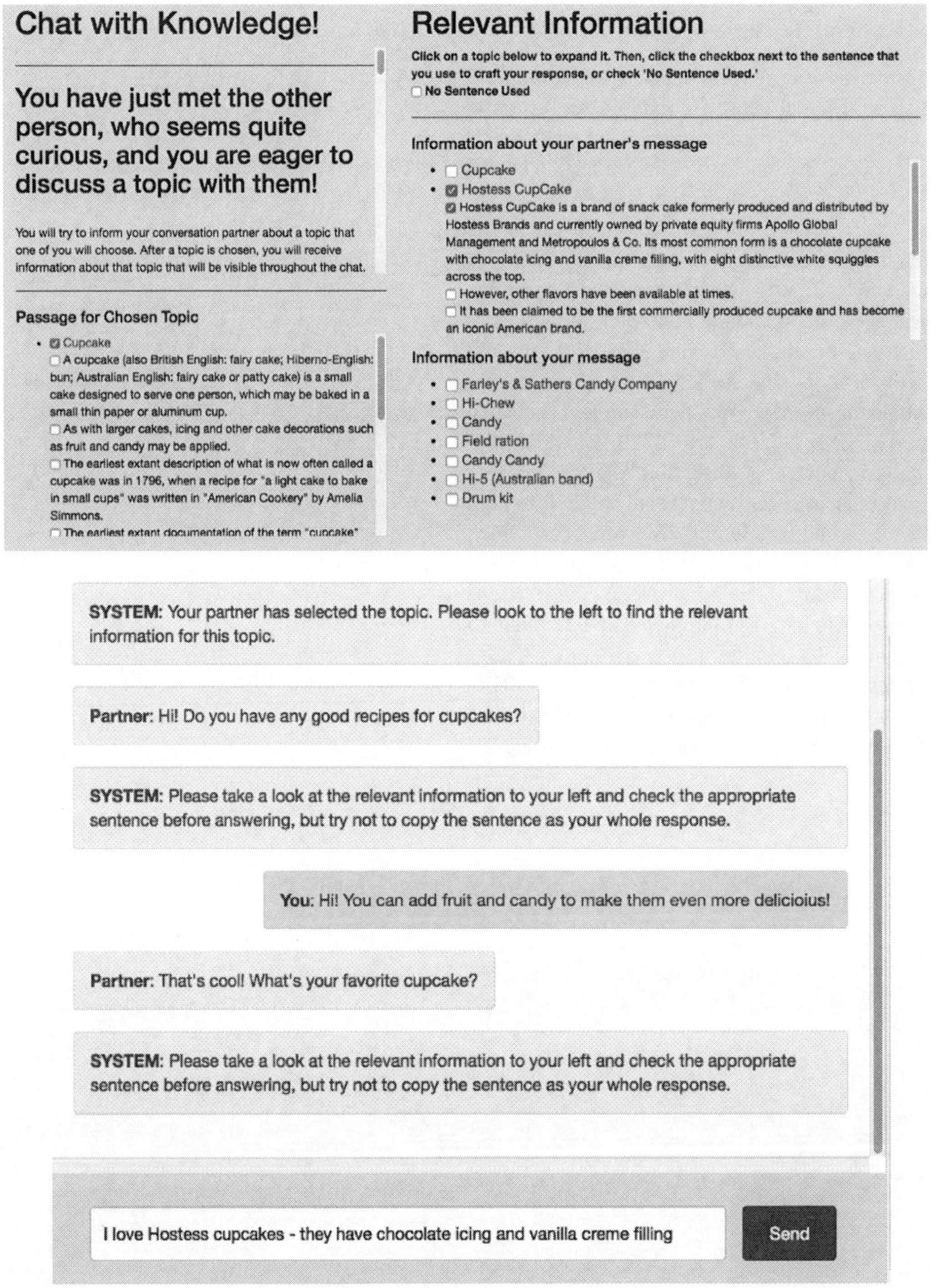

Figure 5: Annotation interface for the Wizard of Wikipedia dataset (from (Dinan et al., 2018))

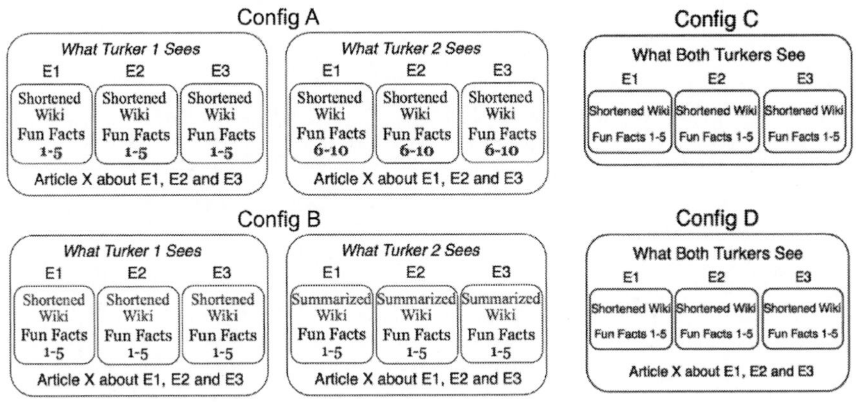

Figure 6: The four knowledge configurations in TopicalChat (from Gopalakrishnan et al. (2019). E stands for Entity.

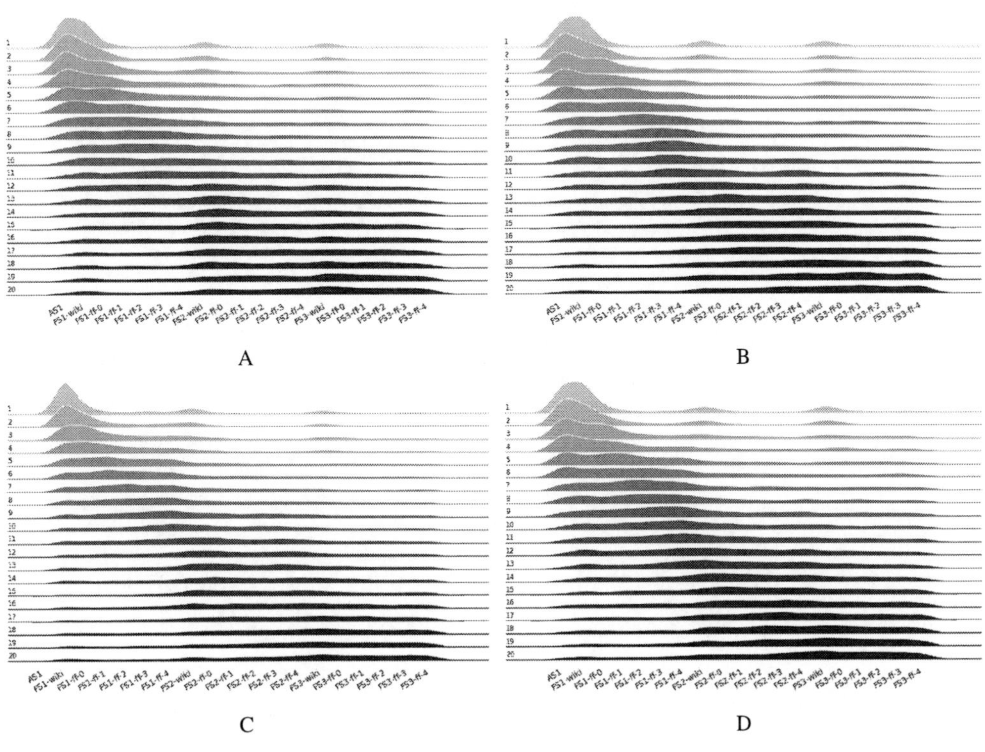

Figure 7: Turn-wise grounding distribution over different knowledge parts (x-axis) for different configurations (A, B, C, D) in TopicalChat train set.

Author Index

Association for Computational Linguistics
209 N. Eighth Street
Stroudsburg, Pennsylvania 18360

ISBN 978-1-7138-8226-8

9 781713 882268

CURRAN ASSOCIATES INC.
proceedings.com